LONDON'S FIRST RAILWAY –
THE LONDON & GREENWICH

LONDON'S FIRST RAILWAY– THE LONDON & GREENWICH

R. H. G. Thomas

'Railways have rendered more services, and have received less gratitude, than any other Institution in the land.'

—John Bright

B. T. Batsford Ltd London

First published 1972
First published in paperback 1986

ISBN 0 7134 5414 8

Printed by Billings, Worcester
for the Publishers
B.T. Batsford Ltd
4 Fitzhardinge Street, London W1H 0AH

ACKNOWLEDGEMENT

The Author and Publishers wish to thank the following for the
illustrations appearing in this book: Trustees of the British
Museum, figs 12, 13, 15-18 and 27; British Railways, Southern
Region, figs 29, 35 and pp. 138, 144, 159, 217 and 219; Sir Arthur
Elton, fig. 31; Greenwich Local History Library, figs. 9, 26, 30 and
37; Guildhall Library, figs 1, 2, 5, 10, 32, 33 and p. 25; Lens of
Sutton, fig. 20; Locomotive Publishing Co., figs 23, 24, 39 and
p. 234; Trustees of the London Museum, fig. 21; Patent Office,
p. 175; Railway Magazine, p. 10; St Thomas's Hospital, fig. 36;
Science Museum London, figs 7, 8, 28, 38 and p. 187; Universitaire
Film, Utrecht, fig. 3; E. N. Walter, fig. 6.

Contents

The Illustrations

4

5

6

Preface

Amid the cheering and revelry of thousands of its citizens, London's first railway was opened by the Lord Mayor on a crisp winter day in 1836; few of those present on that occasion could have foreseen the social changes soon to be brought about by the new mode of transport, or the effect it would have on the growth of the metropolis.

The line between London Bridge and Greenwich was one of the earliest to be built, and many trains had run over it before some of the railway pioneers had reached the height of their fame; but one, Richard Trevithick, had died in poverty and obscurity not far from the railway while it was still under construction. It was built while Parliamentary Reform was still a subject of topical interest and before Queen Victoria began her long reign. When Dulwich, Peckham and Stockwell were numbered among the villages on the fringe of London its trains ran above the meadows of Bermondsey to reach Greenwich, then a town in Kent. Within a few years what is now Greater London was penetrated by lines from all directions, and if in the absence of an overall plan the development was somewhat haphazard, the capital has been, and is still, well served by its railways. Some of the lines have now gone, but those which approach London Bridge Station carry an enormous volume of traffic; by successive enlargements the two lines of the original Greenwich Railway have increased to twelve, and hundreds of trains every day for well over a century have sped along the broad viaduct carrying countless millions about their business or pleasure.

In the following pages the growth of this first railway in London is traced against the background of those other railway companies, then in their infancy, whose affairs influenced the history of the London & Greenwich. Extensive use has been made of the Company's Board Minutes, but since it is obvious from the text where these are the source of information, the list of authorities at Appendix A has not been encumbered with references either to the Minute Books of the Greenwich Railway or to those of associated companies. The Railway received a great deal of attention from a wide range of contemporary newspapers, periodicals and pamphlets, the quotations from which will probably convey something of the atmosphere of the times in which this, and other early railways, came into existence.

The author is indebted to the following, among others, who have kindly supplied information or illustrations, or have allowed him access to archives, family documents and other source material: Dr E. Course, Mr E. Craven, The Earl of Dundonald, Sir Arthur Elton, Bt, Messrs H. Hart, Charles E. Lee, S. G. Ottley, H. Paar, S. H. Pearce Higgins, F. O. Randall, P. Roos, E. N. Walter, the Archivist and his staff at the British Railways Board Historical Records Office, the Librarian of the Guildhall Library, the Scottish Record Office and Mr J. Watson, Local History Librarian, London Borough of Greenwich. He would also take this opportunity of paying tribute to the patience and encouragement of his wife during the preparation of this work.

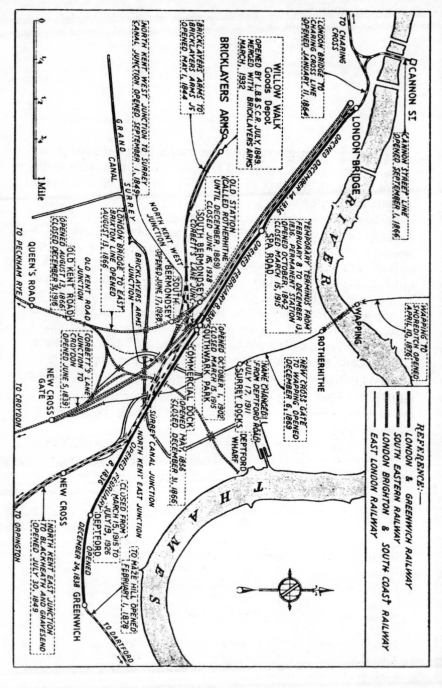

Chronological plan showing development of the London and Greenwich Railways and associated lines.

Chapter 1

The Formation of the Company

THE beginnings of the London & Greenwich Railway go back
to the early years of public steam railways – to the days when the
Stockton & Darlington Railway was still under construction.
When this northern line received its first Act in 1821, it attracted
little attention beyond the area it was to serve, since it was to be
little more than another horse tramroad in a district where such
undertakings were no longer remarkable. When, in 1823, a
second Act authorised the use of steam locomotives, however,
the new possibilities of railway communication became apparent.
The result was the first 'Railway Mania' of 1824 in which, in
just over one month, forty-nine separate companies were formed
for making about 3,000 miles of railway involving some £23
million in capital. Among these early schemes were the predecessors of many great railways – the London & Bristol, the London
Northern Rail-road, the London & Birmingham.

Some curiously prophetic verses appeared in *John Bull*[1] in
1825 which mention both the first Greenwich Railway project
and the schemes for ship canals which then occupied the attention of a man later to become prominent in the affairs of the
London & Greenwich Railway:

Run neighbours, run, you're just in time to get a share
In all the famous projects that amuse John Bull;
Run, take a peep on 'Change, for anxious crowds beset us there,
Each trying which can make himself the greatest gull.

When Greenwich coaches go by steam, on roads of iron railing,
  Sir,
How pleasant it will be to see a dozen in a line;
And ships of heavy burden over hills and valleys sailing, Sir,
Shall cross from Bristol's Channel to the Tweed or Tyne.

A tunnel underneath the sea, from Calais Strait to Dover, Sir,
That qualmish folks may cross by land from shore to shore,
With sluices made to drown the French, if e'er they will come
    over, Sir,
Has long been talked of till at length 'tis thought a monstrous
    bore.

Then a company is formed, though not yet advertising,
To build upon a splendid scale, a large balloon,
And send up tools and broken stones for fresh Mac-Adamising
The new-discovered turnpike roads which cross the moon.

The Greenwich coaches referred to would have been the trains
of the Kentish Railway Company. This concern issued its first
brief notice to the public on 9 December 1824, when applications
for shares were invited, and on the following day an even shorter
advertisement announced that the list was closed. The first
prospectus was issued from 29, Poultry, London, on 18 December;
this stated that early application would be made for powers to
construct a line from London via Deptford, Greenwich, Woolwich, Belvedere and Gravesend, to Strood, Rochester, Chatham,
Faversham, Canterbury and Dover. Branches were to serve Maidstone, Tonbridge, Margate and Ramsgate. The capital of
£1,000,000 was divided into 10,000 shares of £100 and the
engineer was Thomas Telford. The company did not confine
itself to the use of 'locomotive machines' but intended to employ
horses as well. It was asserted that the cost of construction
'...could not exceed £5,000 per mile' for the lines beyond
Woolwich.

It was planned to build the London end first, and to open the
line to Woolwich as soon as it was completed; this was estimated
to produce the greatest profit in proportion to its mileage and
would be earning revenue while the rest of the line was being
built. Of the London–Woolwich section the promoters said

According to the estimate of experienced engineers the expense
of a railway *ought* to be £5,000 a mile; but let it be supposed
that it may require £10,000 a mile to lay down a railway between
London and Woolwich, and that the first portion of Capital
advanced will be £100,000. The number of short coaches running
on this line is 150 per diem. Admitting on the average that these
coaches are only half filled, then receipts for passengers alone will
be £26,000 a year. As locomotive machinery, moving at *twice the
velocity*, and with greater safety, must in a very great degree

supersede the coaches, the Company will probably obtain from passengers alone, independently of the baggage, an income of £20,000 or 20% upon the Capital of £100,000 requisite to carry the railway to Woolwich.

In the *Quarterly Review* for March 1825, there appeared a series of three articles on railways and canals in general, and on the Liverpool & Manchester Railway in particular, in which reference is made to the Kentish Railway, but not by name. The writer questioned the experience of engineers who thought a railway could be built for £5,000 a mile, and expressed surprise that the eminent Telford had associated himself with the project. He went on to say

It is certainly some consolation to those who are to be whirled at the rate of eighteen or twenty miles an hour, by means of a high pressure engine, to be told that they are in no danger of being seasick while on shore; that they are not to be scalded to death, nor drowned by the bursting of the boiler; and that they need not fear being shot by the scattered fragments, or dashed to pieces by the flying off or the breaking of a wheel. But with all these assurances, we should as soon expect the people of Woolwich to suffer themselves to be fired off upon one of Congreve's ricochet rockets, as to trust themselves to the mercy of such a machine going at such a rate. Their property they may, perhaps, trust, but while one of the finest navigable rivers in the world runs parallel to the proposed railroad, we consider that the other twenty per cent which the subscribers are to receive for the conveyance of heavy goods almost as problematical as that to be derived from the passengers. We will back old Father Thames against the Woolwich rail-way for any sum.

The reference to Congreve's rocket is said to have inspired Stephenson to bestow this name on his Rainhill engine of 1829.[2]

In 1825 the company issued another prospectus[3] in rather more guarded terms than the original one; no reference was made to the estimated cost since it was found that the crossing of the Medway and the building of the line from Canterbury to Dover along the hilly route of the old coach road would greatly exceed £5,000 per mile.

Telford does not seem to have been the most obvious choice as engineer since his sympathies appear to have been more with the canal interests than the railways. In 1825 he was advising some northern canal companies how best to meet the threatened competition from the new railways; later that year he withdrew from the Kentish Railway. He was succeeded by Henry Palmer who surveyed the line and whose plan, dated 29 November 1825,[4] shows the railway starting at the Bricklayers Arms in the Kent Road. The main line curved to the north-east and crossed the Surrey Canal just north of its junction with the Croydon Canal before turning southwards again to pass through Coldblow Farm on its way to Lewisham, Lee Green, Eltham and eventually to Rochester. At a point near the Kent Waterworks on the Ravens-bourne, a branch left the main line and ran north to Greenwich, terminating at a station which would have been on the opposite side of the road from the present Greenwich Station. The junction was so arranged that trains from either direction could reach Greenwich without reversing; by this time the idea of taking the line through Woolwich had been abandoned. Palmer had patented a suspended railway in 1821,[5] and in 1824 a railway on this principle was installed in the Deptford Victualling Office of the Navy to replace an even earlier tramway that was in existence there as far back as 1810, when Simon Goodrich visited it and examined the engine.[6] Whether it was the intention of the Kentish Railway to have its line built on this new system, or to run it at ground level with locomotives and horses is not clear.

On 17 February 1826 Parliament was petitioned for leave to bring in the Kentish Railway Bill and a committee was appointed to meet on the morrow to make a preliminary examination of the scheme,[7] and that is the last that is heard of it. The Kentish Railway and many other important lines projected at the same time failed for lack of capital owing to the financial position of the country then, and the only company in the south-east to survive was the Canterbury & Whitstable, which secured its Act in 1825 and was opened five years later.

Although nothing tangible resulted from this first attempt to connect London and Kent by rail, the scheme remained alive in the mind of one man at least; this was Lieutenant-Colonel George Thomas Landmann, RE, who retired from the army by the sale of his commission on 29 December 1824, after having served with distinction in the Peninsular War and later in Canada, where he built brick forts against the threatened invasion by the Americans in the war of 1812. Landmann was born in Woolwich in 1779 and lived on Blackheath during his youth; whether his interest in the district led him to take any part in the formation of the Kentish Railway is not known, but, after he had established himself as a civil engineer,[8] he had plans ready for a line between London and Greenwich which was to form part of a route to Dover, and at this point Mr George Walter became involved in the project.

The second son of a clergyman, George Walter was born in Somerset in 1790; an earlier member of the family had lost £80,000 in the South Sea Bubble, and it will be apparent later that George appears to have inherited this capacity for losing large sums of money. In January 1811 he was commissioned in the Royal Marines and was serving on HMS *Chatham* at the end of the Napoleonic Wars. He had a number of very influential friends and relations, and from 1823 until 1828 he was a member of the Stock Exchange. In 1825 he was a director of the Portsmouth Ship Canal Company, a £7,000,000 project to connect the English Channel with the Thames at Deptford which failed to mature, and in 1829 he founded the General Annuity Endowment Society. With the Hon. Robert Johnston and Abel Rous Dottin, a relation of his, and at that time MP for Southampton, he helped form the Southampton & London Railway & Dock Company with £500 subscribed between them, but for various reasons the venture failed, and when at the third attempt the London & Southampton Railway was launched in 1833 they had severed their connection with it.

In October 1831 Landmann drew Walter's attention to his plans for a London & Greenwich Railway, and a meeting was arranged to take place at the London House of Abel Rous Dottin, 31, Argyll St, on 25 November; this is the first event recorded in the L&GR Minute Books. In addition to the three mentioned, Robert Johnston, Digby Neave, John Twells and A. K. Hutchinson were present. The minutes refer to a notice that had appeared some days earlier in several newspapers[9] announcing the 'London & Greenwich Railway . . . for the passage of Coaches, Chaises, Waggons, Carts and other Carriages properly constructed, and also for foot passengers'. It was envisaged at this time that anyone would be allowed to operate vehicles on the line upon payment of the prescribed tolls, and the foot passengers were to be accommodated on footpaths to run parallel with the railway on either side. About this time Walter's insurance office became the headquarters of the L&GR and he left his other interests to devote himself entirely to the company, of which he became secretary from 1 October 1831.

Colonel Landmann's plan was for a railway running half a mile to the north of the old Kentish Railway's proposed line, and terminating at the foot of London Bridge instead of at the more remote Bricklayers Arms. In the six years that had passed since the failure of the earlier project Rennie's new bridge had been built, and this was opened on 1 August 1831. Access to the City from the south was now better than it had ever been and, to take advantage of this, Landmann produced his plans within a few weeks of the opening of the bridge. From the London terminus the railway ran in practically a straight line to Deptford, where it curved to the north-east before continuing to Greenwich. The L&GR was to run for nearly a mile through a densely built-up area near London Bridge, crossing more than a dozen streets between there and Spa Road, Bermondsey, and for this reason Landmann planned a viaduct to carry the railway twenty-two feet above the ground; an additional reason for the elevated railway was that the land lay below the Thames high water mark, and was naturally marshy. No intermediate stations were provided for originally, and at a very early stage an alternative plan was considered under which the viaduct should extend only as far as the Grand Surrey Canal, after which the line was to run on an embankment descending sufficiently to enable it to pass under Deptford High Street and the Ravensbourne in a tunnel. This was soon abandoned, however, and the original plans were formally adopted by the board on 24 February 1832.

The village of Deptford and the town of Greenwich had a combined population of about 45,000 in 1831, and were both isolated and distinct from London. Greenwich had few industries, but its connection with the Royal Navy was very strong, the whole town being dominated by the Royal Naval College. Ship chandlery and other marine occupations found employment for many of the inhabitants, and the most important factory appears to have been Enderley's rope and sail cloth works to the east of the town. Many large houses existed on the fringe of Greenwich, and near the river were several small alleys bearing curious names and consisting largely of crazy wooden buildings. The park was a favourite haunt of Londoners seeking recreation, and the fairs held there at Easter and Whitsun drew thousands. Of the inns, the Green Man was probably the most widely known outside the town as this was the first stopping place of the Dover

Mail. The Prince of Orange, alongside which the station was subsequently built, is described as having an old world appearance, and seemed to be in the heart of the country. Nearby was a lane called Blue Style in which stood General Wolfe's house, and all around were market gardens, while to the east, in the direction of Woolwich, the cornfields, orchards and woods of Kent could be seen.

Deptford, too, had changed little with the passing centuries, and was said to have presented much the same appearance in the 1830s as it had in Chaucer's day; it had certainly altered little since the time of Evelyn and Peter the Great. It also had strong associations with the sea, for at its famous dockyard many illustrious ships had been built. Away from the river Deptford Broadway had market gardens on either side, and the High Street, then known as Butt Lane, was bordered by hedgerows; Loving Edward's Lane – now Edward Street alongside the railway – ran past a farmhouse on its way to New Cross. Dividing Deptford and Greenwich was the river Ravensbourne, a stream rising on Keston Heath and joining the Thames at Deptford, at which point it was called Deptford Creek. Many thousands spent their last hours in England at the Deptford Emigration Depot, and some of these were to make their last journey here in the trains of the L&GR which brought them down.

The now densely populated district of Rotherhithe was almost uninhabited in the early years of the nineteenth century. Apart from a few houses with large gardens in the Blue Anchor Road and the engine works of Bryan Donkin & Co nearby, this area consisted mainly of marshes intersected by sluggish, dirty streams. Corbetts Lane wound its way northwards through the swampy fields to the St Helena Tea Gardens, famous in 1830, but to disappear in 1881. Even in Bermondsey, although there were more houses, a far greater area of land consisted of gardens, paddocks and pasture.

To the west of Bermondsey, however, the position was very different. For a distance of about three-quarters of a mile from London Bridge a large population lived in the utmost squalor, crowded together in a district which contained an incredible number of tiny courts, alleys and yards. The dwellings were old in 1745 when Rocque made his map of London; nearly a century later they still existed, and frequent outbreaks of cholera there had led doctors and others to suggest schemes of slum-clearance.

As the cost was estimated at £1,000,000, however, nothing was done until the railway cut a path through the middle of the area. Then Gibson's Theatre in King's Arms Yard and the Three Jolly Hatters disappeared, along with the chapel in Dean Street and hundreds of houses, many of them built of wood, in such thoroughfares as Dog and Bear Yard, Naked Boy Alley and Valiant Soldier Alley. Within a few years the whole area had been cleared to provide space for an enlarged London Bridge Station; even St Thomas's Hospital was eventually driven from its ancient site to a new one higher up the river.

One thousand copies of the first prospectus were issued in November 1831, and by 2 December it was recorded that several applications for shares had already been received. Work had been started immediately on the preparation of the Bill for Parliament, and early in 1832 Francis Giles was commissioned to report on the line. He was the engineer who, a few years before, had questioned George Stephenson's sanity in planning to take the Liverpool & Manchester Railway across Chat Moss, but he reported favourably on the L&GR, and his observations were reprinted and distributed to members of both Houses of Parliament and to the principal bankers, among others. This report set forth some of the advantages which the railway would bring to a variety of people, and mentioned the company's intention of letting the arches of the viaduct as barns, warehouses and stables. Local improvements between London and Deptford were promised, including the conversion '...of those vast meadows and market gardens into highly profitable building ground'.

Throughout 1832 meetings were held in the districts across which the line was to pass, and all the advantages that would accrue were duly enlarged upon. At one of these gatherings Robert Johnston said that the stage coach proprietors and Thames watermen were in favour of the railway, although he did not disclose what benefits these particular people might expect to gain from giving it their support. The Greenwich Watermen's Pension Institution was promised £100, payable when the railway had been completed, but the company discharged its debt nearly two years before this time, in April 1836. Numerous advertisements and pamphlets kept the project in the public eye, and among the suggestions they contained was one that the railway could be used to convey fire engines rapidly. The military advantages to be expected when the line was extended to Dover were very apparent to those who remembered the Napoleonic Wars of less than twenty years before. As with other lines then being built, it was even suggested that the L&GR could play a part in the movement of troops within the country in case of civil disorder. There would be fewer accidents on the over-crowded river,[10] less congestion on London Bridge from crowds watching the hundreds of boats plying there, and immense slum clearance. The board was particularly concerned to assure the public of the safety of the railway and frequent reference was made to the elaborate precautions taken to ensure that the trains did not become derailed, or if they did, that they remained up-right and on the viaduct. In those early days derailments were a common occurrence, many having happened on the Liverpool & Manchester Railway, and considerable publicity had been given to these accidents by the opponents of railways.

The prospect of a railway company entering the field naturally alarmed the other transport concerns in the area. Both Deptford and Greenwich were already well served by coaches, horse buses and boats, and as early as 1820 a kind of omnibus known as the 'Long Machine of Greenwich' was plying between that town and London. About the time of the L&GR Act there were proposals to introduce steam road carriages on the route; the London & Greenwich Steam Carriage Company was formed and trials were made with a double-deck steam omnibus, the *Era*. This carriage accommodated six passengers inside and fourteen outside, and travelled at 10 mph. There are some water colours extant[11] of Deptford Steam carriages, 'No 1' which appears to be a two-seater, 'No 2' probably capable of carrying six persons, and a third, the 'Steam Carriage built by Mr Hill, Deptford', appar-ently a four-seater. In each case they required an engine driver who occupied a platform at the rear and a kind of helmsman to steer the vehicle at the front end. They all seem to have been of the most solid construction, and must have weighed as much as a locomotive of those days.

Spirited opposition to the railway came from the famous horse-bus proprietor George Shillibeer, who had introduced this means of transport into central London in July 1829; in January 1834 he abandoned his former routes in favour of a service between London, Greenwich and Woolwich on which he concentrated twenty vehicles, and it was popularly supposed that his action would result in the abandonment of the railway project. A long music-hall song entitled 'Shillibeer's Original Omnibus versus the Greenwich Railroad' said of his buses:

> These pleasure and comfort with safety combine,
> They will neither blow up nor explode like a mine;
> Those who ride on the railroad might half die with fear,
> You can come to no harm in the safe Shillibeer.[12]

Shillibeer's buses did not long survive the opening of the railway, and with the decline of traffic they were seized when their unfortunate owner fell into arrears with his payments to the Stamp Office. A few years later, however, he was back in the transport business, this time as an undertaker, having patented a 'Combined Hearse and Carriage for the funerals of the Poor'.[13]

A contributor to the *New Monthly* not only showed his ignorance of railway travel generally, but that he did not know where the railway he condemned was to have its London terminus, apparently confusing it with the earlier Kentish Railway.

The Greenwich Rail-Road. – As a joke, as a bit of fun, being whisked along from the Bricklayers Arms in the Kent Road to the Hospital Gates, in ten minutes may be all very well, but not for a constancy . . . and there is the absurdity of the whole scheme. If I want to go to Greenwich from Grosvenor Square I must 'first catch my dolphin'[14] by travelling in a carriage, or on foot, to the Bricklayers Arms in the Kent Road, which is half-way for me to Greenwich. There I am to get out of the carriage into another vehicle, and hurled along through the fog and smoke of Deptford Marshes at a tremendous rate, sixteen feet above the heads of my fellow-countrymen, on a thing whence the intervention of a walnut or a schoolboy's marble, will pitch me into the ditches or down the chimney (for all I know) of some respectable greengrocer in Bermondsey, and for what? Why should I be in such a dreadful hurry to get to Greenwich? If I go for pleasure, part of the pleasure is the going; and as for eels and whitebait, which are the only matters of business likely to take a man into the neighbourhood, half an hour gets them ready; and whether I get to the Ship or the Crown & Sceptre – to which, by the way, no railroad can take me – at half past five or a quarter to six, what the deuce does it matter? The calculation of six thousand clerks splashing up and down this iron platform seems not only to be a clerical but a numerical error on the part of the projectors; and we very much suspect, that however the thing may answer as a holiday junket during the fair, it will be found that, in the end, unless the London end of it could really be in London, it will turn out a sad failure.

The journey time by road from Charing Cross or Gracechurch Street to Deptford was at least an hour by the best coaches, and passengers are said to have considered themselves cheated if a stop of ten minutes or more was not made at the Bricklayers Arms en route.[15]

By November 1832 the line had been surveyed and copies of the plan, several yards long, and showing in detail each individual property to be acquired, were deposited with the Clerks of the Peace for Surrey and Kent in readiness for the introduction of the Bill into Parliament during the next session.[16] The Bill was prepared by the company's solicitor and parliamentary agents, and was brought in by Messrs Hodges and William Brougham; it had its first reading on 11 March 1833, and after various amendments had been made by the Lords, the Act received the Royal Assent on 17 May 1833.[17]

A glimpse of the crisis through which the Company had been passing in the months prior to its obtaining the Act was given by George Walter in 1837.[18]

... with the exception of the contributions of a few directors and individual friends, the treasury was empty. The Petition for leave to bring in the Bill, which was left for signature with the Greenwich solicitor, obtained but four signatures of the inhabitants in many weeks, but a sufficient number by me in London in a few hours. The Bill was presented and read a first time; after which a consultation was held, and all agreed in the utter impossibility of proceeding further with it, from the state of the Parliamentary Contract Deed, being only signed for £75,000 out of £400,000. The ridicule attached to my assertion 'that the difficulty should be overcome', made a lasting impression on me, but acted as a stimulant to carry this assertion through. This, however, required no trifling exertions as during the period not less than twenty petitions from local authorities, and persons possessed of property along the line, were presented to Parliament, to be heard by Counsel, against the passing of the Act. So formidable did it appear that the Directors who had lent their names, and occasionally attended a Board, determined to proceed no farther; and it was only overcome by the determination of the Chairman, Deputy Chairman and myself. Our strongest opponents fortunately looked on us as visionaries, theorists, and utterly incapable of making any use of the Act, should it be obtained, and consequently not worth the expense or trouble of opposition; others imposed on us, in our weak state, Clauses in the Act, which, in the execution of the design, greatly embarrassed the Company, and materially added to the expense.

The Parliamentary Contract Deed, or Subscription Contract, was first required in 1813 under Parliamentary Standing Orders.[19] The Third Reading of any Bill for public works was forbidden unless four fifths (sometimes varied to three quarters) of the probable cost of the undertaking had been subscribed under contract. As at that time the subscribers were not required to pay any deposit, the whole business was rather futile. In the case of the Greenwich Railway, 19,400 shares, for which signatures had been obtained, were abandoned as soon as the Act was passed. It was apparently common knowledge in Greenwich that there was some irregularity about the L&GR Subscription List, for a writer in December 1833 threatened to expose the method employed to obtain signatures and publish an analysis of the names.[20]

The first L&GR Act was a very comprehensive document of 110 pages containing 198 Sections covering almost every contingency. If, for example, the bridge over the Surrey Canal should, through falling into disrepair, impede the canal traffic, the railway was liable to a penalty of £10 per hour while the canal was out of action, and if the Ravensbourne Bridge was not raised for the passage of a vessel within ten minutes of application being made, the penalty was again £10. Long before the fencing of railways became general, Section 173 stipulated that the Greenwich Railway was to be fenced, and the old problem of vandalism was dealt with under Section 159; anyone who saw fit to '...injure, break, throw down, destroy, steal, or take away any part of the said Railway or other works...' could be transported for a term of seven years.

Owing no doubt to the reason given by Walter – a belief that the railway would never be built – the Bill had a relatively smooth passage through Parliament, and although the company spent £22,000 in obtaining it, he claimed that it was the cheapest Act of its kind ever to have been passed. The London & Southampton and GWR Acts, passed about the same time, had cost £31,000 and £88,000 respectively, but if the cost is considered in relation to the mileage of the railway, the L&GR Act was anything but cheap.

The company's difficulties were by no means over with the

passing of the Act; in many respects they were just beginning. Walter stated that at this time only £615 had been paid in deposits on the 20,000 shares, and of this amount, £600 had already been spent. A balance of £2,000 was owed by the company, who had only £15 in the bank with which to meet it. The few shares that were out were selling at 10s each, and 19,400 remained to be disposed of. The directors again considered the position and decided that the only course open to them was to pay the expenses of the Act out of their own pockets, and to abandon the undertaking. At this point Walter volunteered to get the unsold shares on to the market, and, with the agreement of the board, he proceeded to do so. By his 'skilful management of the market' he rapidly disposed of the whole balance almost single-handed. He visited agents and brokers in Birmingham, Manchester and Liverpool, paying them commission on the sale of the shares, many of which were taken up by buyers in Lancashire.[21]

Letters appeared in the press, under pseudonyms, but which obviously emanated from the pen of George Walter. 'Peter Fairplay', writing to the *Greenwich Gazette* on 22 October 1833, reminded the public of the blunder on the part of the people of Manchester who originally held no shares in the Liverpool & Manchester Railway, but afterwards eagerly bought them at £200 per £100 share; of the apathy of those in Dublin who had little invested in the Dublin & Kingstown Railway soon to be opened. Of the Dublin line he wrote: 'Like the intended Greenwich Railway, the money has been found by a few London Quakers.' He denied the argument then current, that 'The Wandsworth Railway, established forty years ago,[22] does not pay ⅛ per cent' had any relevance where the prospects of the L&GR were concerned. The profits of the Greenwich line were variously estimated during 1833 as likely to be between £80,000 and £116,800, or 20 per cent to 30 per cent on the original capital of £400,000. These figures were arrived at by taking the combined road and river traffic and multiplying the answer by ten, since the traffic between Liverpool and Manchester, Hull and Selby and other places then served by railways had increased about tenfold.

A number of pamphlets appeared about this time; one, *Observations on the Greenwich Railway in a letter addressed to the Subscribers, by an Inhabitant of Greenwich* was a subtle document, sympathetic to the watermen whose trade had, in any case, the writer pointed out, already been destroyed by the coaches; in favour of the railway if it would fulfil all its promises (repeated in some detail); confident that the company would deal generously with all those whose property it would take; and gently encouraging to all who still opposed or doubted, to accept the railway as inevitable. *The Advantages of Railways with Locomotive Engines, Especially the London & Greenwich Railway or Viaduct*, at a nominal price of 6d, but probably given away with the prospectus, ran to three editions. Here the market gardeners were offered a special service in the transport of manure, which would be conveyed at night at very low rates. It was, of course, never carried either at night or any other time, since the company never catered for goods or mineral traffic, and in any case, this particular commodity was expressly excluded from subsequent toll agreements with other companies as noisome and offensive. A further booklet, *Extracts from Various Publications and Reviews on the London & Greenwich Railway* contained reprints of the favourable references to the company from various sources.

On the day the Act was passed a further prospectus was issued, this time showing a possible extension of the line via Gravesend to Canterbury and Dover. Of the viaduct it said, 'It is contemplated that it will be one of the most durable and splendid structures in the kingdom.' If its splendour has now faded, time has proved its durability.

The possibility of a partial opening before the line was complete and an extension to Woolwich was under consideration at this time, although Landmann was anxious to push the line on to the east through Kent, and he urged the board to apply for powers to do so. It was, however, ultimately decided to extend the railway by forming a series of nominally independent companies, and to limit the L&GR to its original objective, as this offered a better chance of success than would a project similar to the Kentish Railway, which attempted to obtain an Act and raise capital for the whole line in one effort. The L&GR was nevertheless the London end, and the most expensive portion, of a more ambitious plan.

On 10 October 1833 a call of £3 per share was made, and the first payment of interest was announced on fully paid shares; this caused some surprise in financial circles since the company was a long way from earning any revenue, but it was provided for

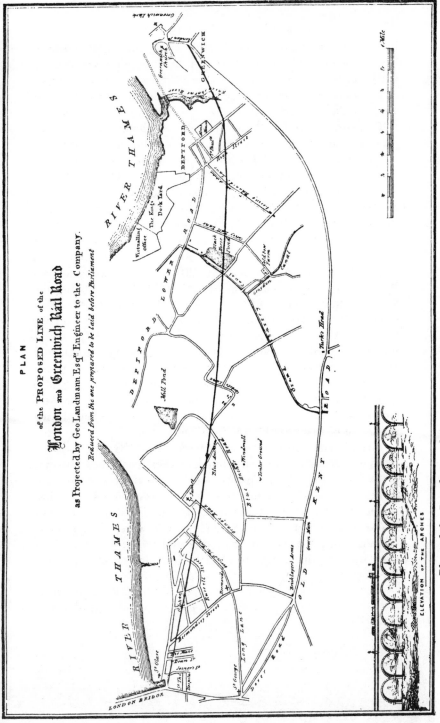

Plan of the London and Greenwich Railway from the prospectus of 1832

in the Act. The company had established an office at 26, Cornhill in the previous May, and Walter had then engaged the first member of its staff, an office boy at four shillings a week; in October a clerk named Horneman was employed at a salary of a guinea per week to help with the shares.

The strong naval and military element among the trustees, directors and officers of the company is evident in its early years. Landmann, Walter and Dottin all had service connections, the latter having been a Captain in the Life Guards. The Royal Navy was always represented on the board, possibly because of its association with Greenwich and Deptford, but more probably to facilitate the company's dealings with the Admiralty, particularly over the matter of extending the line and running it past the Observatory; it was represented by Rear Admiral William Hall Gage, Capt Cuthbert Daly and Sir William Beatty, who was then Physician to Greenwich Hospital, and had, as a naval surgeon, attended Nelson on board the *Victory* at Trafalgar. Of the other directors, John Milroy and John Twells were both also on the board of Walter's General Annuity Endowment Society; Twells was also a banker of considerable standing, being a partner in Spooner, Attwood & Co. The other partner, Matthias Attwood was the L&GR treasurer, and was an influential member of a great banking family. He had been an MP for many years, and his connection with railways went back at least to 1824, when, during the boom of that year he was treasurer to the projected London & Birmingham, Birmingham & Liverpool and Grand Junction Railways. Robert Johnston, who had been concerned in some of Walter's earlier enterprises, was the wealthy and cultured owner of extensive plantations in the West Indies, and had travelled widely on the Continent; he had visited Moscow while it was still smouldering in 1812. He was, however, soon to leave the board of the L&GR and emigrate to the United States. These were some of the men who were to bring the first trains into London.

Chapter 2

The Construction of the Viaduct

SOON after the Act of Incorporation was obtained a Committee of Works was formed to undertake the work of building the $3\frac{3}{4}$-mile viaduct to carry the railway. It was immediately hampered in its task, however, when an attempt was made by one of the directors, the Rev. James Macdonald, to substitute an iron viaduct for the brick structure planned. Macdonald, in conjunction with an American inventor, had secured a patent in 1831[1] for iron railway bridges in which the railway lines formed part of the general structure, being built into the bridge and helping to support it. A model was delivered to the L&GR offices in June 1833, but George Walter insisted on its removal by Bramah & Sons, who made it. Among the objections to a viaduct on this principle, Landmann and Walter maintained that no estimate within £100,000 could be obtained for its construction, it would cost at least £7,000 annually in painting and maintenance, and that between summer and winter it would expand and contract thirty to forty feet in its four-mile length. A certain amount of unpleasantness arose over the rejection of Macdonald's plan, and he was asked to resign from the board.

Meanwhile the Committee of Works had received in June the first tenders for the supply of bricks. It was originally the intention of the company to build the viaduct itself, but in October the committee recommended that the work should be done by contract. Accordingly, Colonel Landmann prepared an advertisement which appeared on 28 October inviting tenders for the construction of that section of the viaduct near Spa Road, Bermondsey.

By 25 November nine tenders had been received, ranging from £10,895 to £7,560, the latter from a contractor called Richardson.

He seems to have nominated the wrong people as referees, however, for when the railway company consulted them, they reported him as unsatisfactory, and the contract went to the next lowest bidder, Hugh McIntosh of Bloomsbury Square, a 'well known builder of public works'. He had originally quoted £7,980, but reduced the estimate to £7,780 on being granted free wharfage facilities on the banks of the Grand Surrey Canal, and in consideration of his being allowed to lay down a tramroad from there to the 'Boundary Ditch', an open sewer between Bermondsey and Rotherhithe.

This contract with McIntosh was for the actual building of part of the viaduct only, the Company supplying all the materials. In actual fact McIntosh eventually built the whole viaduct, but under several separate contracts. In April 1834, for instance, he secured the contract for the section between the Surrey Canal and the west side of the Ravensbourne for £16,245. He also built the temporary stations used at first, but not the permanent ones.

By purchasing the materials itself, the company obtained them more cheaply by reason of the enormous quantities required, and also ensured that, in the event of several contractors being employed the bricks, sleepers, rails, etc., would be of a uniform specification. The first contract for 12,000 yards of rails went to the British Iron Company in November 1834; they were parallel fifty-pound rails of a type just coming into use, and 12,000 cast iron chairs were required for them.

The company and its solicitor were busy acquiring the land over which the viaduct was to be built, and in November 1833 notices to quit within six months were served on the occupiers of all property between London Bridge and Spa Road. The corporation of the City of London was also notified 'that the company would require a piece of ground at or near London Bridge' – which eventually cost them £7,550. By May 1834 notices had been served on all the tenants down to Deptford. In many cases agreement could not be reached between the company's solicitor and the owners, and the cases were then taken to court. Many owners placed an exaggerated valuation on their property, and some of the cases from Bermondsey were tried at the Town Hall, Borough, on 27 and 28 January 1834; they were generally reduced to about one-half or less of the amount claimed. In all nearly five hundred separate interests were affected by the property along the line, and in the next few months thirty juries were empanelled to hear cases which were disputed.

In December 1833 the directors invited the fourteen-year-old Princess Victoria to perform the ceremony of laying the first brick, and the Duchess of Kent wrote from Kensington Palace accepting the engagement on behalf of her daughter, if the function could be '...delayed until April or May next'. The board agreed, and a special trowel for the occasion was ordered.

In the meantime the materials for the viaduct began to arrive in large quantities, and on 8 February 1834 the Committee of Works made the following report:

On Wednesday last Mr McIntosh's men commenced the work near Corbetts Lane, Rotherhithe, and by Thursday evening the whole of the work was marked out; on Friday the excavations for receiving the foundations of the piers was commenced, and will be proceeded with till the whole shall be completed.

The spectacle of hundreds of men digging holes in the ground appears to have had as strong a fascination for Londoners of the early nineteenth century as it has today, for thousands gathered daily to watch the contractor's men excavating the foundations of the viaduct. Unfortunately owing to the illness of Princess Victoria, the royal ceremony never took place. Instead, the first brick of the great viaduct was laid in the open country near Corbetts Lane on 4 April 1834 by Colonel Landmann himself, at a small ceremony of which no account has survived.

The viaduct was started near Corbetts Lane as this point was somewhere near the centre of the line, and no demolition work was necessary in the area. It was also near to the Surrey Canal, at which point the bricks and other materials were being accumulated. The grey bricks used for the arches were of very good quality, and were sent up by the bargeload from the Kentish brickfields near Sittingbourne. The company was soon using bricks by the million, and a short while after the work had begun their price rose in the London area owing to a temporary shortage caused by the demands of the railway. Within a few weeks 400 men were at work on the viaduct, and 100,000 bricks were being laid daily.

In fact more bricks were going into the Greenwich Railway viaduct than had ever before gone into a single piece of work, and the company was purchasing them in 1834 at about thirty-

four shillings a thousand; it paid two shillings a square yard for
the immense quantities of cement that were also being used. At
the same time it was selling large quantities of old building
material from the demolished houses.

Once building operations started, it was essential to obtain
possession of some property quickly, and the engineer and other
officers of the company were exposed on several occasions to the
risk of violence from groups of occupiers who objected to moving
when required to do so. Walter mentions the difficulties encountered in Bermondsey in '... superintending the plans of laying out the line of road through the most horrible and disgusting
part of the metropolis, and during the period when the cholera
was raging in that particular neighbourhood'.[2]

A contemporary description of the works appeared in a letter
published in the *Greenwich Gazette* of 10 May 1834, from a
correspondent who signed himself 'Common Sense'.[3] 'It's a fine
evening,' said his wife after tea, 'let us take a view of the Greenwich Rail-road works'; whereupon they wandered down Penny
Bundle Lane, between the hedgerows of rural Deptford, to the
accompaniment of the nightingale's song, in the direction of the
canal. Here they saw the '... barges waiting to be unladen; large
masses of bricks, sheds, train roads, small waggons, and, in the
distance near St Helena Gardens, this undertaking in progress'.
The writer supposed that the parallel lines, twelve paces apart
and cut in the turf, marked the course of the railway, but was at
first puzzled by the sight of the transverse pits, five paces by
eleven and several feet deep; they were all full of water from the
swampy ground. On discovering that loads of shingle, lime and
cement were shot into these pits, and that these materials, com-
bining with the water, formed an enormous concrete block for
the foundation of a pier, he was filled with admiration at the
brilliance of the engineer. For a disinterested, and somewhat
bewildered layman, the writer displayed an astonishing familiar-
ity with technical data in concluding his letter with a few remarks
on the tractive effort developed by the engine *Victory* on the
Liverpool & Manchester Railway.

In the spring and summer of 1834 work went on rapidly in
the country near Corbetts Lane, to the east of which point about
a hundred piers had been erected by May. These must have
presented a curious appearance, since they were merely plain
brick walls, parallel to each other and about eighteen feet apart,

stretching away in a straight line for about a mile. By September the arches between fifty-two of them had been completed.

At the end of 1834 there were two separate stretches of the viaduct built, one on each side of the Surrey Canal, and in January 1835 the skew bridge over the canal itself was built.

A curious provision of the Act of 1833[4] empowered certain local parish committees to suggest alternative plans to those of the engineer for bridges across roads in their areas. The viaduct was brought up to, and left standing, here and there at a road, while these committees and their surveyors considered the relative merits of brick, stone and iron bridges. A writer in the *Railway Magazine* of October 1835 suggested that the committees might consider bridging the gaps left in the viaduct by attaching balloons to the trains and floating them across.

The iron bridges demanded of the company over Bermondsey Street and High Street, Deptford, caused some delay owing to the slow delivery of the parts from the foundry at Dudley. In August 1836 some ironwork was on the ground, but the rest was still on the road from the midlands. The Bermondsey bridge was not completed until December 1836, and caused the postponement of the opening to London Bridge by six weeks.

The engineer and contractor encountered considerable difficulties in places from the very swampy nature of the soil; it was reported that '... such is the nature of the ground upon which the contractors have to erect their buttresses, that in many places there is as much brickwork below the surface of the ground as there is above'.[5] So bad was the ground in winter that it was almost impassable except on horseback, and Walter, who spent most of his time on the works, kept two or three horses for this purpose alone. It was also found desirable to make liberal donations to the men employed on the works at this time to encourage them in their exertions.

Many of the hundreds of labourers employed by McIntosh were Irishmen, and large-scale fights used to break out at weekends between them and his English employees in the neighbourhood near London Bridge, where they lodged. This led to their segregation, and a small L-shaped alley off Battle Bridge Lane, Tooley Street, still bears the name 'English Ground', bestowed upon it at that time; 'Irish Ground' is a short distance away.[6]

Progress was checked by the very severe winter of 1834-5, heavy gales delaying the delivery of bricks by river, but by 4

April 1835, exactly a year after the first brick had been laid, 422 piers had been built. By July there were 500 piers, including about 300 upon which arches had been built. A single line was by that time in position over the finished section, and labourers were busily hauling up baskets of gravel ballast by rope and pulley along the structure. Mid-September saw the completion of 540 arches, and the single track extended over two miles of viaduct; six hundred men were engaged upon the work at this time.

The comparison between the London & Greenwich Railway and an ancient Roman aqueduct was first drawn by a member of the Clarence Club, who had seen one of the pictures of the railway lying on the table in the clubroom; the impression persisted for many years, and in Gilbert's *Railways of England* of 1839, the resemblance between the railway and the viaduct of Segovia is mentioned.

Throughout the summer of 1835 bricks were being accumulated along the banks of the Ravensbourne in readiness for the commencement of the section between Deptford and Greenwich. Work on this end of the viaduct began in October 1835, nearly all the ground having already been cleared. In the autumn of 1835 it was still hoped that the railway would be open for traffic by the Christmas of that year.

About this time a man named Finch claimed, at the local Petty Sessions, that his property[7] had been forcibly entered by 'a great number of workmen', who had the company's authority to 'oppose force by force'. McIntosh's foreman intimated to Finch that he could bring up another 500 men if necessary. It was claimed that compensation of £3,170 was outstanding, but the magistrate pointed out that the company was entitled to possession by Act of Parliament, and that compensation would be paid afterwards. Actually it had been settled some time before the case was heard, and no damages were awarded against the company.

The first arch to be occupied was one near Corbetts Lane, let by Walter to a Mr Smith in May 1834 for £30 per annum. This was probably the first arch to be completed, since the work had only been going on for a month. The directors had other plans for the arches, however, and at a board meeting on 7 June they resolved to fit up one of them as a dwelling house. Although the idea of houses in a railway viaduct may seem a little odd now, the scheme was not an unreasonable one then.[8] It was a plan to provide accommodation for the families whose houses had been demolished to make way for the railway, and whilst the company was under no obligation to rehouse the people concerned, it could have done so to its own advantage, and to the advantage of those who had been accustomed to the squalor of Bermondsey.

It was not until 1835 that two demonstration houses were completed in the viaduct at Deptford, a few arches to the west of the station. Each house had six rooms, and they were described as being small, but neat and comfortable; their natural resemblance to a row of caves was concealed behind their square, plastered fronts which faced on to the south footpath. The cottages were lit by gas, and the rooms were heated by gas stoves; there was also some form of gas cooker provided. This extensive use of gas was not so much for the convenience of the occupiers as for that of the passengers above, who would otherwise have been annoyed by the smoke issuing from a row of chimney-pots along the line; incidentally, gas did not come into general use for cooking until some forty years later.

On 12 March 1836 George Walter let one of the cottages for £20 a year. It did not prove easy to let the rest, however, and in February 1837 it was stated that '... the speculation has failed, for it was found that no sooner does a heavy shower fall than the water filters through the crown of the arches'. What happened to the people who had to move to make way for the railway is not recorded, but they certainly did not go to live beneath it.

The board decided in November 1837 that, as the cost of keeping the gas constantly burning in the cottages was very great, it should be discontinued, and that they should be closed. By February 1839 it appears from a report to the directors that only one house was then tenanted, and that as a beershop.

The company had received an offer of several thousand pounds for the whole of the arches, which would then have been sub-let, but the offer was unwisely declined on the grounds that they could more profitably be let separately; this supposition proved to be false, and there was never any noticeable enthusiasm on the part of the business men of the time to acquire these premises, partly owing to the noise set up by the trains travelling frequently over the stone-sleepered track above. By October 1839 about fifteen were occupied as shops and storehouses between Bermondsey Street and Dean Street, near London Bridge, and by 1842 only fifty-two had been let out of about 850 available.

An early printed form of agreement for the letting of an arch provides for the tenant to '...fit up and enclose the said arch from the Railway Path at his own expense...', and to keep the interior in good repair; the standard rent, printed on the form, had been reduced to £7 per annum.

The arches were linked together, usually in pairs, by small transverse arches which could be bricked up if necessary. It seems, however, that many of the tenants did not stay long enough to warrant their taking much trouble to install fittings in the arches, merely renting one for a short period for some particular purpose. Thus the *Morning Herald* of 1 August 1835 reported that some had been taken for 'houses of entertainment', whatever that rather general term might imply, and in August 1836 the large arch which crossed Parish Street near Bermondsey New Church, was used for the exhibition of a 'Travelling Hop Garden'. What must have been an unusually interesting auction was held in Arch No 55, near Crucifix Lane, London Bridge, on 9 June 1843,[9] when two nearly new locomotives built by Rennie were offered for sale. It has not been discovered who they were built for, or by whom they were bought, but they had nothing to do with the L&GR. Long before the trains started running overhead, another arch had been successfully converted and let; this establishment, The Half Way House, is still discernible, but is no longer a public house.

Southwark, being the most convenient part of London for the delivery and storage of Kentish hops, had long been the centre of the trade. With a view to encouraging the transport of hops by train when the South Eastern and Brighton lines had been completed, the London & Greenwich Railway, in 1836, proposed to remove the Hop Market to the arches of the viaduct near London Bridge. These were either too damp or not large enough, however, for soon afterwards a large warehouse was built adjoining the viaduct on the north side, with its frontage in the Maze.

A feature of the original Greenwich Railway was the roadway and gravel footpath to run parallel to the viaduct, and on each side of it, from end to end. This road was to serve the dual purpose of providing access to the arches and of being a fashionable thoroughfare; at a toll of 1d per person, a considerable revenue was expected by the company. The idea of these footpaths was probably suggested by the 'Halfpenny Hatch', a similar toll-footpath in the neighbourhood,[10] which is said to have produced £5,000 a year. The company had at one time intended to reserve the north side for carriages and the south side for the 'esplanade', but there seems to have been some difficulty in coming to a decision, for the matter was still in doubt in 1836.

The first section of the footpath was opened to the public on 4 September 1834, from Corbetts Lane to Deptford; six months later an ornamental arched entrance to the Deptford end was built. This was on the south side of the viaduct; the road on the other side was, for the time being, reserved for the transport of materials used in building the viaduct, and a temporary tramroad was laid along part of it.

As further stretches of the viaduct were completed the road was made up, sometimes on one side, and sometimes on both, and saplings were planted at regular intervals. It was bounded on the outside by a row of shrubs and small bushes, and at intervals there were signboards indicating the way to London and to Greenwich.

The original pathway was two or three feet below ground level, and gave the viaduct a more lofty appearance than it presents today. It was found, however, that persons using this sunken footpath could not see over the top of the boundary wall, which replaced the hedge of shrubs, and that in consequence it was not so popular as had been anticipated. Colonel Landmann arranged to pay one shilling a load for rubbish to be shot on to the path to raise its height, and said that he expected before long that these persons would be willing to pay the railway at the same rate for permission to dump their rubbish on its property.

A special general meeting of the shareholders was held at the City of London Tavern on 21 November 1835 to discuss the question of raising a loan to meet the cost of land purchased in excess of the actual requirements of the company for its viaduct. A clause[11] was inserted in the Bill of 1833 compelling the company to purchase the whole of any property on the line of the railway, if required by the owners to do so, even if only a small part were needed. The company possessed many such plots adjoining the line, and the directors were of the opinion that the value of this land, estimated at £90,000, would appreciate considerably once the railway was working. If, then, they could raise sufficient money to enable them to retain the land, they could sell it at a great profit later.

This meeting also considered the cost of building the railway. The original estimate had, by the end of 1835, been exceeded by £37,000, and this was attributed by Landmann to the fact that '... every possible depredation is committed on the company's property'; trees were uprooted from the boulevard, the quickset hedge forming its outer boundary was destroyed as soon as it was planted, and a band of watchmen had to be employed to protect the works and locomotives. 'Indeed,' he added, 'the first machine had hardly been placed upon the railway before attempts were made to injure it.' The receipts from the footpath had by that time totalled £600, but the cost of policing it and the works had been over £800. Where the railway ran through pasture land, a paling fence, five-feet high, with 8ft five-bar gates was erected at first, but this did not prove satisfactory, and eventually it was decided to build a brick wall four feet high along the whole length of the footpath, at a cost of £20,000.

A printed report of the meeting of 21 November was sent out to the shareholders, and included with it was a copy of the engineer's report of 18 November 1835. In this report, Colonel Landmann stated that 4,000 yards of the line was finished, 1,800 yards not yet started, and the rest (about 800 yards) in course of construction; 660 arches had been finished, and about 240 remained to be built. Deptford and London Bridge stations and inclined planes, the arches over the canal, and all other expensive works had been completed.[12] It was to be discovered later that the expensive works were by no means finished, and the stations at Deptford and London Bridge were not the permanent ones.

At ten-past-seven on Sunday evening, 18 January 1836, the neighbourhood of Bermondsey and Tooley Street was aroused by the crash of the last two arches falling in at the unfinished end of the viaduct. The work here had been held up pending the demolition of some old houses that stood in the path of the railway, and on the previous day the workmen had removed the shoring from the end arch to make room for a stack of bricks. No injury or loss of life resulted, but this may not have been the case had the collapse taken place a few hours later, for it was the practice of boys and men who were too poor to obtain lodgings to sleep at night beneath the viaduct. The newspapers on the following day reported the incident under headlines announcing that the Greenwich Viaduct was falling down.

In February 1836 the line between Spa Road, Bermondsey, and

Deptford was opened, but at the London end the works went forward slowly during 1836 for a number of reasons. In the first place, the materials required had to be brought up from the canal, now 1¼ miles distant from the actual building operations. At London Bridge itself there was some difficulty in constructing the inclined plane as this had to be carried over the old Flemish Burial Ground. The Act of 1833 had stipulated that this should be done by one single arch to be constructed without any piers resting on the burial ground itself. It was found to be impracticable to make one arch, however, and after some delay an agreement was entered into between the company and the parishes on 28 March 1836, under which the approach was to be built on a series of arches. The railway undertook to provide free access to the vaults and graves, and to allow burials to continue, on the understanding that any digging which had to be done should be performed well away from the piers supporting the arches. Many years later disputes were still occurring over this piece of ground; ultimately the company paid the expenses of providing a new burial ground for the two parishes at Snow's Fields nearby, and of the removal thereto in 1842 of all the remains buried in the old ground.

In 1836 the company found itself with its capital sunk largely in surplus property, and at the same time faced with a debt of £20,138 owing to McIntosh. The contractor, reasonably enough, required some security before proceeding with the work, and deeds of property worth £40,000 were lodged with him under a Deed of Security on 2 July 1836. The value of the surplus land did not appreciate noticeably, however, and the nearer it was to the line, the less desirable it seemed to be. Early in 1839 the company decided to sell the spare ground it did not expect to need for any future widening of the line.

Rumours about the instability of the viaduct were started in 1837, and the board asked James Walker, then engineer to the Kent Railway, to make a report. Walker, accompanied by Colonel Landmann, surveyed the line in August 1837, and his opinion was that, whilst the railway was not perfect, few such works were. As the board had pressed Landmann to hurry on the work, some of it had suffered, and about a mile of the viaduct had not yet been pointed. Some of the arches were not properly curved, and four had been so unsymmetrical that they had been taken down and rebuilt. He added that several more had been fitted with iron tie-bars from wall to wall, and that the arcade under London Bridge station leaked badly. Like those of most other railways, the cast-iron chairs were too light and thin, and in consequence the rails were loose through many of the chairs having broken, causing much clattering and rattle as the trains passed over them. He did not like the stone sleepers, and recommended that they should be replaced by wooden ones. Walker considered the viaduct to be quite safe, however, and remarked upon the boldness of the company and its engineer in undertaking a work of such proportions.

There was about a mile of the viaduct at the London Bridge end which had been filled in with loose rubble instead of concrete, and it was here that the transverse tie-bars referred to in Walker's report were used, after the brickwork had settled down and several cracks had appeared in the structure. Colonel Landmann reported in November 1837 that 293 arches had been secured in this way, and that a further twenty-three needed attention. No doubt the knowledge that these precautions were being taken gave rise to some of the rumours about the viaduct in the first place. The company did not worry unduly about the broken chairs reported by Walker, but steps were taken to replace them in April 1838, after Hayton, the Inspector, had found 987 broken ones between London Bridge and Deptford, and had reported to the board on the state of the line.

Walker's report was printed and a copy sent off quickly to each shareholder. This appears to have settled any doubts that might still have been entertained about the safety of the viaduct, but behind the recommendation that wooden sleepers be substituted for the stone ones employed lies the clue to the whole trouble. In another pamphlet which came out at about the same time as the Report, *An Exposure of the Costly Fallacies of Rail-Road Engineering . . .*, the only fault that the writer could find with the London & Greenwich Railway was that '. . . the rails shake loose with a solid arch beneath them'. Shortly afterwards the company decided to use no more stone blocks.

The use of granite blocks instead of wooden sleepers was not by any means confined to the L&GR; they were used almost exclusively on the Grand Junction, Clarence, Leeds & Selby, Newcastle & Carlisle, and Stockton & Darlington Railways, whilst among others, the North Union and London & Birmingham Companies used them extensively.

Many engineers favoured stone on the grounds of economy, for granite blocks were virtually indestructible, whilst the absence of any reliable system of treating timber to prevent decay meant the frequent renewal of wooden sleepers. The process known as 'Kyanizing', described at the time as the impregnating of the wood with a solution of arsenic, was only just being introduced in the late 1830s; this was an expensive and untried method, but it became widely used later.

Nevertheless, the cost was enormous; the L&GR paid 12s 6d each for granite blocks of four cubic feet volume, having decided against the employment of Portland and artificial stone at 5s 4d and 7s per block respectively. The immense quantities required – it was estimated that the London & Birmingham alone needed three quarters of a million – led to the search for substitutes, and in December 1836 a Mr Thomas Parkin of Dudley, lecturing to the Southwark Literary Institution, described his plan for substituting 'vitrified earth' for granite. His system provided a continuous bed which supported, in a groove, a wooden bearer on which the rail was mounted. The report[13] states that '...he had been allowed to try his system upon a part of the London & Greenwich railroad, and with complete success' – and also at half the cost at which the company had laid its line with granite blocks. In a letter he refers to the railway laid down in Duke Street, London Bridge during October 1836; how he came to get permission to lay it in a public street is not clear, unless it is a reference to a part of the Greenwich Railway footpath near Duke Street.

On most of the lines where stone blocks had been laid down, they were set in the earth; on the L&GR they rested directly on the brickwork of the arches (except where it was necessary to have a layer of sand below to bring them up to the correct level), and all the vibration set up by the trains was transmitted straight to the viaduct. Equally serious was the damage caused to rails, chairs, wheels and axles by the rigidity of the track, and the discomfort caused to the passengers travelling over it. Loch, writing in 1839, compared the smoothness of the Belgian Railways (which had, no doubt, profited from the experience of the English ones), with '...that thumping which distinguishes the Greenwich as well as the Liverpool Railway'.[14]

It was originally thought that the blocks alone, surrounded with ballast, would be sufficient to preserve the gauge, and no transverse ties were provided. This proved not to be the case, however, and on 14 January 1837, within a month of the opening, the board ordered that the spaces between the blocks and the parapet wall be filled with concrete, which had the effect of making the permanent way part of the viaduct itself.

In 1838 it was decided that the unfinished part of the line beyond Deptford should be laid on wood, although the Company had already bought the 26,000 granite blocks required for the whole line. The Eastern Counties Railway purchased 1,000 in 1838 at about half their original price, but hundreds were left lying between Deptford and Greenwich for a long time after the viaduct was finished. Between 1840 and 1842 the London Bridge-Deptford section was relaid and all the old stone blocks taken up. These were piled in great stacks on the banks of the Ravens-bourne and by the side of the Surrey Canal until, in June 1842, 20,000 were bought by the London & South Western Railway for £2,225, delivered 'under the crane at Nine Elms'. Several thousands remained, however, and occasionally shareholders would ask why they had been taken up, as stone sleepers were still being used on the Birmingham and London & Brighton Railways. In fact they have not all disappeared yet, for some may still be seen near the road bridge which crosses the ends of the platforms at New Cross Gate Station.

After the partial opening of the railway, the apparent neglect on the part of the company to finish the works to Greenwich was contrasted in the press with the scenes of activity a few months before on the main section of the viaduct.[15] Despite the company's promise in May 1836 that the line would be completed from London Bridge to Greenwich within three months, given good weather, two-and-a-half years were to pass before it was actually finished.

After long negotiations with the Turnpike Trustees, Landmann's designs for a single-span iron bridge to cross Deptford High Street at right-angles was agreed upon. By January 1838 the side walls of the bridge were built, and the cast-iron pillars were on the ground in readiness; soon afterwards the bridge was erected by a Mr Harvey for £100, after McIntosh had lowered the road under a separate contract. Like the bridge at Bermondsey Street, it was of cast-iron girder construction, supported by six cast-iron doric columns on each side in a row by the edge of the pavement.

The track across Bermondsey Street Bridge was carried on 12in by 12in oak longitudinal sleepers, but over Deptford High Street it was laid on large flat stones, since this was thought by experience to be a better method than the former. A wooden screen high enough to hide the chimney-tops of the locomotives was erected on each side of the Deptford bridge, to prevent horses in the street below being frightened by the sight of the trains;[16] its unsightliness was contrasted with the 'light, handsome iron railing' on the Bermondsey Street Bridge.

The bridging of the Ravensbourne, although the stream was but a few yards wide, proved to be another problem which took years to solve. The company was permitted under its Act to build a fixed bridge only if it had the consent of all the occupiers of wharves and quays to do so. If it failed to obtain such consent, then a swivel-bridge or a drawbridge was to be built. In June 1835 the railway abandoned an amended Bill it had prepared concerning the Ravensbourne bridge, and it had then to rely upon obtaining the consent of the parties interested, as it wished to avoid the trouble and expense of a movable bridge. The consent was not forthcoming, however, and the company, believing that no swivel-bridge would be firm enough, discussed the possibility of tunnelling beneath the river. The question then remained in abeyance for over a year, and when it arose again in August 1836 a firm known as Kingsford & Co unsuccessfully sought an injunction to restrain the railway from building any kind of bridge.

The Ravensbourne crossing affected the whole of the works between Deptford and Greenwich, for until it was decided whether to go above or below the stream it was not advisable to erect the Deptford High Street bridge, or complete the viaduct.

Colonel Landmann was instructed by the board on 17 September 1836 to give his immediate attention to the question of the bridge, and '... to ascertain the mode of crossing the River and the Canal between Brussels and Antwerp, which is reported to the Directors to be both cheap and permanent'. A drawbridge was eventually decided upon, and so far as can be traced there was at that time no similar structure in existence on an English railway.[17]

Even when the bridge had been designed, further delay was caused by the difficulty of providing machinery to work it. In the meantime the construction of the line from Deptford was proceeding rapidly, and during March and April 1838 most of the arches up to Blue Stile, Greenwich, had been built behind a screen of old houses, which were then pulled down to make room for Greenwich Station.

Towards the end of November the bridge was at last finished, and it was described at that time as consisting of two arches, one of which was a drawbridge of 26 feet span, and the other a wooden arch. The drawbridge opened in the middle, each part being lifted slowly by a crab, and strong sliding rods steadied it at the top, making the whole structure very firm. Each of the flaps was balanced by counterweights hanging from chains over pulleys, and the mechanism is said to have required eight men to work it.[18] By some extraordinary oversight the lifting machinery fouled the line by projecting one inch too much on either side; this was not discovered until the directors made an inspection of the line, and their special train was held up while the ironwork was 'filed away'.

A separate lifting footbridge on the south side of the viaduct carried the footpath across the Ravensbourne; it replaced a temporary wooden bridge forming part of the footpath, which was erected in April 1838, and there was an even earlier foot-bridge opened in December 1836, and used by 'many thousands' on Christmas Day.

A Deptford Creek toll bridge had existed for years before the railway came but, as the railway footpath provided the shortest and most direct way to Greenwich, few people used the old bridge after the footpath was opened. The bridge company, fore-seeing this, had secured a clause in the railway company's Bill for compensation. In 1837 the third Greenwich Railway Act,[19] which dealt entirely with the Creek Bridge, was passed, under which the railway had to pay the bridge company the difference between its total annual receipts and £2,325, its former average yearly income. The railway company was in turn empowered to charge a one-penny toll for the use of its footbridge.

The first rails used on the Greenwich line, those between London Bridge and Deptford, were $\bot$-section; the surface width was only $1\frac{1}{4}$ inches, since the distance between the outer edges of the rails was 4ft 11in. These rails were secured by wedges to cast-iron chairs, 9in by $4\frac{1}{2}$in, the chairs were fixed by four-inch iron spikes driven into oak plugs in the stone sleepers, and felt pads were fitted between the chair and the stone block.[20]

Soon after the railway was opened it was reported that the rails used in the western half were of good quality and had suffered little wear and tear; from about 1½ miles east of London Bridge, however, there was '. . . a change for the worse in the manufacture, or welding of the iron, and considerable defects already appear in many of them'. The company therefore decided to adopt a heavier rail for the Deptford–Greenwich section, in view of the many breakages that had occurred on the older part of the line, and reversible rails of 85lb per yard were used there. This rail became standard for the whole railway when the original line was relaid.

On 4 September 1838 four directors, Miller, the new L&GR engineer, and Fox, the resident engineer of the London & Birmingham Railway, went down the line to examine the works, particularly the laying of the rails on wooden sleepers between Deptford and the Ravensbourne

. . . when their attention was forcibly directed by Mr Fox to the circumstances of the sleepers being laid longitudinally as well as transversely instead of the latter mode alone, which is the proper one. Mr Fox assured the Directors that the London & Birmingham Railway Company had tried the former method and were necessitated to abandon it and take the rails up again. Colonel Landmann . . . observed that the late Board of Directors had so ordered contrary to his own opinion, and as a proof of this he said he was now constructing a railroad in the North of England of some considerable extent[21] which he was laying on transverse sleepers . . .

A week later Landmann reported that he had inspected the tracks of the London & Birmingham and Great Western Railways, but could see no advantage in altering the London & Greenwich sleepers, since the expense had already been incurred. He also pointed out that trains would not run at high speed between Deptford and Greenwich, and the board thereupon ordered the work to continue.

Some years later Landmann described the Deptford–Greenwich line as being laid on the GWR principle,[22] with 12in by 12in longitudinal timbers spiked on to 10in by 6in cross sleepers, the latter about four feet apart. The gauge was maintained by iron ties, and the track was ballasted to a depth of two feet. Bridge rails were used on part of this section, and on 2 March 1838 McIntosh was trying to obtain from 'Mr Brunnell' the rails for completing the line. It is very doubtful if Brunel would have been in a position to supply rails to the London & Greenwich, or any other railway, in March 1838, since a delay of several months in the delivery of rails to the GWR itself was retarding the progress of that line.

When finally completed in 1838, the viaduct consisted of 878 arches,[23] most of which were of 18ft span; they were 28ft wide and 22ft high. The only gradients were 1 in 756 and 1 in 1232, near Spa Road on the London Bridge side. Distance-posts, marked in large figures, were placed at quarter-mile intervals.

Parapet walls 23in thick, 4ft 6in high and 3ft 2in from the rail, ran the whole length of the line on both sides, and as the space between the line and the wall was purposely made so small, recesses were placed at every twelfth arch, into which the policemen, platelayers and others could retire. In several of these recesses 'sentry boxes' for the signalmen were erected, and in these was kept 'certain apparatus to raise up the wheels of the carriages in the event of any unforeseen casualty'.[24]

Colonel Landmann had not decided upon the best method of drainage when the viaduct was planned and consequently, when finished, the structure had two distinct systems with minor modifications in some places. In the stretch of line eastwards from Spa Road an open brick surface drain was built into the bed of the viaduct along the centre of the 6ft space between the tracks; the water from this was discharged down vertical drains built into the large piers, and ran out through holes in the base of these piers. In the western portion, which was built a little later, the rain was carried off by small transverse drains to the end of each pier, and this method, proving to be the more satisfactory, was eventually adopted. In order to protect the arches from the rain, those beyond Deptford were asphalted before the permanent way was laid.

Landmann departed on a number of occasions from the provisions of the Act. His Bermondsey Street Bridge was of two thirty-foot spans instead of one span of sixty feet, and his rails were of $1\frac{1}{4}$-inch tread instead of $2\frac{1}{4}$-inch. He also ignored the clause requiring crossings every half-mile, as he thought this number unnecessary and dangerous.

Considering that Colonel Landmann had had no opportunity of observing the effect of running a railway on a brickwork viaduct until his own plans had, at considerable trouble and vast expense, been carried out, it is remarkable that the venture proved as successful as it did. From the engineering point of view, there was the one serious weakness arising from the decision to employ granite blocks and this led to endless trouble until the line was relaid. The unsuitability of these blocks did not become apparent until over two miles of the line had been laid with them, and the trains started running. Even then it was not immediately realised that the loose and broken rails and fractured axles and wheels were largely caused by these blocks. Gradually, too, the vibration transmitted to the viaduct itself began to affect the brickwork, particularly that of the drain running between the two lines of rails, and the water which it should have carried away seeped instead between the loosened bricks to dampen the arches below. By this time it was too late to remedy the situation without taking up the track and delaying the final opening of the railway.

Chapter 3

The Opening of the Railway

I T W A S the original intention of the company in 1833 to build and open the L&GR for traffic by Easter 1835, but if this proved to be impossible, to open the section between Spa Road and Deptford then, and to finish the ends of the line afterwards.[1] Locomotives and carriages had been ordered in good time, and in the summer of 1834 it seemed quite possible that at least the partial opening would take place.

The railway was in fact opened to visitors in July 1834, and its first income was derived from the pence they paid for being allowed on the works to watch the building operations, and to walk along the top of the completed length of viaduct. A few months later the first engine and a number of carriages were exhibited in some of the arches and earned the company a small sum before they even turned a wheel. The company seems to have realised early the value of encouraging the public to take an interest in railways and their equipment, and direction boards were erected at various places showing the way to the gates for genuine visitors. There were also the familiar notices against trespassing, and it is of interest to note that the cost of engaging in this pursuit remained steady at forty shillings until 1965.

In July 1834 the company's first superintendent, a Mr Twaddle, was appointed at £50 a year. As at that time there was hardly any line to superintend, his job was that of guide to the visitors, for it was he who received the admission fees, and the few shillings arising from the sale of peat excavated by McIntosh's men.

Announcing the arrival of the first locomotive in February 1835, the *Public Ledger*[2] stated that many thousands visited Manchester and Liverpool from London and elsewhere solely to ride on the railway; the people of London would soon be able to satisfy their curiosity without going two hundred miles to do so, however, as it was expected that the Greenwich Railway would be open by Easter. The company itself still hoped in March to start a service between Bermondsey and Deptford the following month, and an extra 150 men were taken on to hurry the work forward; it was found to be quite impossible to complete even this portion of the line in so short a period, however, after the delays that had occurred. Instead, crowds from Greenwich fair swarmed over the viaduct on Easter Monday, complaining afterwards that having paid sixpence and walked a long distance down the line, they had either to climb down a narrow ladder or retrace their steps.[3]

On Easter Sunday nearly ten thousand people walked along 'the London & Greenwich Mall', and about £50 was taken in tolls. Soon the fame of this footpath had spread to different parts of the Empire. A Calcutta newspaper informed its readers that '... the south side of the Greenwich Railway is planted with various forest trees, and forms a delightful walk for the citizens of London.' The reason for this slight exaggeration was rather more obvious than the trees were; a railway was being promoted in India at the time by Walter – the Calcutta & Saugor Railway.

During 1835 the progress of the railway was followed with keen interest by the general press and by the technical journals. *The Times* was a strong supporter of the London & Greenwich Railway, and the *Mechanic's Magazine* made regular reference to the progress of the undertaking. The company naturally had no control over the editorial policy of these papers, and this led it to found the most famous of all early railway publications. *The Railway Magazine*, or *Herapath* as it soon came to be called, was first issued in May 1835 as part of a campaign being waged by George Walter to maintain the value of the company's shares, and he wrote later that 'the establishment of the Railway Magazine cost me upwards of £100.' The first volume was dedicated to 'Abel Rous Dottin, Chairman of the London & Greenwich Railway', and contained a good reproduction of the very fine print of the railway near Corbetts Lane; the title page carried the company's motto – *vires acquirit eundo*.[4]

The original *Railway Magazine* ran for ten months, and then started again with 'Volume 1, New Series' in March, 1836 under the editorship of John Herapath.

During the summer of 1835 hundreds of people climbed Nun-head Hill, then quite pastoral, to obtain a view of the whole length of the line. There can be no doubt that the viaduct, parti-cularly when new, was an impressive sight, although the London end of it could not be distinguished, being lost in a maze of small streets and alleys. In August 1835 it was still possible for a writer to say of the Greenwich Railway arches: 'The country which they overlook is very rich, and is almost wholly laid out in vegetable gardens. These will probably disappear ere long before the en-croachments of brick and mortar...' Only a few years were to elapse before his prophecy was fulfilled, although the last market garden in Deptford lingered on until the 1920s.

On Whit Monday, 8 June 1835, the first experimental trains were run between Corbetts Lane and the Grand Surrey Canal, a distance of three quarters of a mile. These trials were held to test the viaduct and track, and to run in the locomotives and carriages; they also served to familiarise the public with railway travel, and, as a subsidiary object, to enable vibration tests to be conducted on behalf of the proposed Greenwich & Gravesend Railway whose line would have passed near the delicate instru-ments in the Observatory.

No charge was made to travel on the trains, and such was the fame of many who gathered round the viaduct at that time that it became fashionable to be seen on the railway. For a few weeks in the summer ladies made up parties to ride in the carriages, although Lady Hardy could not persuade Nelson's old friend to venture into one; Sir Thomas declined to go at any price, saying it was a needless risk to run.[5] The trials were made at weekends for the general public, and on Thursdays for the more distin-guished guests – Sir John Rennie, Professor Airy the astronomer, Charles Babbage the mathematician and Mr Toplis, vice-presi-dent of the London Mechanics' Institution and the inventor of an early machine-gun were guests of the company. Groups of foreign visitors, members of the Society of Friends and parties of Cambridge scientists all found their way there, as did several MPs, the Swedish ambassador and the Prince of Orange and suite. There were always some directors and shareholders in attendance.

As more track was laid the trials extended to the Blue Anchor Road, Bermondsey, but they were brought to an abrupt end on 12 November, when the first accident occurred. The incident was reported in *John Bull*,[6] a periodical notoriously hostile to the railways, on the following Sunday.

The loss of life upon the favourite toy from Liverpool to Manchester has already been terrific. Mr Huskisson was the first martyr to this favourite absurdity; and the last splendid exhibition took place only on Thursday, upon the new Tom-foolery to Greenwich, when in the outset 'by some accident', one of the carriages, in which a party of noodles ventured themselves, was thrown off the rail, but although it ran a vast many yards, no serious accident occurred. How lucky! Nobody killed the first day of trial!

The derailment was the result of a broken axle, and was the first of many from the same cause over the years. Landmann said afterwards that it was the axletree of the engine that had fractured, and that he was glad that the occurrence had taken place, since it demonstrated that '... the engine could get off the lines without any injury being produced thereby'.

Some modifications were made to the engines and carriages after the accident and the trials were resumed on 18 January 1836 when vibration tests were made with instruments placed at the end of Glebe Meadow to measure the effects of running an engine, tender and six carriages over the arches.[7] A month later the line was partially opened.

After the L&GR had been authorised, several other companies had been formed to construct railways that were to join it; these are considered later, but may be briefly mentioned here; they were the London & Croydon, Deptford Pier & Junction, Westminster Bridge & Deptford, and London & Gravesend.

The progress of these four companies during the year 1835 affected the development and completion of the L&GR itself, for their affairs were all at different stages. The London & Croydon Act was passed on 12 June, and by 12 October the ground at the London end near Corbetts Lane, where it was to join the Greenwich line, had been staked out; the Deptford Pier & Junction and the Westminster Bridge & Deptford, both of which were to join the Greenwich at Deptford Station, had not progressed as far, while the end-on extension of the line from Greenwich to Gravesend was not prospering at all. While the fate of the Bills was in the balance the board could not have the stations at Deptford and Greenwich completed.

The company was naturally anxious to complete and open the line as quickly as possible, since by a combination of the efforts of George Walter and the declared intention of a number of other railway companies to apply for powers to use the Greenwich viaduct, the stock of the company stood high at the end of 1835. However, the L&GR had, at this time, to approach Parliament for powers to raise additional capital, and this would quickly bring about a fall in the value of the shares, if not accompanied by some prospect of the line opening. At the general meeting in November the question of a partial opening early in the New Year was broached, but opinion among the shareholders was divided. Walter was in favour of opening a part of the line as soon as possible, however, and in this he was supported by those who desired their company to have the distinction of being the first to operate in London. The publicity value of being the first railway to run trains in the capital had not escaped Walter, and other lines fast approaching completion might easily have forestalled the London & Greenwich, had its opening been delayed very much longer.

The company's original share capital of £400,000, together with an additional £133,333 which it had raised by mortgaging the viaduct, had practically been spent; this amount of over half-a-million pounds was the total authorised by the first Act, and a further one was necessary before the remaining sum of £150,000, estimated to be the amount required to finish the railway, could be raised. The meeting agreed to the board's proposal that powers should be sought to increase the capital, and the Bill, prepared during 1836, was passed on 8 June 1837.[8]

As the main section of the viaduct was nearing completion some changes among the board and officers of the company took place. On 14 November 1835 Mr Beeby, a director, resigned, and George Walter was appointed resident director. About the same time John Yonge Akerman was appointed secretary, and William Stephenson became clerk of the company. A new superintendent, Lieut Simpson, had already been appointed, and in January 1836 his salary was increased from £70 to £100 per annum.

The decision to open part of the line was taken after the general meeting referred to above, and the first train left Deptford for Spa Road at 8am on Monday 8 February 1836; the event passed almost unnoticed in the press. The *Railway Magazine* of 1836 reported that 'This railway has at length commenced running for pay, though only about $2\frac{1}{4}$ miles in the middle of it, from Deptford to Bermondsey Street, has been finished'. The trains did not run to Bermondsey Street, which is three quarters of a mile nearer to London Bridge, until October 1836; the distance between Deptford and Spa Road was about $2\frac{1}{2}$ miles.

The first timetable, published in various newspapers on 13 February showed 'A Train of the Company's Carriages' starting hourly from Deptford from 8am to 5pm, and from Spa Road from 8.30am on the half-hour, to 5.30pm; the fare was 6d. Among the papers in which the timetable appeared was *Aris's Birmingham Advertiser*; since it could have been of little use to the people of Birmingham, it was evidently a convenient means of informing the company's shareholders in the midlands that their railway was a going concern.

During the first week the line was open passengers amounted to about 700 a day, producing an average daily income of approximately £17. By the second week their numbers had increased to about 1,200, and after the first month's working 20,412 passengers had been carried. As the summer approached the experience of a train ride became more popular; during the second and third months it was open the railway carried 25,465 and 40,492 passengers respectively. The last figure includes 13,000 who travelled on one day alone, Whit Monday, 1836. The London & Greenwich shares reached their highest value in March, being quoted at £32.[9]

The train service was maintained by one engine and three sets of carriages, the engine taking the trains in turn from one end of the line to the other. The second engine appears to have been held in reserve or to have worked on alternate days at first. As there were no signals, and the gas lamps to be erected along the viaduct were not yet in position, the trains did not normally run after dusk. During the first few weeks no trains were running on Sundays, and those who found the footpath rather tame – or too crowded – were allowed to walk along the track on payment of a small charge.

The editor of the *Railway Magazine* asked how the directors, who '... keep up their police, keep men to receive tolls, and to shew the carriages, the arches, the railway etc. for profit on a Sunday, and very properly so, can have any qualms as to allowing an inanimate machine to roll over the railing [sic] on that day for the convenience of the Public.' The reason, as he afterwards discovered was a shortage of locomotives; only one was at work with a seven-carriage train for the Easter Monday traffic.

By May there were at least three engines on the railway, Messrs George Forrester & Co having delivered one about that time, and the trains now ran every half-hour from 8am to 7pm. It was stated that carriages were always in readiness to take passengers from Deptford to Charlton or Woolwich, or from Bermondsey to Town; stabling was available at Deptford for gentlemen coming from the country. A Sunday service started on 29 May, and as it was a fine, moonlit night, the trains ran until 10pm. It was said that '... the directors intend on all occasions to prevent their men being employed during Divine Service on Sundays, as they have engaged two pews at St James's Church, Bermondsey, expressly for their accommodation, and have intimated their wishes, that those who are in their employ should be constant in their attendance at Church.'

The company was confronted with peculiar difficulties in operating its first trains from the very nature of the railway itself. Elevated on a narrow viaduct that could carry only two tracks, the only space available for shunting was at London Bridge and Greenwich, where there was provision for three or four lines, but neither of these were ready when the service started in February 1836. The L&GR, therefore, adopted the system known as 'fly-shunting', which was fairly widespread at the time and had very probably been observed by Landmann or Walter on some of the northern railways. It had the merit of enabling three trains to be worked by one locomotive, and as applied to the Greenwich Railway, it took the following form:

1   Just before the train reached the facing points at the approach to Spa Road the guard, who was in charge of the first carriage, at a signal from the engine driver 'cast off' the train by releasing the rope by which it was attached to the engine, and he, together with the other guards along the train – one to every two carriages – applied their brakes.

2   The engine, now released from the train, ran to the points and was diverted to the south line.

3   The points were changed as soon as the engine had passed over them and the train, now slowing down, ran straight on to stop at the station on the north line.

4   The engine driver applied his brake as soon as he had crossed to the south line, and stopped his locomotive at the head of the waiting train, to which it was then coupled by the rope.

5 The engine was then reversed (or put into forward gear if it had been running in reverse), and it took the second train to Deptford; here a similar performance took place, resulting in the third train being brought up to Spa Road, thus completing the cycle.

The incoming train had, of course, to be transferred to the other line in the meantime, and several men were available at each end of the railway for this purpose. Whether they moved the train back across the points and then forward again on to the opposite line by a windlass or capstan and rope, or whether a small stationary steam engine was employed is not known definitely; it is possible that steam engines were used, since the company had bought two or three by this time.

There would always be one train waiting at Spa Road and another at Deptford, whilst the third would be either at one of these places or travelling between them.

The L&GR intended running its trains on the left, as most railways did, and trailing points were installed at intervals along the line. The operating system adopted, however, required facing points, so the up and down lines were simply reversed as a temporary expedient, and the trains ran on the right. The fact that they continued to do so for over three years was the result of the delay in finishing the line to Greenwich, and the alteration to normal running was only made shortly before the London & Croydon trains came on to the line in the summer of 1839, although the method of working the trains was modified as soon as more engines became available.

At the London end of Spa Road Station a barrier of stone blocks was placed across the north line to provide a primitive buffer stop for up trains; a similar arrangement was made at Deptford for both lines, as an overrunning of the station here would have deposited the train into the High Street, the bridge over this road not then having been built.

Exactly one month after the opening of the line, on Monday 7 March 1836, a fatal accident occurred at Spa Road Station to an intending passenger, one Daniel Holmes, who was waiting with others on the track for the 3.30pm train to Deptford. As the train from Deptford came up the other passengers climbed on to a narrow platform provided as a safety measure, but Holmes remained on the track, watching the incoming train. The engine was approaching much faster than usual because its brake had failed, and the driver's attention was distracted by Holmes, to whom he was shouting; consequently the engine, diverted to the south line, collided with the stationary train waiting there. The impact sent the waiting train several yards along the line, and caused a number of passengers already in it to sustain minor injuries. Meanwhile the up train, continuing along the north line without the engine, struck Holmes and killed him almost instantly. The occurrence does not seem to have affected the service or the driver very much, for he and his engine took the down train away to Deptford shortly afterwards. This driver, Thomas Millender, was the first engine driver in London; he had previously been on the Liverpool & Manchester Railway for seven years, and thus also must have been one of the most experienced drivers in the country at that time.

The unfortunate duty policeman, who only just managed to save his own life by leaping on to the platform, was dismissed for failing to give warning to the passengers in time, and a letter from George Walter, who saw the accident at Spa Road, referred to the great difficulty his men had in keeping people back out of the way of the trains, and drew attention to the penalties for trespassing on the line.

The great popularity of the railway during the first summer of its existence was due largely to the wide publicity the undertaking had received in the press for nearly four years. Although when travelling between London Bridge and Greenwich today one might well wonder if the writers could have been referring to the same railway, no doubt their descriptions were true enough at the time, after making allowances for a certain amount of enthusiasm nearly always present in articles of this nature. The following extract is from an article of 1834:

The view commands St Paul's, the Tower of London, the winding of the River to Greenwich, and all the commercial activity of the shipping to the north. Eastward there is Greenwich College, Deptford Dockyard, and all the picturesque woody scenery on the heights of Blackheath. The green Surrey hills on the south, and the more contiguous cultivated fields extending to the Kent Road and the Surrey Canal complete one of the most delightful views near London.

Nearer to London Bridge, however, the prospect was not so

pleasing; in the course of an article on the Eastern Counties
Railway, a writer in *Bentley's Miscellany* of 1837 mentions the
traveller's first glimpse of London from the trains of the Greenwich Railway as the line '... swirls above the tragic dens of
Rotherhithe and Bermondsey'.

Even the first fall of snow on the railway was noted by the
press. After remarking that the northern railways were little
affected by snow, it was stated that the Greenwich line was not
impeded in any way, as the parapet walls prevented the formation
of drifts.

The railway was brought to the notice of the sporting community in the summer of 1836, when, during the Lee Race Meeting in July, the 'Railroad Stakes' was run. George Walter refers
to the 'Railway Cup' in connection with the Lee Races, which
cost him, personally, £25. The Lee, Lewisham, Greenwich and
Eltham Races of 18 and 19 August included a race for the 'Railway Plate of 50 sovs. value. . . . This plate, being a gift to the
fund, will be embellished with a representation of the London &
Greenwich Railway, and the train thereupon.' The design was
probably taken from the popular Corbetts Lane view. Walter
also mentions the Shooters Hill Races, which cost him a further
three guineas, although whether he put up this rather modest
sum as a prize or backed a horse with it on behalf of the company
is not stated.[10]

As soon as the engines started running on the viaduct complaints reached the company of red-hot cinders being thrown
down causing small fires, and the fire insurance premiums on
properties along the line were increased. Passengers also complained of the sparks, but they received little sympathy from the
local press; one paper suggested '... that the driver should play
upon the passengers occasionally with a hose, or that a man in
asbestos breeches should sit on the funnel to keep the sparks in'.
A House of Lords Select Committee [11] in June 1836 was concerned with the danger of fires started by sparks from locomotives
and cinders dropped along the track from the ashpans; in the
case of the L&GR the parapet walls were considered sufficient
protection from the latter. Rennie was one of the witnesses, and
he referred to a 'Hood or Cullender' on top of the chimney, made
of wire, used by both the Greenwich and Liverpool & Manchester
Railways. Evidence was also taken from a Greenwich Railway
fireman, John Walker, who joined the company on 8 February

1836 after serving two years with the Liverpool & Manchester, where he had often had his neck and clothes burnt by sparks and cinders until wire guards were fitted to the chimneys. He stated that the Greenwich engines could run faster than they did, but that the manager would not allow it. A few years later, when the London & Croydon engines began to run on the viaduct, re-newed fears were expressed about the danger of fires, since these locomotives, being more powerful than those of the L&GR, threw their sparks farther afield.

During 1836 Walter gave evidence on the Brighton and London & Dover Railways' Bills, in each case assuring the House of Lords Committee that the London & Greenwich Railway could carry all the trains that the others could possibly send over it. His anxiety to secure the tolls that would accrue from the use by these lines of the Greenwich viaduct led him to make some extra-vagant assertions as to its capacity; one train a minute, he said, could leave London on its single down line.[12]

In a pamphlet published shortly before the railway was opened a writer noted that the estimated cost was £85,000 per mile, and that '...no such work can have the slightest chance to succeed'. He suggested that if the London & Greenwich remained the only railway in London, it might pay 'as a holiday plaything for the people', but that the other lines, when built, would compete for this privilege; the theory was then developed that lines costing only a quarter of the amount per mile would charge only a quarter of the fares prevailing on the Greenwich Railway, and the town of Greenwich would therefore lose visitors and trade by having a railway. He concluded his remarks on the Greenwich Railway by saying '...it is clear that this railway is amongst the most monstrous abortions that folly ever yet has caused to be brought into the financial world.'[13]

While the trains were running between Spa Road and Dept-ford, work went on at the London end of the line, and on 30 September 1836 it was announced that the trains would run to and from Bermondsey Street from 10 October; passengers used London Bridge Station from that time, and walked along the viaduct to Bermondsey Street, about 300 yards. By this time more than 300,000 people had travelled over the line.

It became obvious in the autumn of 1836 that the section of the line from Deptford to Greenwich was still a long way from being ready, and it was decided to arrange for the official opening of the London Bridge to Deptford portion to take place on 1 November. Invitation cards were prepared, but at the last moment the Bermondsey Street bridge was not ready, and the opening was postponed only five days before it was due to take place. So short was the notice, in fact, that caterers and entertainers who had been engaged were notified by newspaper advertisements.

The people of Greenwich evidently regarded the opening of the line to that town as imminent at this time, for a letter signed 'A Mourner' appeared in a local paper on 5 November;[14] the writer referred to '... this infernal Greenwich Railway, with all its thundering steam engines and omni*busters*, just ready to open, and destroy our rural town of Greenwich with red-hot cinders and hot water . . . too late . . . what have we let come amongst us?' Under the heading 'The Folly of Railroads' another letter was printed – 'verbatim et literatim' as the editor said, in order that the full depth of feeling therein expressed might be preserved.[15]

Greenige Ospittel
Octobur 10

Mister Editter –
        i no youre verry parshal to this countery and Wont see the place Cutt Up by these Raileway roads, its a imposishun and deservs exposur – besydes – what do you think Sir – The Greenige Homtribusses and Stagis will giv you a ryde for half an nour or three quatters, for six pense, but thes ralerode peopl dont give you no more than ten minnits of it – You jist git into there carridges and wiz gos the steme and their you are at Deptfurd in 10 minnites – i like the ould fashened way sir and plente of ridin for my monny not to bee wisked along in sutch a fluster that you cant enjoi nothin at all

Youer umbel st
betty Cringle

The *Railway Magazine*, however, said rather pompously 'We are by no means pleased with this Company for not having opened their line.'

A committee of three directors, Thomas Philpotts, Sir William Beatty and Capt. Page, was appointed on 19 November to supervise the arrangements for the opening of the railway, and on 3 December advertisements in the morning and evening papers announced that the ceremony would take place on Wednesday

14 December. Digby Neave, one of the directors, resigned on 26 November, and George Money was elected in his place.

The Company issued a notice on 13 December, in which the arrangements for the following day were briefly outlined:

Opening of the London & Greenwich Railway. Notice is hereby given that the Carriages will start as usual from their respective stations on Wednesday the 14 instant until 10 o'clock, and from that hour till 2 p.m. the railway will be closed for the ceremony of the opening, after which the trains will proceed as usual. Tickets of admission to the opening will admit at the station, either at London Bridge or Deptford.
No 26, Cornhill.   J. Y. Akerman. Secretary.

The tickets mentioned, of which a few examples still exist, were issued to any shareholders who applied for them, and to numerous others whose presence at the function seemed desirable.[16]

The railway was duly opened by the Lord Mayor of London, the Right Hon. Sir Thomas Kelly, on the appointed day, and the best account of the affair was that published in *The Times* on 15 December; it is from this article that the following extract is taken.

The completion of this undertaking as far as Deptford was celebrated yesterday by a public opening at which the Lord Mayor and several other of the civic authorities attended. The bridge end of the railroad was tastefully decorated with flags and banners of various devices. An awning with three tiers of seats was erected at each side of the road at the bridge end, for the accommodation of those who wished for admission to the carriage trains, and also for those who came merely as spectators to see the trains go off and return. Under one part of the awning a military band attended which continued to play several national airs. It was expected by those who had tickets of admission that on presenting them at the gates they would have places assigned to them in some of the carriages of the trains, but this was not the case, and the ticket-bearers as they arrived took their stations near the carriages or under the awnings at either side so as at last to form a very dense crowd. The tickets announced that the trains would start exactly at 12 but at this hour there was no symptom of readiness. There were, it was true, three rows of trains consisting of 8 or 10 carriages (each capable of holding with ease 20 persons), but the 'steamers' had not come up. It was then announced that the trains would not start till 1. It was, however, half-past 1 before the Lord Mayor and his suite arrived, and in about 10 minutes afterwards the first train with the carriages containing his lordship and several other members of the Corporation, the Directors and their friends etc. started. In a few minutes after the 2nd train set forward, and the others (five in all) followed with their appended carriages.[17] The speed of the several engines had already been tried on the railway, so that no competition was necessary on this occasion, and none was attempted. The first train starting some minutes before the others was of course soon a long way in advance, but after a short time it halted; the second train then moved on and passed the first at a very rapid pace and then pulled up, allowing the third, fourth and fifth to pass it in succession. It was so arranged, however, that the train conveying the Lord Mayor etc should arrive first at the Deptford end of the line. When his Lordship alighted he proceeded to the Board Room under the archway of the road where an address was presented to him from the Directors thanking him for his patronage and support of the undertaking. His Lordship returned thanks, after which the procession proceeded back to London in the same order as that in which it came. The rate at which the carriages proceeded in their way downwards could not be fairly taken as a test of their general speed as each train had a stoppage of 2 or 3 minutes at intervals. The greatest rate of going of any of the engines did not much exceed 20 miles per hour but the mean rate was not more than 16 miles per hour.

On the arrival of the several trains at Deptford the occupants of the carriages were allowed to get out, but here the arrangements fell far short of what we expected for no preparation was made for their return. Many who had got out in the hope of being present at the presentation of the address to the Lord Mayor, and others who wished to regale themselves at some of the neighbouring inns at Deptford could not, from the density of the crowds below the railway, get out, and on retracing their steps to the railway they found it a work of still greater difficulty and danger to return to the carriages from which they had alighted. Many who had taken the precaution of observing the name of the engine which drew the train, and the number of the carriage which brought them down, got back in the line between two trains, but were told by the conductors that they could not return by that way without great risk, for that the trains would return immediately. In consequence of this many persons who had come down by the trains, went on to Deptford and from thence to town by the coaches. We do not blame the Directors for this. It was perhaps unavoidable.

Throughout the whole line the bells of the Parish Churches by

which the rail-road went rang merry peals. The house tops on
both sides were teeming with spectators who loudly cheered as
the engines passed. Comparing the sensation which the traveller
feels on this road, as compared with other rail-roads, we may
state that owing, no doubt, to the whole road being over archways, there is a rumbling noise which is not heard on other roads.
Much of this, however, is obviated by the construction of the
carriages.

The directors, apparently, did not expect such large crowds
on a December day, but the weather was fine, and the Lord Mayor
had just previously announced his intention of attending the
ceremony in state. In addition, there were various other attrac-
tions; for instance, a certain Mrs Graham had offered to make an
ascent in her balloon to mark the occasion. The accounts vary
somewhat with regard to the military bands present on that day;
the Grenadiers, Coldstreams and Scots Guards are all said to
have performed at the opening ceremony, together with a band
in the uniform of Beefeaters which played while seated on the
roof of one of the carriages going down to Deptford. It is fairly
certain that there were at least two bands, one at London Bridge
and the other at Deptford; and that one of them was that of the
Coldstream Guards, since a letter from Sir William Gomme
giving permission for this band to perform is still in existence.
There are also references to the trains being started by signals
from a bugler, and to the firing of cannon as they left.

The *Morning Advertiser* stated that the delay at the beginning
of the ceremony was caused by the late arrival of the Lord Mayor,
who had kept the directors waiting for over an hour. One or two
other minor points are mentioned in this account: the hastily-
constructed bench which collapsed at London Bridge under the
weight of spectators, and the total absence of accommodation for
reporters. The latter was an inexplicable lapse on the part of
George Walter, who was generally very conscious of the value of
publicity, and presumably accounts for the fact that in all the
London newspapers, apart from the two mentioned above, the
opening was either completely ignored, or was dismissed in about
three lines.

The men employed in building the London & Croydon Railway were given a day's holiday, and were assembled at Corbetts
Lane, where the junction with the Greenwich Railway was later
to be made. Another line which was then expected to join the

London & Greenwich also celebrated the occasion: 'The line of junction of the Westminster & Greenwich Railway with the London & Greenwich Railway was marked out by small flags in the vicinity of the Deptford Depot.'

There were some 1,500 passengers in the five trains, or about thirty-six to a carriage; the less exalted of these '... found seats in them how they could, and the remainder were obliged to stay behind'. The Lord Mayor's train was drawn by the locomotive *Royal William* and reached Deptford at about 2pm. After receiving the address from the directors and one from the rector of Deptford, he went, with the Lady Mayoress, to inspect the works at the Ravensbourne. He was then conducted through the '... extensive workshops under the railway ...', and was very impressed with the machinery therein, which he likened to that at Portsmouth Dockyard.

On their return to London the Lord Mayor and four hundred guests were entertained to dinner in the Great Room of the Bridge House Tavern, Southwark. A. R. Dottin, the chairman of the company, presided and, apart from the loyal toast, all others were to the success of the railway. The Lord Mayor's speech is interesting for the forthright manner in which he stated the objects of the business community of London, and how the new railway would contribute to their attainment. An illuminating passage runs

... the great object which the new railway will effect is that of economizing time; the great characteristic of modern commercial life is the value set upon time; time constitutes wealth, and any diminution of its expenditure is a fresh creation of that which it is the main object of all commercial communities to obtain in the greatest abundance.

Other speeches that evening referred to the railway as the 'toll gate of Europe', and reference was also made to the proposed extension to Westminster Bridge. Mr Dottin in his speech said that sixty million bricks had been used in the viaduct, and that their manufacture had provided work for hundreds of poor people in the Kentish brickfields. A spirit of high optimism prevailed at the dinner, and the festivities were kept up to a late hour, Mr Walter taking the chair after the departure of the Lord Mayor and Mr Dottin.

Meanwhile on the railway the trains had resumed their half-hourly service in the afternoon, and when darkness fell rows of coloured lamps were displayed along the whole length of the viaduct. The stations were specially illuminated and exhibitions were held at London Bridge and Deptford. Among the exhibits at Deptford was the latest invention of Lord Dundonald, a model of a 'submarine destroyer called a naval torpedo'.[18] A firework display concluded the programme of the opening celebrations, but the shows and illuminations were continued into the New Year. The story that bands continued to play the trains in at the stations until the traffic was established, when they were replaced by barrel-organs, is probably apocryphal.[19]

Chapter 4

Early Years on the
Greenwich Railway - I

THE successful opening of the major part of the line in 1836 must have given Walter and Landmann considerable satisfaction, since they were about the only people whose confidence in the project had never faltered. Writing in 1837 of the early days of the railway, Walter said: 'This railway was the first attempted in the South of England, and consequently subjected to all the ridicule which ignorance, malice and those whose interest it would affect, could suggest.'

Exactly what Walter knew about railways before 1831, when he became interested in the Southampton line, and then in the London & Greenwich, is not clear, but it was probably not very much. A Committee of Accounts minute dated 28 June 1833 states that

Mr Walter, having returned from Manchester and Liverpool on the 27th instant, reported that he had visited the Railroad, where he was received in a friendly way, and every information was given him as to the manner in which they kept their books and carried on their business, and that he has brought the forms of their waybills, etc.

When giving evidence in 1836 he was asked what experience he had of other railways as an engineer, and he replied 'I have seen the Liverpool & Manchester Railway, and passed over it several times.'[2] He said that he had devoted many years to the study of railways, but his interest was in the financial, rather than the engineering aspects.

After his appointment as resident director in November 1835, he appears to have controlled the Greenwich Railway almost single-handed He organised the repair shops at Deptford, super-vised the conversion of the carriages, was constantly on duty on the line in 1836, attended board meetings when he could spare the time, and was in complete charge of the staff. The staff seem, on occasion, to have questioned his authority or ability, for the following order was issued on 9 March 1837:

It having been reported to the Board that the Company's servants employed on the railway have at various times evinced a spirit of insubordination, the Directors think it necessary to state: –

1st;   that Mr Walter having been appointed by them Resident Director, . . . all orders emanating from him must be con-sidered as the orders of the Board.

2nd; That the Engineers, Cheque-takers, Police and Collectors are to attend to the verbal orders of Mr Walter in all matters relating to the affairs of the Company . . .

3rd;   That any Engineer, Cheque-taker, Policeman or Collec-tor, or others in the Company's employ, disobeying these orders shall be summarily dismissed the service of the Company.

By order of the Board,
J. Y. Akerman, Secretary

In addition to his duties on the line, he also acted as a kind of public relations officer, writing letters to *The Times*, and other papers whenever it was necessary to refute some charge brought against the company. His position as resident director did not entitle him to vote at board meetings, however, and officially he had no seat on the board. Neither did he in fact reside upon the railway, since no accommodation was provided by the com-pany, and he was often referred to as the managing director by the staff.

Neither Walter nor Landmann ever intended the London & Greenwich Railway to be complete in itself, and its extension eastwards, eventually to Dover, was their ultimate object. To this end attempts were made to form a company in 1833 under the title of the London & Gravesend Railway by Walter and others of the Greenwich Railway, with William Green as secretary and Colonel Landmann as engineer. In March 1834 ambitious plans to extend the line to Folkestone were published, and for a time the line became known as the 'New Kent Railroad'.[3] Towards the end of May a meeting under the chairmanship of Green was held at Dover to enlist support for a line via Gravesend, Maidstone and Ashford to the port, and in June Colonel Landmann was being referred to as the engineer to the 'Continental Railway Company'. The company, however, decided against asking Parliament for such wide powers in one Bill, and it reverted to the London & Gravesend Railway.

The first official meeting of the Gravesend Railway Company was held at 26 Cornhill, the office of the L&GR, on 28 October 1834, and a prospectus issued on 19 November gave the capital as £600,000. Walter, Twells, Dottin, Beeby and George Money all accepted directorships on 22 November, but Dottin declined to become chairman.[4] The new company formally approached the Greenwich Railway in November 1834 on the question of tolls for running trains through to London Bridge, and the board stated that it would accept two thirds of the fares prevailing on its own line. This is the first reference to tolls in the L&GR records; the minute books of a few years later contained little else but references to this thorny subject.

In January 1835 advertisements appeared in the newspapers inviting those interested to apply to the company for a 'Lithographed Plan and Section' of the proposed line, and on 13 February a large print showing the intended ornamental viaduct across Greenwich Park was advertised as obtainable from booksellers in Greenwich.

It is said that George Smith, the company's architect, had copies of this print prepared in order to make the public familiar with his scheme for taking the railway through Greenwich Park on a viaduct, rather than running beneath it through tunnels, but that a representative of the Admiralty objected to its use as propaganda, and all copies of it were ordered to be destroyed.[5]

The possibility of the extension of their railway to Gravesend was favourably received by the majority of the people at Deptford, who welcomed it as a means of bringing trade to their 'populous parish, which, since the peace has suffered considerably by the reduction of various government establishments'.[6] Early in 1835 the company issued a folder entitled *Reasons in Favour of the Greenwich & Gravesend Railway*; the ten points which followed included engines standing by with steam up to convey couriers or urgent state messages etc. The Bill received its First Reading on 7 April 1835.

There was, particularly in Greenwich, a strong minority who opposed the railway, and perhaps in the belief that the original

Greenwich Railway had succeeded only because of the apathy of its opponents, they made sure that the Gravesend Bill should not slip through Parliament for want of effort on their part to prevent it. Early in 1835 a list of 'Reasons against the Greenwich and Gravesend Railway Bill' was printed and circulated, and by May a second series of fourteen 'More Reasons . . .' was published. When the catalogue of reasonable objections had been exhausted it was urged that this main line railway should not be built because '. . . the colonnade underneath the viaduct will afford opportunities to the holiday-folks and the frequenters of the park to practise indecencies'. The king, the Princess Sophia Matilda (a ranger of Greenwich Park), numerous MPs and others received petitions against the Bill. The local press, strangely enough, resisted the Gravesend Railway as vigorously as it had supported the London & Greenwich.

In the face of all this hostility the Bill was withdrawn, but the scheme itself was not abandoned, and in July 1835 experimental borings were made near Greenwich Park to see if a tunnel would be practicable. In September a prospectus was issued in which it was stated that the deposit of £1 had been paid on all the 30,000 shares; the facts were, however, that few shares had been allotted, and that deposits totalling only £1931 10s 0d had been received, most of which amount had by then been spent.

In the autumn of 1835 it was decided to form a new company with the provisional title of the Greenwich & Gravesend Railway, and its first meeting was held on 13 October; the old company was formally dissolved and all its papers transferred to the new one. On 18 November a notice of the intention of the company to apply for an Act appeared in the *Railway Gazette*.

It was during the latter half of 1835 that the various tests for vibration were conducted on the Greenwich Railway, ranging from a glass of water placed on a stone sleeper to elaborate calculations with special instruments and columns of mercury.[7] On 2 July Landmann made some experiments on the Liverpool & Manchester Railway and discovered that the vibration set up by trains of 120 tons travelling at twenty-five miles an hour was perceptible nearly 1,000 feet away; but as there was no indication that the ground structure there was the same as that in Greenwich Park, and the trains were about five times as heavy as any that he would have permitted to run on the Greenwich viaduct, the value of the tests was rather dubious. Professor G. B. Airy stated on 4 February 1836, however, that in his opinion no inconvenience to the observatory would result from taking the line past it and across the park, if the Astronomer Royal was empowered to signal all trains to stop for one minute twice each evening, while certain readings were being taken, and the company gave a written undertaking to stop its trains at any time.[8]

To placate the Naval authorities, the company hinted in February 1836 that it intended placing '...niches at stated intervals between the massive piers . . . wherein are to be placed busts of our most celebrated bygone Admirals, leaving vacant ones for the reception of future naval heroes', the whole to be surmounted by '...a colossal statue of his present Majesty, in full Naval costume'. This failed to make the slightest impression on the Admiralty, however, but it gave the local press another opportunity to ridicule the railway company; 'Gravesend Rail-road. – Instead of some future Nelson leading his men to victory with the rallying cry "Death and St Paul's", it will be "Here goes for a hole in the Gravesend Rail-road".'

The Bill was given its First Reading on 18 February 1836, by which time the company had become the London & Gravesend Railway. The usual flood of petitions against it were received, and on 29 February it was decided by 177 votes to 63 to postpone the Second Reading for six months; the Bill was virtually thrown out, and the local newspapers recorded the fact with great satisfaction.

Without waiting for the outcome of the Greenwich & Gravesend Bill, Walter, Green and the L&GR Directors launched the £1,000,000 London & Dover Railway on 4 November 1835. This was described as a 'continuation of the London & Greenwich and Gravesend Railways', and was to run from Gravesend via Maidstone and Ashford, to Folkestone and Dover, with a branch to Canterbury.

An extension to Dover would not have been considered at that particular time had not the South Eastern Railway's prospectus appeared at the end of October, and immediately imperilled the chances of the Gravesend Railway. The project was dropped in February 1836 on the failure of the Gravesend Bill.

With a degree of persistence which must have astonished their opponents, the promoters refused to abandon the Gravesend extension line, and the two companies opposed the South Eastern Bill when its committee was appointed in March 1836. On 12

April they amalgamated as the Kent Railway, with six London &
Greenwich directors and a nominal capital of £2,000,000. At this
time Landmann withdrew from the project, and James Walker
became engineer. The committee reported in favour of the South
Eastern line as the best one to Dover, and on 28 May the Kent
Railway issued a prospectus proposing a line to Ramsgate, via
Sittingbourne and Faversham; the plans for the Dover line were
abandoned. James Walker and his assistant Alfred Burgess
carried out their survey of what was now, in effect, a North Kent
line to Ramsgate, in September. By the end of the year opposition
to the line was again being organised in Greenwich, and the company decided in December 1836 to seek powers for a junction with
the L&GR at Deptford.

By this time, just as the L&GR was officially opened, there had
been four separate companies formed to undertake its extension,
behind all of which was the figure of George Walter. The affairs
of these concerns, however, were to contribute to his downfall at
the very time when he might have expected some reward for his
efforts.

Three Grenwich residents who opposed the Kent Railway discovered that there were irregularities in the Parliamentary Subscription Contract, and as a result of their petition an official
inquiry was held in March 1837 into the subscription lists of this
and a number of other railway companies.[9]

During this inquiry it was disclosed that William Green and
Walter had procured the signatures of hundreds of people who
were alleged to be willing to take up shares in the various companies by fraudulent means, although their object was not to
defraud individuals, but to satisfy what was, in their view, an
absurd and unnecessary Standing Order of parliament. Green
had persuaded many people to sign the deed under the impression that it was a petition in favour of the railway, inserting
various amounts against their names later. He also employed a
man named Costello who produced a number of poor stock-
jobbers, shoe-makers, and other characters who might easily have
found a place later in the pages of Dickens and Mayhew; styling
themselves 'gentlemen', and with no qualification other than the
ability to write their own names, they signed the deed for sums
ranging from £7,500 to £12,500. They then disappeared into the
lanes and alleys of the City each four shillings the richer, and in
ignorance of the fact that Green had authorised Costello to pay

them five shillings.

Walter persuaded many of his friends and business associates to sign; Akerman subscribed for £2,500, Henry Watkins (a book-keeper on the L&GR earning £100 per annum) for £4,500, and Effingham Wilson, the bookseller at the Royal Exchange, for £10,200. Landmann was down for a modest £6,000. Any likely passengers Walter met in the London & Greenwich trains were invited to call at the Cornhill office to see the large model of the Kent Railway there, and if they became subscribers, they received a print of the railway.

At this time Walter was also a director of the Preston & Wyre, Salisbury & Exeter and Calcutta & Saugor Railways, and various people connected with these companies became involved in the Kent Railway. Thus Peter Hesketh Fleetwood, MP, of the Preston & Wyre was a director of the Kent company, as also was George Money, a wealthy barrister and former Accountant General at Calcutta.

Despite the exertions of Green and Walter, by February 1837 only about two-thirds of the £2,000,000 capital of the Kent Railway had been underwritten, and Walter himself signed the deed for the balance of 33,000 shares, i.e. £660,000. Of the company's 100,000 shares, 31,926 had actually been applied for, and the £2 deposit had been paid on only 1,444.

Although no legal proceedings followed the inquiry, the disclosures reflected no credit on Walter's reputation; he and Green seem to have borne all the responsibility for practising a deception which must obviously have been well known to many others at the time. Since the committee was not concerned with the London & Greenwich or Preston & Wyre Railways, the methods by which their capital had been raised were not revealed. Somehow Walter had managed to raise about seventy per cent of the Preston & Wyre capital in London during 1835, and his efforts on behalf of the Greenwich Railway during the previous year have already been mentioned.

Just as the findings of the committee of inquiry into the subscription lists were published, Walter claimed the sum of £9,700 from the L&GR. Most of this represented the expenses connected with the disposal of the 19,400 shares of the company in 1834, but £200 was the cost of obtaining signatures to the subscription contract. Walter contended that the arrangements that resulted in this expenditure were known to the original board of directors,

and were made with its full authority and approval. In view of
the company's desperate need of money to build the viaduct in
1834 and 1835, it is unlikely that any director would have questioned his methods of raising the capital, particularly as he himself advanced the money to pay the brokers' commission. The
directors in office at the time he made his claim, however, denied
all knowledge of the arrangements, and decided to submit his
account to the shareholders at the general meeting then
imminent. A week later, on 20 July 1837, Walter resigned his
appointment as resident director and A. R. Dottin also resigned
from the chairmanship; John Twells, the original deputy chairman had resigned in June.

The company's financial position had worsened by the early
part of 1837, and with its capital gone in building and equipping
the railway, the board had for a period to rely upon short term
loans from its wealthier members to meet its commitments. Thus
John Yates[10] alone lent the company more than £5,000 between
January and July.

The special general meeting was held the day after Walter
resigned, under the chairmanship of Sir William Beattie, when
the shareholders were informed that the railway could not be
completed until a further £45,000 had been raised. At this the
meeting became very hostile, and a committee was appointed
consisting of the eight principal shareholders. In this frame of
mind the proprietors were in no mood to consider Walter's claim,
and it was promptly rejected.

The committee examined the books for six weeks, and on
30 August another special general meeting was called at the City
of London Tavern to receive their report. In this document they
criticised the board for failing to employ auditors, and for placing
too much reliance upon Mr Walter. The directors declared that
they had dispensed with the services of auditors on grounds of
economy. Walter was refused admission to this meeting because
his shares were not properly registered, and he suffered the
humiliating experience of being forcibly restrained from entering by police stationed at the door.

A few weeks afterwards Walter published a pamphlet[11] on
the subject of his claim – the first of several – in order '... that the
name of one who is descended from one of the most ancient and
highly connected families in the Kingdom, should not be handed
down to posterity tarnished in its association with this "Monu-

ment for future ages", as the Chairman styles the Rail-road'. In this pamphlet, which is probably a fairly accurate statement of the case, he attributes the attitude of the company to the ill-will of the Rev. J. Macdonald, who took this opportunity of discrediting him because of his opposition to the iron viaduct scheme of 1833. Various figures are quoted which are of little consequence now, but one is inclined to agree with Walter's assertion that his salary of £500 a year was '... wholly inadequate to the expenses which I incurred during my exertions to forward the works night and day, and working the railway'.

Widespread regret was expressed at his decision to resign; press reports referring to the dispute described him as the man '... without whom this important fabric had never been heard of...', and the cancellation of his free pass was regarded as '... a paltry step for a body of gentlemen appointed to so important a trust'. Instead of charging him sixpence to travel on the railway '... as if he were a stranger...', they should have applied themselves to finishing the line; 'their apathy or want of knowledge to proceed exceeds all belief'.[12] In May 1838 the influential people of Deptford gave a dinner in Walter's honour,[13] and presented him with a silver chalice in acknowledgement of the benefits his project had brought them; eighteen months later the following advertisement appeared in the *Railway Magazine*: 'Railway Medal. – The Committee of "those connected with the Greenwich Railway" beg to announce to subscribers, that the medals struck in honour of Mr Walter, the late Resident Director, are now ready for delivery at Mr Law's, 68 High Street, Borough.'[14]

Meanwhile the dispute continued, and Walter's solicitors claimed £25,000; the board resisted the claim and in March 1839 action to recover a reduced amount of £15,541 was taken. The directors were advised by counsel that they were not legally liable, so the question was referred to a special committee under Mr Yates of the South Eastern Railway who, in September, found that Walter was entitled to £2,500. Apparently in the expectation that the company would accept the award, Walter abandoned his original claim, and accepted £41 13s 4d due to him as salary – an amount that was not in dispute – and gave a receipt which was afterwards produced as evidence that nothing further was owing to him. At a general meeting held on 28 September 1839 Yates proposed that the board release Walter from liability to pay £5,550 on shares he held, and that the company pay him

£2,500 in addition. George Money, the chairman, agreed to cancel Walter's debt, but opposed any payment to him, and only five shareholders voted in favour of the full proposal made by Yates. Walter thereupon revived his original claim, and the case dragged on until 1840, when a new committee of three directors and four shareholders, one of whom was nominated by Walter, reconsidered the matter. In August it reported entirely against the claim on legal grounds. Walter was present at the meeting when the announcement of the committee's decision was made, and he accepted the verdict with dignity and good grace; he stated, however, that he and his family were ruined by the company's action.

Several magistrates, MPs and bankers sent a strong recommendation to the Board of Trade that Walter be appointed one of the new railway inspectors in December 1840;[15] the board decided, however, to appoint its inspectors from the Royal Engineers. The following year a group of shareholders attempted to get Walter reinstated on the Greenwich Railway, on the grounds that the company would never prosper until he again took charge of its affairs; another group supported the same object from the fear that, if he did not return, his constant attacks on the board would ruin the company. He had at that time addressed a pamphlet to the shareholders containing fourteen *Hints on the Management of the Greenwich Railway*. Several of the points he raised were dictated by his own curious obsessions, but others were sound, and within a year or two had received attention.

When Walter was promoted from secretary to resident director in 1835, his place was taken by John Yonge Akerman. He had been an accountant until 1832, when he became secretary to William Cobbett; on the death of Cobbett in 1835, Akerman came to the L&GR, at the age of twenty-nine. When first appointed he received only a nominal salary, barely enough to cover his expenses, and continued to do so until the railway was completed.[16] Akerman was a member of the Society of Antiquaries, his particular subject being numismatics, upon which he wrote some thirty books,[17] but he left no account of the Greenwich Railway. At a general meeting in February 1842, when the discussion turned to some cracks which had appeared in the viaduct near London Bridge, he was accused by a shareholder of being more interested in the arches of Rome than in those of the railway. Akerman filled the office of secretary for over nine years.

The board decided to abolish the office of superintendent in December 1837, at that time filled by a Mr Simpson, and he was accordingly asked to resign. The decision was taken as an economy measure and also to stop many 'irregularities' for which he was held responsible. For some time there had been considerable waste, and loss of materials from the stores. Three months later a general inspector named Hayton was appointed at £250 a year, but he held the position for only a few months. On the appointment of a new board of directors he was succeeded in August 1838 by George Mackay Miller.

Miller was born at Pentonville, London, on 7 December 1813, and after a course in mathematics at University College, was apprenticed to Lloyd's of Southwark, mechanical engineers and millwrights. Here he worked at the bench and in the drawing office until the firm closed down, when he went to work under Albinus Martin, then manager of Lord Balcarrie's iron works and collieries, at Wigan. After a short time Martin introduced him to Mr Dixon, then resident engineer on the Manchester end of the Liverpool & Manchester Railway, who engaged him as an assistant in the drawing office. He then went to the London & Birmingham Railway, where Robert Stephenson appointed him to the drawing office at St John's Wood, and he afterwards superintended forty-eight miles of that railway as assistant resident engineer, until the line was opened to Boxmoor. During the course of his duties there he appears to have made the first through journey by rail from London to Birmingham. It was upon Robert Stephenson's recommendation that he became resident and locomotive engineer to the Greenwich Railway at the age of twenty-five.[18]

The directors, justifying Miller's salary of £300 a year, increasing by £50 yearly, said that he had, within a few months of his appointment, saved the company thousands of pounds. Until he came to an arrangement with Gregory, the superintendent of the London & Croydon Railway, to have one Sunday off duty in every three, he worked seven days a week, and at times far into the night. He supervised nearly everything that was done on the line, and after the normal traffic ceased at about 10pm, he had the engines running until one or two o'clock in the morning 'for the attendance of the rails'. He guided and advised the board on practically everything but finance; he planned and supervised the building of stations, kept the locomotives in good condition and took over the carriages. The staff, the train service and the ordering of materials were all his concern. In effect, he ran the railway as Walter had done before him, but with greater efficiency, until he resigned in the summer of 1844; his salary was then only £400 a year, the annual increments of £50 having ceased after the first two years.

There was a marked change in the character of the company after the resignation of Dottin, Twells and Walter. Little more is heard of grandiose plans for extensions, and the emphasis is first on economy and then on efficiency. The affairs of the company were conducted in a very haphazard way at first, and there was a dangerous tendency for such things as new locomotives to be ordered verbally by Walter without reference to the board, if he happened to be too busy to attend the meeting that week.

Towards the end of 1837 several economies were made, and in November a new board was elected under the chairmanship of Mr George Money. The shareholders, having been shaken out of their complacency by the Walter inquiry, repeatedly raised complaints about the conduct of the company's business, one of the criticisms being the delay in finishing the line; another was the very considerable excess of expenditure over the original estimate.

The dividend for the year 1837 was 3 per cent, the amount the company was authorised to pay, regardless of earnings, while the line was still uncompleted, but a disappointing figure in view of what the shareholders had been encouraged to expect. Theirs was one of the few railways that paid any dividend at all, however, the only others that year being the Liverpool & Manchester (9 to 10 per cent) and the Stockton & Darlington (6 per cent).

In August 1838 William Shadbolt became chairman of an entirely new board. He had taken no interest in the affairs of the L&GR before this time, and he knew nothing whatever of its history. He appears to have known nothing about any other railways either, for he admitted complete ignorance of the contest over the various Brighton lines of 1836, a subject which was very fully reported in the press, and upon which several pamphlets had been published.[19]

About this time Colonel Landmann, the main part of his work being finished ceased to be the company's engineer, but was retained as consulting engineer at £100 a year. Several parts of the railway remained unfinished, the stations being at that time merely temporary halting places; the company decided, however, that the architect and the superintendent between them were capable of finishing the works, which, in due course, they did.

The directors, accompanied by the engineer, inspected the new works as far as the Prince of Orange Tavern, Greenwich, on Tuesday 4 December 1838, travelling down in two carriages from London Bridge at 1.15pm. The event is described in the minutes as the private opening of the line. Their train was drawn by the new engine, No 9, and there was a small celebration at Greenwich.

The public opening of this final section of the line, to a temporary terminus at Church Row, Greenwich, took place on 24 December. Contemporary accounts of the event are in marked contrast to those of the opening ceremonies of two years before. 'On Monday morning last . . . opened all the way to Greenwich . . . no procession, no band of music, fluttering of banners or directors . . . all went off quietly.'[20] Large crowds watched the arrival of the trains at Greenwich, and for the drivers and firemen, the occasion was marked by the distribution '. . . of new pilot coats bearing the initials of the Company upon the collar'. The journey time from London Bridge was eighteen minutes, and each train was met by omnibuses for Woolwich, Blackheath and Lewisham at a fare of 6d.

The company had distributed fifty-thousand handbills advertising the opening of the line, promising new carriages in the near future, and announcing the revised fares to take effect from 24 December as follows:

Fares: – from the London Station to Deptford or Greenwich, or returning from either, First Class Carriage, 1s; Second Class Carriage, 8d.

Observing that the directors had some anxiety as to how the public would receive the rise in fares, a report went on to say that no mention had been made of what was to be charged to Deptford (in itself an incorrect statement), '. . . the fare turning out to be, when the passengers came to pay, 8d to Deptford also, being a rise of 2d on the previous fare'. The first passenger that morning 'was a shilling one', and therefore not affected by the increase, but the next three refused to pay 8d to Deptford, '. . . and like independent, monopoly-hating Britons, turned away and went per coach'. This report continues:

The passengers are now placed in separate carriages – those for Greenwich being in the last carriage and those for Deptford in the first; when the carriages arrive at Deptford the passengers for that place are bundled out with as much rapidity as possible; and the trains run (or rather walk) on to Church Passage, Greenwich, where the remainder of the passengers get out, and go down a flight of wooden steps and across a marsh of loose, wet, and muddy gravel, when they arrive at the Greenwich Road, and may get into the town as fast as they please.[21]

In 1839 letters began to appear in the railway journals from shareholders. At first they usually contained suggestions for improving the position, such as the running of carriages or buses from London Bridge to the City in conjunction with the train service. By 1840 *Herapath* and the *Railway Times* were receiving a flood of indignant letters about the way in which the company was being managed. One of these, suggesting that the railway '... must have been begotten in sin', went on to give a short history of the undertaking. The arches, it said, '.. were neither covered with cement nor asphalte, and to this hour leak like drip stones'.

Among the more serious suggestions was one urging the company to run goods trains, whilst another was that one locomotive contractor should work all the Greenwich and Croydon trains, and later, those of the Brighton and Dover Railways also. A group of shareholders in the four companies terminating at London Bridge Station suggested an amalgamation of them all under the title 'The Great South Union Railway Company'.

A special general meeting of shareholders was held at the George and Vulture Tavern, Cornhill, on 3 December 1840. Few attended the meeting, but those who did registered their lack of confidence in the board, and laid charges of corruption against it. Among other things, they called for an inquiry into the activities of George Miller, who was supposed to have had interests in some of the firms which supplied plant and materials to the company, but who, in fact, had no such business connections apart from his interest in Fox's Patent Switches. Various directors were said to have had financial interests in Kyans Anti-Dry Rot Company, and in ironworks, engineering companies and asphalt concerns. The fact that some of the directors held only the mini-

mum number of shares, and 'privileged' (preference) shares at
that, was a cause of dissatisfaction to the holders of ordinary
shares. The company had to find large sums to meet the interest
on loans made by the Joint Stock Bank, and this absorbed most
of the profits; the fact that Shadbolt was a director of this bank
caused further acid comment.

The expenses of running the L&GR were high in relation to
the receipts; a considerably longer line would have required little
more staff or equipment, except at holiday times. The hundred-
odd trains that ran a total of over four-hundred miles each day
between London and Greenwich would earn less between them
than one train on the London & Birmingham or Great Western
Railways, despite the fact that the Greenwich line carried more
passengers than most of the main lines put together in the
thirties. The number of passengers in itself resulted in the rapid
wearing-out of the carriages, the process being hastened somewhat by certain of its patrons on their return from Greenwich
Fair. The company published some figures in October 1840
showing that its trains had run 570,305 miles, carrying 5,787,240
passengers, from 9 February 1836 to 30 June 1840.[22] For some
time, however, the railway had been losing passengers to
Wheatley's buses, and it was said that 200 people used the buses
daily in preference to the dirty and worn-out carriages of the
London & Greenwich.

The misfortunes of any passengers unlucky enough to become
delayed on the railway soon found their way into print; the
following is from one of the first letters printed by *The Times* in
which any criticism of the railway was voiced:[23]

Greenwich Railway

Sir, I went yesterday by the above Railway, and as they profess
to go every quarter of an hour, I was at their London entrance
at about 35 minutes after four, hoping to leave at the quarter to 5.
I bivouacked about 5 minutes over a coke fire, when the person
who received the checks said (alluding to the engine) 'Here she
comes', and I was directed by another person to get into a
carriage. I did so. It soon filled, and it was presumed that the
train would have started. Five o'clock came – a quarter after
passed – still we were all kept at London. On asking the cause
for not going, no satisfactory reason was given. Passengers were
still arriving; sixpences were taken; continued application was
made for seats in the overloaded carriages, and, at half-past-five

we moved. Having proceeded about 200 or 300 yards, the whole train returned to hook on to the half-hour train (the half-past-five), and we got to Deptford, after a very slow passage, at a few minutes before six.

It is understood that an accident occurred by the breaking down of an up-town train; and what I complain of is, that knowing that assistance was sent off, no intimation was given to those who might be in a hurry, no explanations, no apology for the delay, except, on arrival at Deptford an assistant accounted for the delay by the train being overloaded.

...the concern has got your money, and then they laugh at you. Should this be?...

A glimpse of the scene at the London Bridge Station is given in the Parliamentary Committee evidence of 1840, when the question of the traffic congestion in the roads leading to the City and Westminster was raised. The company would not allow carriages, hackney cabs and the like to stand in Dottin Street, and they formed a cab rank in what is now Borough High Street almost at the foot of London Bridge itself. When the whistle of an approaching train was heard, the drivers whipped up their horses, and a kind of chariot race in Duke Street and up the inclined plane ensued. The station itself was small enough, but there was even less space in Dottin Street, so the iron gates were opened, and the vehicles all crowded on to the station where, apart from the arriving train which had stopped some distance away from the station entrance, there were few obstructions, and no platforms to complicate matters. Here the passengers either transferred themselves to the cabs, or jostled their way off the station in a stream down the incline, while the vehicles that had taken up passengers turned round in the station and made their way down Dottin Street also. Cabs and carriages arriving with passengers were allowed to go straight on to the station, but not to wait there once their passengers were discharged. During rush hours the uproar may be imagined, and perhaps St Thomas's Hospital had some reasonable grounds for resisting the railways' proposal, then before Parliament, to treble the area of their activities.

During the early years of its existence the Greenwich line carried an enormous number of passengers to and from Greenwich Park throughout the summer months. The great crowds that attended the fairs held there at Easter and Whitsun often got out of hand, particularly while waiting to enter the stations, and extra police were usually on duty at London Bridge and Greenwich.

At Easter 1837, before the railway was opened throughout, it was reported that travellers had to wait for half-an-hour in a crowd to reach the railway at Deptford, and then travel seventy-five to an open carriage up to London. Conditions had hardly changed by Easter 1840 as the following extract shows.[24]

At the London Terminus of the Railway the gates were surrounded by multitudes, many of whom having waited half-an-hour and more, left in the hopelessness of obtaining a seat by the trains, which, crammed almost to suffocation, pelted up and down the viaduct as fast as possible.

For those fortunate enough to have reached Greenwich, the return journey by night seems to have been even more hazardous. Unable to return to London by coach or river, 'Miles's boy' – whoever he may have been – in desperation tried the railway

... the Directors of which promised the deluded multitudes conveyance 'to town till two in the morning'. Vile mockery! Miles's boy, who can make his way anywhere and everywhere, did succeed in braving the horrors of the 'Middle passage' to the paying counter; thence by a series of furious charges, forced the defile of the check-taker, fought his way through the Bolan Pass on to the platform amid shrieks and cries that might have appalled the victors of Cabul. Once in twelve minutes a signal was given, and then woe to those who had soft corns or soft ribs; Miles's boy has neither, but he can feel for the victims of railway management thus cruelly situated, and heartily wisheth that a half-dozen of Directors could have been got into the melee – they would have received no more than their deserts. Whew-ugh-ugh-ugh-ugh, and our 'hell in harness' is off, Tooley Street is reached – the gas illumination of 'Greenwich every ten minutes' glitters in lying brilliancy at the terminus, and ere midnight Miles's boy again greeteth the Strand...[25]

One feels that he might at least have given the railway credit for bringing him back before midnight, which is more than the coaches or boats were capable of doing.

Both Greenwich and Croydon fairs were at the height of their popularity about the time when the railways to these places were opened, but they declined very rapidly after a few years. The railways in general were largely responsible for the failure of these old-established fairs, and many others farther afield, in consequence of the wider scope for recreation brought about by the introduction of cheap travel.

Towards the end of 1840 *The Times* opened a campaign against inefficiency on the railways, and its readers tumbled over themselves to submit examples of alleged abuses from which they had suffered. One correspondent contributed the following in support of a previous writer's exposure of the 'trickery and humbug connected with the class of carriage known as the "catchpenny sixpenny" '.

The Directors stick up large placards about town 'Go by the Greenwich Train, fare 6d' . . . they have got one carriage or van only stuck up in the middle of the train, without any covering to it, sometimes (in wet weather) 2 inches deep in water, having two or three short rough seats resembling huge salt boxes, such as might have been seen about a century ago in the chimney corner of old farm houses; and into this van – which may be more fitly described as a large, square, filthy dogs-meat cart – all the flats are crammed in one indiscriminate heap.[26]

Another outraged member of the public wrote, in 1840,[27]

. . . you run from your residence with great haste, to catch a train – fancying that you are rather late. Within a short distance of the terminus you catch sight of a railway clock. It happens to be just 4 minutes slower than your watch. It *must* be right you think, because it belongs to a railway company. Deluded with that notion, your run subsides into a walk, and you arrive at the booking office just in time to pay your money, get your ticket, and see the train start without you. You complain to the police constable; he points you to *another clock* which is just *5 minutes faster* than that downstairs. You have, therefore, to cool your heels, and your temper, for a quarter of an hour, under the shed, and, when you start, have the gratification of seeing a number of people who have been similarly deceived, gazing at the train that leaves them behind.

The clock at Deptford Station is even more eccentric still. Sometimes it is 10 minutes in advance of its lingering brother at Greenwich; sometimes it is as much behind it; and occasionally it is self-willed enough to refuse to go on at all . . .

I am sir,

One to whom a quarter of an hour

is always of consequence.

One would imagine that, of the five-million-odd passengers,

some must have been satisfied, but the only one who appears to have recorded the fact in 1840 was a German, who probably visited London in 1839, and described the railway to his countrymen the following year as

... a picture of variety and beauty equal to anything to be found in the world. The view of the River, stretching away to the horizon, and glistening between the hundreds of ships and boats upon it, was contrasted with the houses immediately below, their roofs dark, sooty, without any bright spot or decoration, gloomy, mostly low and small.

Referring to Greenwich fair, the writer says,

Most odd is the atmosphere on such days, in the company of several thousand above the housetops, with the merrymaking of the Cockney 'day out' below ... a railway carriage full of busker musicians immediately behind the tender at the beginning of the very long train ... the incomprehensible roar, the product of a hundred various craft above the shouting of skippers, the hoisting of sails, the creaking of cables, the sound of oars, the groaning of cranes, the rattle of machinery, the lushing of waves through the ruddergear, the hammering noises on board and on the quays, makes a wonderful accompaniment to the music, and to the hissing and snorting of the iron horse.[28]

A strange mishap involving the 9pm up train occurred on 15 March 1841, the contemporary accounts of which throw some faint light on the working of an early railway.

By some casualty of which no explanation has been given, the up train was thrown off the line of rails, and some of the carriages were drawn across the line of trams used for the down conveyance. The engineer and stoker blew out the fire, and the passengers were at length, after much alarm and excitement, handed out of the vehicles, and shown to a lateral staircase from the foot of which they might thread their way through the dirty streets of the neighbourhood. On the remonstrance by an MP who happened to be a passenger, one of the attendants consented to light the passengers on their way by the line of the railroad; and on their arrival at the terminus it was found that the attendants were in ignorance of the accident, and were preparing to start a train downwards.[29]

Arising out of this accident, the case of *Shillibeer* v. *the London & Greenwich Railway* was tried at Croydon on 23 August 1841.

Whether the plaintiff was the omnibus proprietor or any connection of his is not known, but he was travelling in the 9.30pm up train when it stopped near Blue Anchor Road because of the obstruction caused by the engine and carriages of the previous train lying across the track. He, with the other passengers, alighted from the carriages, and tried to get down into Blue Anchor Road, but, the door at the foot of the stairs being locked, they returned to the viaduct, and walked along the track. The ballast on which they had been walking did not continue over Bermondsey Street bridge, however, and at this point Shillibeer with eight or ten others fell into a pit between the rails and injured themselves. The conductors said that they had ordered the passengers to sit quietly in the train, but they refused, and became very violent, kicking the carriage doors until the conductors were compelled to let them out. They then told the passengers to go down the steps to Blue Anchor Road,[30] and that their fares would be refunded the next day; the passengers all insisted on walking along the line to London Bridge, however, and '...threatened to knock the conductors' heads off when an attempt was made to restrain them'. Shillibeer was awarded £25 damages.[31]

In the early days of the railway its footpaths were very popular, and in one week in August 1838 they produced £53 in one-penny tolls. The company discovered at this time, however, that some persons were driving carts along them, so posts and a wicket gate were put up near the Blue Anchor Road. Where the path ran across the Surrey Canal the company decided to have some sort of protective arch erected, but they ended by having a watchman stationed there instead.[32] The paths now ran almost the whole length of the railway, from the Maze, near the end of London Bridge Station, to Blue Stile, the site of the original Greenwich terminus. The boundary wall and the avenue of trees were not continuous, and by 1840 Landmann said that the paths were 'not much frequented'. In order to preserve the footpath as a private road, the company closed it once a year, half being closed on one day, and the other half the next.

The meadows and gardens between Bermondsey and Deptford did not long survive the opening of the railway; by August 1839 it was reported that the '...intermediate space is almost covered with houses'.

The company seems to have drawn up a set of bylaws some

time between March 1839, when the secretary said there were
none, and 29 October 1840 when reference was made in a police
court to one against drunks travelling in the trains. On that day
a man was fined £1 (or fourteen days) for causing a disturbance
at London Bridge by hindering '...persons passing from the turnstile where the money was paid, to the carriages'. Whilst being
led off the station down the incline, he struck the policeman, and
was thereupon arrested.

Although it drew the line at drunkenness, the board permitted
smoking in some of its carriages at least from an early date, if not
from the opening of the line. In March 1838 the company was
advised to 'suffer nobody to get into the trains with long pipes
and cigars – ladies do not like to enter their drawing rooms per-
fumed with tobacco'.[33] This appears to refer to first-class
carriages; but while other companies were then attempting to
stamp out the practice, which many of them had previously con-
doned, the London & Greenwich extended the facility to second-
class passengers in September 1842.

It was suggested in 1838 that 'on Sundays and evenings, when
the trains fill fast', closed carriages should be reserved on some
trains for ladies only, as the passengers who filled the open ones
were generally drunk. There is no evidence that the suggestion
was actually adopted. At this time the van and fly drivers, who
were usually waiting about at the Deptford Station took to amusing themselves by calling 'No sir, you are too late', or 'Run, my
man, or you will lose the train' to dignified but gouty old gentlemen hurrying towards the station.[34]

The first mails to travel by train from London were carried
by the Greenwich Railway, and within a month of its opening a
contract was entered into between the company and the GPO
for the conveyance of 'an additional Post Office bag'. There was
also under consideration a plan for sending the French mails
from Greenwich '...by powerful steam boats every evening at
9pm'. They would have reached Boulogne at 7am the next morning, and have been delivered in Paris thirty hours after leaving
Greenwich. In June 1839 the company '...agreed to take three
bags per day at £60 a year for the Twopenny Post Office'.

It is most probable that the company established the first Railway Lost Property Office in London, amongst the various other
things initiated by it. At the end of the first year's working from
London Bridge it seems to have accumulated quite a collection

of lost property at its headquarters, and the board decided on 22 December 1837 to place the following advertisement in *The Times*:

Several articles having been found in the Company's trains, parties owning the same are requested to apply at the Company's Offices, London Terminus, when they will be delivered on a proper description being given.

The board minutes refer to some books and documents which are, unfortunately, no longer to be found. One of them was a complaints book, the contents of which were read at each weekly board meeting; another was a book kept by the secretary, in which each director made a report on the line when he took his turn in making the daily inspection instituted in February 1840.

The terms 'luggage' and 'parcels' were interpreted rather loosely by the passengers, who took large quantities of merchandise with them on the trains, and very soon a considerable traffic in fish developed between Greenwich and London. In February 1842 the board directed that payment was to be obtained for luggage where practicable and the transport of fish in its new carriages was prohibited. A few months later, however, it was stated that the amount of £7 a week received from the carriage of parcels was not worth while.

Apart from some ballast waggons, which were acquired for the widening of the line and disposed of when the work was finished, the L&GR possessed no goods waggons of any description, and it was probably the only railway in England from which such vehicles were completely absent. The company did possess some 'garden carts' in 1837, but these were road vehicles, and were probably used by the railway for its own purposes, or in construction. They bore George Walter's name, and as he had an office in the City, payment of certain City tolls was thus avoided. On the removal of his name from one of the engines, following his resignation, he insisted on its removal also from the company's carts.

With railways opening in all parts of the country, each usually under several separate private Acts of Parliament granting powers and imposing restrictions of a widely differing nature, the government decided that some degree of uniformity and control was necessary in the interests of public safety, and the first general Act for regulating railways was passed in August 1840. This Act established the Railway Department of the Board of Trade, empowering it to call for traffic and accident returns, and to forbid the opening of any new line until authorised by its newly-appointed inspectors. The London & Greenwich, in common with all the other railway companies eventually started to make periodical returns of passenger and goods traffic mileage etc., but unlike most of the others, it could not state precisely how many miles its trains had run in the period covered by the return '... as extra trains run on Sundays and holidays, the number of which is not exactly known'.[35]

The Railway Department was not very happy about some of the practices employed in operating the Greenwich Railway. Even though they differed from the methods of other lines, however, they had proved satisfactory on this railway, and the company was not disposed to alter them; the Board of Trade had no power at first to compel them to do so.

After a fatal accident on the Sheffield & Rotherham Railway in July 1841, caused by running an engine in reverse, the department wrote to the London & Greenwich expressing its concern '... at learning that it is the practice of the London & Greenwich Railway Company to run their trains in one direction with the tender foremost ...', and requested that steps might be taken to discontinue the practice, '... although it may hitherto have produced no serious michief'.[36] The railway had no means of turning its engines at that time, and even if it had, it is unlikely that it would have gone to the trouble of turning them at the end of each short journey; they always ran down to Greenwich tender first, and continued to run in this manner.

Another long-standing practice on the Greenwich Railway was that of locking the carriage doors; this again did not meet with the approval of the Board of Trade. Miller had pointed out that the trains ran so close to the parapet wall, that it did not matter whether the doors were locked or not; those on one side could not be opened in any case. He also argued that

... danger would result from leaving the passengers the discretion of quitting the carriages should the trains stop on any part of the line, as the distance being short, on a stoppage occurring, passengers almost always evince a desire to leave the carriages and walk the remaining part of the journey, and thus they, by the frequent passing of trains, might be run over, the railway being built on arches, and enclosed with parapet walls on either side.

On the evening of 13 June 1842, Major General Pasley, '...unknown to the policemen as the Government Inspector of Railways...', rode on the London & Greenwich Railway, and afterwards made a report in which he observed that

...no prudent person would go out of the carriages on the near side if left open, as there is hardly room for a very thin person between them and the parapet wall; and even persons of this description, if wearing clothes, etc., might thereby become entangled, and liable to some serious accident if standing there when a train passed them.

If General Pasley had known the Greenwich Railway's passengers as well as Miller knew them, he might have realised that they were not all prudent persons. However, the Board of Trade pondered over the matter for nearly a month before they intimated to the company that '...their Lordships, after having consulted Maj. Gen. Pasley, are of opinion that it would be desirable that the practice of locking up the passengers should not be persisted in'.[37] The directors accordingly gave instructions that the doors be left unlocked in future.

The train service on the Greenwich Railway improved from one in each direction per hour in February 1836 to one every half-hour by May, and eventually to one train every fifteen minutes in December. Sunday trains had started in May 1836, but with an interval from 10.30am until 1pm. By the end of the year weekday trains ran from 8am until 9pm, and Sunday trains from after Divine Service until 10pm. In January 1837 the train speeds were given as 15 to 20mph on the down line and a maximum of 30mph on the up line.

On 23 March 1839 the board altered the regular service to a train in each direction every 20 minutes, but put on extra trains between 8 and 11am and 4 and 7pm at intervals of ten minutes before and after the regular trains, thus providing a ten-minute service during six hours of the day; these extra trains ran at a higher speed than the normal ones, and carried only first-class passengers at a fare of one shilling; the alteration did not prove justifiable, however, and the 15-minute service was resumed after a fortnight, to continue unchanged for many years.

At holiday times and on Sundays in the summer, the timetable was suspended, and the trains started as soon as they were filled, often at six-minute intervals during the peak periods. They were also lengthened, sometimes to nine carriages; the engines could have taken thirteen if the company had had the coaches available, but six trains of nine carriages each was about its limit in this direction.[38] At these periods the trains often ran until 2am.

The directors resolved at a board meeting on 10 June 1837 to run trains all day on Sunday, a decision by no means universally popular at that time. However, the trains were run without a break on Sundays for about two years, and then on 27 May 1839 they decided 'that it is the duty of the London & Greenwich Company to endeavour as far as lies in their power to set an example to the Metropolis of respect for the sanctity of the Sabbath by ceasing to run their trains during the time which is universally set apart for Morning Worship.' A copy of this statement was sent to the London & Croydon Railway, due to open in about a fortnight, and they agreed to conform although they had little choice in the matter so far as running over the Greenwich viaduct was concerned.

The rather unnatural quiet which descended upon London Bridge Station on Sunday mornings is described in a letter to *Herapath* of 14 December 1839.

I will . . . describe what took place at the Tooley Street Station on Sunday the 1st instant. On arriving at the gates at a quarter before one o'clock ,I found them shut, and a large assembly of upwards of 100 persons standing shivering in the cold (or rain had it done so), but no notice was put up as to what time the train would start; indeed we might have stood if a gentleman had not arrived who was immediately admitted, and who, having gained an entrance, stood provokingly picking his teeth, whilst we were left to look on, and do the best we could. We soon observed that this toothpicking gentleman was the Managing Director, who had just left a good luncheon, but not his church, though the appearance of things at the station would imply that all things had taken rest, and the persons employed there sent to church; but we were undeceived by a man in a box reading a paper. Thus we stood in the open air, not admitted even under the covered way, though that was erected by the former Managing Director for the accommodation of the public. Well, at one o'clock the gates slowly opened, and the parties were admitted as gradually as possible. Not a single individual, however, was present to tell them which were the carriages they were to go into, and we supposed the people were all gone to service. The man reading the newspaper when applied to did not know which were the carriages. So we got into the first that presented itself, and the train seemed to consist of upwards of twelve carriages. All this time not a word was spoken – everything was as still as death; and the parties kept crowding in and asking if this was the right train, which no-one could answer. Presently the stillness was slightly broken by the asthmatic breathing of what we supposed to be the engine, and a gentle motion indicating that something was going on; and we actually did not know till the last minute whether we were right or not; and the only indication which we had that we were to move at last was the slamming of the doors, but no 'all's right' or other notice of such a dangerous mode of starting. Presently we began to move, and at a quarter past one, by the wheezing sound, guessed we were in motion by steam; but that was so slow that at no time did we exceed 7 miles per hour; and when we arrived at the Greenwich Station it wanted a quarter to 2, being half an hour going the line.

The writer went on to say that the return journey was just as slow, his train having been delayed at Bermondsey by a down Croydon train '...whether on the same tram or not I cannot say'.

In December 1840 the London & Croydon Railway, apparently not having made itself familiar with a recent Act of Parliament, ran a train on Christmas Day between 11am and 1pm. The Greenwich secretary promptly drew their attention to section 18 of the Act, pointing out that they had rendered the London & Greenwich liable to a fine of £10.

Two additional trains each day were run from May 1844; one left Greenwich at 7.25am, calling at all stations, and the other left London Bridge at 10.15pm, also for all stations. The latter was for first-class ticket holders only.

A correspondent in 1839[39] suggested that the railway should hold trials to ascertain how many trains it could run at the same time. He argued that the more trains that passed a certain point, the safer it would be, '...as the vigilance of the switchman can never relax'. There is no record that the company ever tested this theory. It did, however, somehow contrive to maintain its fifteen-minute service all through the three-and-a-half years from 1841 when the line was in a constant state of upheaval from the building of the new viaduct,[40] the relaying and asphalting of the old line and the enlargement of London Bridge Station, and despite the influx of increasing traffic from the other railways; and during those years extra trains were still run on Sundays and holidays.

Chapter 5

Early Years on the
Greenwich Railway - II

T H E company intended, from an early date, to have the viaduct illuminated at night by gas lamps, and it referred to this project in pamphlets issued long before work on the railway was started. When, in 1834, it was decided to convert some of the arches into dwellings, and later, the possibility of so converting the whole viaduct was considered, the prospect arose of an immense consumption of gas along the railway. In 1835, therefore, a separate company, the Greenwich Railway Gas Company, was formed. The nominal capital was £20,000 in £1 shares, and the six directors were all members of the Greenwich Railway board. George Landmann was the engineer and J. Y. Akerman the secretary.

A prospectus of 1836[1] stated that

This Company has been formed for the purpose of providing the gas which will be required for the London & Greenwich Railway and the works connected with it, whether for the supply of the Lamps on the Railway and Footpath, or for warming and lighting the Cottages and Shops under the Railway, by the use of Gas Stoves, or for the supply of the gas cooking apparatus which will be adopted in the cottages.

Whishaw[2] in 1837 wrote that the whole viaduct was then '... furnished with gas light, the effect of which on a dark night is peculiarly striking'. To Londoners, unaccustomed to the lighting of streets outside the centre of the town, this straight, regular display of yellowish, flaring gas lamps nearly three miles long and visible for almost the whole way must have been impressive.

The real purpose of these lamps, set at intervals of about

22 yards, was not primarily to add beauty to the London scene at night, but to make it possible for the police to signal the trains during the hours of darkness by the same methods as they used in daylight. There were over two hundred lamps between London and Deptford, and the task of lighting them each evening, and of maintaining them, must have been a heavy one.

Since the project of creating some thousands of consumers fell through with the abandonment of the scheme for using the arches as cottages, the gas company was a failure financially, and an attempt was made early in 1838 to reconstitute it as the Deptford, Rotherhithe & Bermondsey Gas Light & Coke Company; the prospectus[3] of this concern refers to the gas works established on the banks of the Ravensbourne at Deptford, and reference was also made to the '.. mains already laid from Deptford to London Bridge' as the means of supplying gas to Bermondsey and Rotherhithe. It was also suggested that 'by the erection of Coke Ovens a ready supply of that material for the Engines of the numerous railways now forming in the locality must be a source of considerable profit...'.[4]

The original gasworks occupied a site between Creek Street and the west bank of the Ravensbourne, reached via one of the arches of the railway known as the 'Gas Arch'. A water-colour of 1841 shows the exterior of the works, and an entry in the Deptford Rate Book of 1843 mentions Retort Houses, Warehouses and a Wharf at 'Creek Street, London & Greenwich Railway'.

The lights went out on the viaduct for the last time one night in April 1838, for on the sixth of that month the board resolved '... that the gas lamps between the two termini be for the future discontinued'.

The idea of illuminating railways at night possibly originated on the London & Birmingham Railway, for in January 1831 it was stated that the company '... contemplate lighting the road in winter by gas, coal being procurable much of the way, and the by product, coke, will be useful as fuel'. There is some evidence of its application to inland waterways at an even earlier date.[5] The principle was developed on the Greenwich Railway by George Walter, who was still advocating it in 1840 when he suggested that some recent accidents might have been prevented

... if all railways starting from the Metropolis ... were properly lighted with gas within three or four miles of their respective stations at least, ... With this in view, some years since I got gas works erected for the cheap supply of lights to the Greenwich Railway . . But this safety principle was abandoned, from mistaken economy . . . that the public might travel in the dark over elevated viaducts and bridges . . .

The fares on the London & Greenwich Railway fluctuated considerably, since they were varied by the board frequently to meet the changing circumstances of the company. When competition from other forms of transport threatened the railway, either reductions were made, or increases were imposed to compensate for the loss of revenue from decreased traffic. The state of the carriages also influenced the fares; as they grew old and dilapidated, the tendency was to reduce the fares, but when new ones had to be provided an increase was considered justifiable to help pay for them.

On the opening of the line from Spa Road to Deptford in February 1836 a uniform fare of 6d was charged, there being no distinction of classes. By October, however, many more carriages were in service, and with the extension of the line to Bermondsey Street, the following scale of fares became effective:

	s.	d.
1st Class	1	0
2nd Class	0	9
3rd Class	0	6

The above is from an early fare-bill, of which there were at least two varieties. One is printed in black on blue-green paper, about 3in by 4in, and the other is rather larger, on white card printed in blue. The latter was probably either framed for exhibition at the stations and in the carriages, or distributed to local shops for display.

In December 1836, on the opening to London Bridge, the fares between there and Deptford were unchanged;

	s.	d.
The Imperial Carriages	1	0
Mail	0	9
Open carriage or omnibus	0	6

Free Tickets (not transferable) may be had at the Company's Offices, 26 Cornhill:

Imperial Carriage	£5 per quarter
Mail	£4 „ „
Omnibus or open carriage	£3 „ „

These 'Free Tickets' are believed to be the first railway season tickets ever to have been issued.

This second fare table appeared in the form of an advertisement in many London newspapers, and also as a poster, about the size of a newspaper page. The latter were printed in black, some on yellow paper, and some on white, and they had a rough reproduction of the familiar view of the railway crossing Corbetts Lane, but with the picture laterally reversed.[6]

On 1 May 1837 the third class was abolished, and the fares became 1s first and 6d second class. The local press thought that the third class should have been retained at a fare of 4d '... to accommodate the poorer classes'. The open third class carriages were kept in reserve for use at weekends and for the Greenwich Fair trains, but the fares were the same by either closed or open carriages; they were known officially as 'Second Class, Open'. At this time it was decided to take first class passengers only after 10pm, or at least to charge 1s each, whether the appropriate carriages were provided or not. For the next eighteen months no alteration was made in the maximum and minimum fares, and the board refused to increase them when requested to do so by a deputation from the Greenwich Steam Packet Company in February 1838.

In December 1838 50,000 handbills[7] were printed advertising the opening of the line to Greenwich, due to take place a week later, and announcing the new fares 1s first class (unchanged), and 8d second class. While these fares were still in force, it was stated in a mileage return to the Board of Trade that the rates were:

1st class	4d per mile
2nd class	
2nd class (open)	2d per mile

First class fares were thus charged on the basis of the railway being three miles long, and second class on its being four miles.

By December 1839 the quarterly season tickets had been discontinued, and the company refused an appeal by a number of regular passengers to restore them. Increasing competition had affected the railway by this time, and in an attempt to increase the traffic, third class open carriages were reintroduced in mid-1840 at a fare of 6d, on weekdays only.[8]

At a general meeting held in February 1841, George Walter

addressed the shareholders on the question of fares and locomotive expenses. It had been proposed to abolish the first class
fare of 1s, but he did not agree with this on the grounds that many
passengers would prefer that class '...in consequence of not
wishing to mix with the different characters on the line'.

When the first trains of some new composite carriages went into
service a further alteration in fares was made. From 1 January
1842 the first class was reduced to 9d, the second class discontinued
and the third class left at 6d. During the next month the following rates for children were announced:

Children in arms, under four years	Free
„ under ten years	2nd class fare
„ over ten years	Full price

This is the first reference to children's fares, and the concession
applied only to those who travelled first class.

On the suggestion of Miller, it was decided in June 1842 to
run special trains between 10 and 12pm at 50s per train, each
person over fifty paying one penny; this was in addition to the
10.15pm first-class-only train. There followed a certain amount
of unfavourable comment to the effect that the railway closed its
gates promptly at ten o'clock, and would rather turn intending
passengers away than carry them for less than first class fares.

Until 1840 the fares were for journeys over the whole length
of the line. In a return made to the select committee on railways
of that year the secretary stated: 'Some of the passengers only
go to Deptford, a distance of little more than three miles, but the
fare being the same as to Greenwich (and there being no separate
tickets given), the Return is made for the whole distance.'

By 1841, however, differential fares had been introduced, and
were given in the Railway Almanac for that year as:

	1st	2nd	3rd
To Greenwich	1s	8d	6d
To Deptford	9d	6d	4d

The fares introduced in January 1842 do not appear to have
been economic, for on 13 September the Board decided that they
were to be increased to 1s and 8d respectively. As there were still
some old carriages in service, however, the increase was delayed
until 10 October, by which time they had all been replaced,
either by new coaches or by respectable ones borrowed from other

railways. The new fares between Deptford and London Bridge were 9d and 6d, and for the first time separate fares were given for journeys between London Bridge and Spa Road – 6d and 4d, first and second class respectively.

The board had been urged in the previous April to issue return tickets at the single fare, in accordance with the practice adopted by the Hull & Selby Railway, in order to meet the increasing competition from river and road traffic.[9] Several new steam boats had recently been put into service, and the fare on these between London and Greenwich was 4d. The directors considered the suggestion, and did in fact introduce return tickets in October 1842; no reduction was made, however, and the fares being just double those for a single journey in each case, they did little to increase the number of passengers. Some passengers soon discovered that they could take return tickets from Deptford, and return to Greenwich; on this being reported to the board, notices were posted at the stations threatening the offenders with prosecution. As an experiment the rates for return tickets were revised in January 1843; they were issued from all stations, except Spa Road, at a flat rate of 1s 6d first class and 1s second class.

In August 1843 the fares were altered again to arrest a decline in traffic following the reduction of the bus fare from 1s to 6d. The first class fare was reduced to 8d '. . . either to or from Greenwich, Deptford, the Spa Road or London, with return tickets for the day at 1s each'; the second class was reduced to 6d, with returns at 10d. Annual tickets at 12 gns. and 10 gns. respectively were also considered. Further, the restoration of third class open carriages at a fare of 4d, but with no return tickets, was recommended as soon as suitable carriages could be obtained.

The reductions in the first and second class fares were made five days later, on 20 August, and the secretary prepared and signed in advance twelve annual tickets of each class. Miller was sent off to Derby at once to borrow some third class carriages from the North Midland Railway, pending the construction of new ones, and on his return he said that he could start running them on 29 August.

With the introduction of the new scale of fares in August 1843 the company dropped the practice of charging different amounts for travel between intermediate stations and the terminus. The system had never been wholly satisfactory on the L&GR because it had not been adopted completely.

No further drastic changes were made by the L&G Railway. In January 1844 the second class annual tickets were reduced to 8 gns, and the fare by the special down train at 10.15pm, which had remained at 1s, was reduced to 8d; the extra charge which holders of day return tickets had to pay for travelling by this train was also abolished. In April the board decided to suspend the issue of return tickets on Whit Monday and Tuesday.

The results of the reduction in fares of August 1843 were not very encouraging; to the 31 December an additional 151,947 passengers had been carried over the corresponding period of 1842, but the receipts had fallen by £966.

If the board had adopted all the suggestions it received from helpful or disgruntled shareholders, its fares would have been more confusing than they were; a typical letter of 1840 ran

If it should be thought inconvenient to have Third Class passengers mixed with those of other classes, let every alternate train be a third class at not exceeding 5d each passenger, (the room to each passenger being economised as much as possible, and the carriages being made plain, without covers, which would prevent the more respectable classes going by them).[10]

There were various reasons for all the changes made from time to time in the fares on the L&GR. The railways could, of course, vary their rates at that time without consulting any authority, and legally, they were not obliged to provide trains at all. The Greenwich Railway Act of 1833, in common with others of that period, merely provided for the building of a 'railroad'. George Walter, when appearing in 1836 before a committee of the House of Lords on the London & Dover Railway Bill, was asked: 'Have any persons a right to run carriages on your road, paying tolls?' to which he replied: 'They have, the same as on all railroads.' To the next question: 'May I start a carriage if I please, by payment of the tolls?', he answered 'Yes.' Had it been feasible for private trains to have been run over the line, the company would have had no control over, and little interest in, the fares charged, so long as it received the toll from the operator of the train service. As the company itself provided the trains, it naturally made whatever charges it thought would yield the greatest profit for the time being.

It is interesting to note that the Greenwich Railway regarded a part of the fare received as a toll paid by the passenger for passing over the line. Thus, the fares of 1838-40 were analysed as follows[11]

	Charge for locomotive power and carriages.	Toll for each passenger.	Total fare.
1st Class	9d	3d	1s
2nd Class	5d	3d	8d

The 1833 Act provided for a maximum fare for all classes of passengers along the whole of the railway, or any part of it, of 1s 6d each, '... including the use of the company's carriages and locomotive power...'; if they provided their own engines and carriages, the maximum toll was 9d.

The directors of the L&GR held firmly to the opinion that fares should be related to the cost of constructing the line, and as the Greenwich Railway served an area of high, and rapidly increasing population, so the costly viaduct was necessary to carry it; but it was precisely in such a locality that alternative forms of transport were already long established, and their competition for the traffic effectively kept the railway fares down.[12]

A small fraction of all railway fares in those days represented Railway Passenger Duty, payable by the companies to the Treasury. This was provided for by an Act of 16 August 1832,[13] and was the same rate for all classes of passenger, viz. $\frac{1}{8}d$ per mile. At first a composition of the tax was permitted in order to encourage the railways, particularly the short lines, in their earliest years. The L&GR made its first payment to the Stamp Office on 12 March 1836; the amount of £28 18s 9d paid, represented the 20,412 journeys over the length of line then open during the first month's working. The company in fact paid duty at the full rate for the first year, but then, on petitioning the Treasury, it was allowed to compound for £400; in 1839 it commenced paying at the full rate again.

In the matter of tickets the L&GR did not, for obvious reasons, follow the example of the main line railways which at that time used printed paper tickets and counterfoils completed in handwriting by booking clerks. Instead, it adopted, in a modified form, the procedure used on the Dublin & Kingstown Railway, where silver-nickel tokens were issued; on the Irish line, however, the class of travel was inscribed on the token, but none of the surviving examples of Greenwich Railway tokens give any such indication.

Known variously as tallies, tokens and countermarks, this form of ticket is the oldest known, its use having been traced back to the ancient world. The name cheque, or check-ticket was often indiscriminately applied to these tokens and to paper tickets, although the terms belong properly to paper tickets with counter-foils.

In July 1835 the company ordered a 'Tale Register for 10,000 persons' from Messrs Stevens & Sons, Engineers of Southwark. This was probably a rack for storing the tokens (or 'tallies'), with some device for counting or recording the number issued, but nothing is known about it except that it cost £15. In 1836 the first class passengers received paper tickets, showing the number of the carriage and seat to be occupied, and an example of one of these old tickets exists. It is of dark orange-red paper measuring $2\frac{3}{4}$in by $1\frac{1}{2}$in, printed in black.[14]

The tickets and tokens were issued by booking-clerks, or money-takers as they were usually called, and taken at the barrier by collectors, or cheque-takers, before the trains were entered; as the choice of destination was limited, and while the fares were the same in any case, there was no necessity for passengers to retain their tickets during the journey.

The board thought its receipts were below what they should have been and in December 1837 it decided to install turnstiles at the stations '. . . as a check on the money-takers', similar to those then used at Vauxhall and Southwark Bridges. On 9 February 1838 Colonel Landmann was asked to have the turnstiles sited, and boxes were erected for the men who were to work them. They came into use in February 1838.

At first the turnstile system applied only to third-class passengers, and at Deptford, as at London Bridge, first and second class passengers entered the station by different gates; by 1843, however, all passengers used them. It is believed that the London & Greenwich was the first to use turnstiles, although the practice spread to other lines.[15]

In December 1838 the directors investigated the system of fare collection employed on the buses, and three months later placed orders for 97,000 paper tickets with J. Wertheimer & Co, printers, of London Wall, at about 8s per thousand. Season tickets were of the printed card variety, and the Committee for Working the

Line suggested in February 1842 that books of first-class tickets be issued, in order to save the money-takers and the passengers time and trouble. They were to be paid for in advance, and to be valid for six months, but there is no record that the recommendation was actually adopted.

An order for 5,000 metal tokens was given to Messrs Thomas Dowler & Co, medallists, etc., of Birmingham, in June 1840, but there is no evidence to show which of the three principal varieties this order covered. The following description of the examples of tokens that have survived is taken from various sources; the design is the same on both sides in every case:

1   Copper, 34mm diameter. A flying horse (Pegasus) running to left. 'London and Greenwich Railway Company'. (Said to be rare; some 'silvered' examples exist).

2   Design and size as above, in lead.

3   Design and size as above, in brass.

4   Design and size as above, in thick, pale pink cardboard.

5   Copper, 28mm diameter. Arms of London and Kent on an ornamental shield. 'London & Greenwich Railway Company'. Legend begins at bottom, and is continuous round the edge. (Said to be a more common type; some 'silvered' examples exist).

6   Copper, 26mm diameter, milled edge. Design as above, but legend begins at top right and continues round edge to top left.

The traces of 'silver' remaining on some of the specimens is in fact tin. On 13 July 1839 a board minute refers to '... copper cheques sometimes mistaken for coins . . . to be tinned over'. What probably happened was that passengers sometimes foisted halfpennies and pennies on to the collectors, and kept their tokens for another occasion; the difference in diameter was negligible, Nos 1 to 4 above corresponding to the penny of that time, and No 5 to the halfpenny.[16] The milled edge of No 6 was presumably provided for the same reason.

The metal tokens appear to have been used continuously for third class passengers, and intermittently for the other classes. Although the various types of token were not very distinctive they could have been used by most passengers since they came on to the platforms through different waiting rooms, doors and turnstiles according to the class of travel they had paid for. It is, however, difficult to see how they could have been used when differential fares for intermediate stations and return tickets were introduced, and other arrangements must have been made for these journeys. Third-class travel over the whole length of the line, in any case, accounted for most of the journeys made over the Greenwich Railway.

It appears that by 1844 the offices of money-taker and collector were combined. At that period each money-taker had a float of £4, but they were responsible for making good any losses arising from mistakes in issuing tickets, or in '... the turn of the turn-table', which suggests that they had control of the turnstiles themselves.

On the opening of the railway 'Free Life Tickets' were pre-sented to the more distinguished guests; these were of silver, 39mm in diameter, and were engraved with the name of the recipient. In January 1838 the board granted a free pass to Superintendent Mallalieu, of the Greenwich Metropolitan Police, and in June 1839 the directors of the Greenwich and Croydon Railways exchanged ivory passes enabling them and their respective engineers to travel over each other's lines. Examples of the above are extant, as also are silver directors' passes and engineers' tickets in brass; the latter bore serial numbers. All these special passes had the Corbetts Lane view engraved on the obverse, and carried various inscriptions on the reverse.[17]

No contemporary evidence has come to light concerning the use of platform tickets on the Greenwich Railway, but an article written seventy years ago refers to the public being admitted to London Bridge Station on payment of one penny '... to see the trains start'.[18]

The records of the L&GR contain some fragments of information about the men who worked on the line from which it is possible to get a glimpse of the activities of those first London railwaymen.

At the beginning the company employed only one or two clerks, and the first men to work on the railway were those employed by McIntosh, of whom there were more than 600 at the period of greatest building activity. In addition to these, a great number were employed indirectly, the brickmakers and lime-burners, the bargemen, and those engaged in demolition work. The employment afforded to such large numbers of men by the new railways was frequently commented upon in those days, and the Greenwich Railway was congratulated from time to time on the way in which it was relieving unemployment in the district.

The first applicant for a job on the L&GR had his case entered in the minutes of the board in May 1834; he wanted to be a watchman, and soon afterwards was engaged.

The minutes of the Liverpool & Manchester Railway record that in October 1835 that company was asked by the London & Greenwich directors for particulars of the salaries paid to various classes of employees, and the details were supplied by their treasurer. It was the custom at that time for railway companies to seek information from the Liverpool & Manchester Railway; its position as the first important line in the kingdom gave it considerable prestige and authority, and it seems to have been very willing to give the other lines the benefit of the experience gained by its three or four years seniority.

A description of the railway just before its official opening in December 1836 mentions those of its servants with whom the public was likely to come into contact;[19] these were the police, of whom there were thirty, and the conductors and carriage-men, numbering twelve. The conductors, or guards as they were soon to be called, wore a dark green uniform with brass buttons bearing a design incorporating the arches of the viaduct, while the collectors wore blue frock-coats with silver lace, with caps to match. Policemen and pointsmen wore tall hats with waterproof crowns, and long cutaway coats; they were also supplied with greatcoats by the company, and the police were issued with truncheons. Except in the case of the police, the original uniforms were not replaced, although the company continued to supply its outdoor staff with 'rough weather coats'.

At the opening of the railway the total establishment was about 150, with a weekly wages bill of £260, but when the line had been in operation for about a year the first reductions in staff were made; sixteen artificers, three policemen and five junior conductors were discharged in November and December 1837, but at the same time an inspector was engaged at £1 per day. The police on the L&GR came and went as the traffic rose and fell; as Easter 1838 approached, four extra constables were taken on for the week to control the passengers who would be crowding the trains from 8am until 2am the next day; these were virtually Special Constables. During 1838 four more brakesmen went, and the hours of those remaining were increased to ten in the summer months, and 9 hours 40 minutes in the winter, at 3s 6d per day. The 'Hammer Man' at Deptford Works had his wages raised from 2s to 2s 6d a day at this time.

Among some amusing suggestions made by the *Kentish Mercury* in March 1838 on the management of the railway, were these, directed at the staff:

Some of the trains have three steps, and the conductors should always let the whole of them down – all ladies are not fond of displaying the beauty of their legs and ankles.

Order the conductors not to press the ladies' fingers and stare them full in the face when they hand them into carriages – it may some day or other lead some gentleman or other to the necessity of giving the offending party a kick, somewhere or other.

The conductors and engineers should be more guarded in their conversation (particularly at the Deptford terminus) – all that falls from their lips is not fit for 'ears polite'.

From all accounts the ears of any traveller in that neighbourhood should long have been attuned to the vigorous English of watermen, and coach and bus drivers; perhaps a higher standard was expected of railwaymen.

Until they were dismissed in September 1838, the company had a grade of employee known by the curious name of 'Hook Rope Men'. They had no distinctive uniform, but were supplied with rough weather coats, as were the drivers and firemen. One was stationed at each end of the line, and their job was to detach the engine from its train, upon its arrival at London Bridge or Deptford, and to re-couple it by means of a tow-rope. The engine then proceeded to tow the train into the station, running itself on the adjacent line to which it had been diverted, the points afterwards being restored before the train at the end of its rope reached them. This arrangement left the engine free to take another train back immediately, without the necessity of pushing the carriages, and superseded that of fly-shunting. The practice was fairly general at that time; on the London & Croydon Railway the men were called 'Tail Rope Men', and in June 1840 one of them, with the driver of the engine *Sussex*, was held responsible for damaging two carriages of a train borrowed from the Greenwich Railway, by getting the rope caught on the water-crane.

The hook rope men went from the London & Greenwich during an attempt to work the line more economically. The carriages were fitted with improved brakes at this time, and the company intended replacing the small staff of conductors and brakesmen attached to each train by one man. Commenting on the proposed new arrangement, the *Kentish Mercury* predicted a hectic and somewhat hazardous life for the guard:

...no conductors to the trains, no brakesmen to attend to the breaks [*sic*] . . . no persons to attend to the hooking or un-hooking of the engine . . . the new man will have to see all the passengers into the carriages, then to fasten up all the doors and put up all the steps to the different carriages, and see all safe for starting; then to give the word and off the trains go. Arrived at the other end . . . he must ease the carriages, preparatory to stopping them with the 'new break'. He must then take the pin out that connects the engine with the train, and hook on a rope to the engine, that it may continue to drag the train after it (the engine) has gone off that line of rail to take back the next train. The man must then jump off the train, and run ready to break his neck to un-hook the rope again, and coil it upon the train. He then stops the train completely with the new break...[20]

The first engine drivers on the Greenwich Railway came from the Liverpool & Manchester in 1835 and 1836, and they presumably trained others as the need arose. It was said of them 'In experience they cannot be outstripped, having been on the Liverpool & Manchester at the opening, in the days of the *Rocket*',[21] and on the dismissal of one of them in October 1837 the London & Croydon directors told their engineer to interview him with a view to retaining his services for their line; this was nine months before their first locomotive was delivered.

A brief entry in the minutes of 8 February 1842 records the board's decision to pay all the drivers and firemen a bonus, as there had been no delay to any train in the previous six months. This was certainly an achievement worthy of recognition, for the service then in operation would have required more than 20,000 trains to run during this period; moreover, builders were at work enlarging the viaduct, the original lines were being taken up and re-laid, and there were Croydon and Brighton trains running on the Greenwich rails.

By June 1839 there was probably a certain amount of casual labour employed on the railway, for there were comments on the 'shoal of needy looking men' waiting for employment outside the offices at London Bridge on Tuesdays and Saturdays, when the board meetings were held.

The establishment in 1840,[22] excluding the engineer, secretary and clerks, was 105, made up as follows:

5	Collectors	3	Coke and water fillers
22	Police	4	Cleaners
5	Porters	4	Fitters
7	Pointsmen	1	Millwright
12	Guards	5	Smiths
3	Watchmen	2	Boiler-makers
11	Waymen	1	Joiner
8	Engine drivers	4	Carpenters
8	Firemen		

The wages of an engine driver were £2 per week, and those of a fireman £1 2s 0d; on the advice of Miller the board raised the pay of the latter to twenty-five shillings a week, exclusive of Sundays, in November 1840.

The company seems to have been a good employer by the standards of over a century ago, for whilst it would condone no negligence, it treated its steady and reliable men well, and on occasion, generously. There are instances of rewards being paid to men who had, by their vigilance, prevented accidents on the line, and the board usually paid the full wages of men who were absent on sick leave, if the illness was attributable to their employment. Several cases are recorded of the directors agreeing not to deduct the pay of policemen and others who had caught colds while on duty.

The payments made to the dependents of those of the company's servants who were killed on the railway were at the discretion of the board, and generally amounted to between one and two months wages. In April 1839 a brakesman named John Ferneaux was killed at Greenwich when a down train ran over him, and £5 was paid to his widow by the board; in addition a subscription list was opened at Greenwich Station by the passengers, and rapidly filled. On 9 January 1840 another brakesman was killed; the records state that this man, Thomas Hayward, passed along the outside of a carriage while the train was running, and slipping off, fell beneath the train which ran over him. The company paid his burial expenses of £6 and gave £5 to his mother.

On the whole the company was fortunate in the men it employed. From 1836 until 1845 there was no accident serious enough to cause the death of a passenger – although of course, some were killed and injured through their own fault – and many millions had been carried in those nine years. Colonel Landmann, in evidence before a House of Commons Committee in 1840,[23] stated that the running of trains on the London & Greenwich Railway was eight to ten times more frequent than on the Liverpool & Manchester line. The trains were sent off at intervals behind each other – very short intervals at holiday times – and it was the responsibility of the enginemen, the switchmen and the police to ensure that they came to no harm. That there were so few accidents, even when other railways started to use the already congested Greenwich lines, says much for the efficiency of the staff.

The company naturally had some irresponsible characters in its service, until it discovered who they were. Almost as soon as the line was opened a fatal accident occurred, and the report of the inquest gives an insight into the early working of the line.[24]

The inquest was held at the Railway Beer Shop, High Street, Deptford, on William Sadler a brakesman who was killed near Deptford Station on Monday afternoon 24 January 1837. Benjamin Dawson, one of the engine drivers from the Liverpool & Manchester Railway, was driving the *Victoria* with the 4.15 from London Bridge, and on approaching the points outside Deptford Station, the train was cast off by Sadler, who was the brakesman on the leading carriage. On reaching the points the engine was derailed and the driver called back to the brakesmen on the train now following closely to put down their brakes, but they could not stop in time, and several carriages were thrown off the line by the impact. Sadler jumped off the footboard of the first carriage just before it was derailed and was crushed between the train and the south parapet wall of the viaduct. Another brakesman saw that the points were incorrectly set and that the point-shifter, Paull, was absent. He was, in fact, in the Brown Bear opposite the station with a friend, having arranged with the fireman of the *Dottin* that the latter would attend to the points in his absence. Jackson, the fireman, had seen the 4 o'clock train in, and expecting Paull back any minute, had returned to his engine without resetting the points; neither man had told Acting Serjeant Baker, in charge at Deptford, of the arrangement or sought his permission. Both Jackson and Paull were dismissed, but the pointsman was acquitted of wilful neglect as he had made some provision for his duties during his absence.

In November 1838 a collector was dismissed for striking a passenger, and a policeman who was present at the time of the assault but took no action, was reprimanded. This was a bad month for collectors and policemen, for a few days later Collector Groom and Constable Sinclair forced a Mr Kirby and his sister to pass through a turnstile together. The board received a very indignant letter from the victim of this curious incident, and the result was the dismissal of Sinclair, the collector this time getting off with a warning. This same policeman Sinclair seems to have been a reckless individual, for on 11 November 1836 he had jumped up behind the 7.30 train to London after it had started, intending to get off at Spa Road Station, where he was to go on duty. As there were no passengers to put down at Spa Road, and the driver had not seen Sinclair get on to the train, he did not stop. The policeman, therefore, jumped off as the train went through the station at full speed, hit the parapet wall, injured his face and head, and was picked up later unconscious.

A good deal of responsibility rested with the police, particularly with those known as train serjeants. The one at Deptford, for instance, was empowered to alter the times of the trains if he thought it necessary to do so. There was also a visiting serjeant who travelled on the trains and kept control over the constables. The switchmen were largely responsible for regulating the time interval between the trains, and for this purpose the company supplied them with '... time-pieces at £4. 10s 0d each ...' in May 1839. In earlier days the drivers had gauged their speed and timed the trains from two church clocks visible from the viaduct, those of Deptford Church and Bermondsey New Church.[25]

By the end of 1839 there were no police on the footpath by the railway, a circumstance which led a correspondent to complain in the *Railway Times*[26] of the unprotected state of this path; he added that '... boys, and indeed grown up men, resort within the enclosed walls with guns and pistols, and discharge them altogether recklessly at birds on the wall and ground.'

As the L&GR had sought advice from the Liverpool &

Manchester in its early days on the question of staff, so it in turn was asked for information as to hours of work and salaries by the London & Croydon Railway in 1839. The detailed reply shows that the clerk's day started at 7am and the office remained open until midnight. Five money-takers were employed at 30s per week, two each at London Bridge and Greenwich, and one at Deptford; these had to find securities of £200. There were '... two Brakesmen or Guards to each train, who also act as Conductors'; their wages were £1. 4s 6d per week. Each station had two superintendents whose duties were '... to inspect the trains, close the carriages and report time'; three of these received £100 a year, whilst their assistants were paid twenty-six shillings a week. Finally, the salary of the company's accountant, who incidentally, supplied all this information, was £250 per annum, increasing yearly by £25, to £500.

It will have been noted that there is no reference to station-masters in the foregoing pages; in fact, this particular appointment appears to have been unknown on the Greenwich line. London Bridge and Deptford stations were originally in the charge of police serjeants, but in January 1839, after the opening of Greenwich Station, three inspectors were appointed to these duties; one of them, Bishop, was formerly 'cash-taker at the Creek Bridge, and one of the most obliging and attentive men the Company ever had upon their line'. These inspectors were promoted to superintendents a few months later, and each was provided with an assistant. The stations themselves were, in effect, police stations, even having the outward appearance of such, for in January 1838 the board resolved: 'That a blue light be kept burning at each end of the line until the trains cease running at night', i.e. at London Bridge and Deptford stations.

Among the records is an old book, found at Deptford Station in 1952, containing entries of the dates and times the Ravensbourne Bridge was lifted; pasted in the cover is the following document:

London & Greenwich Railway Office,
London Terminus, 5 March 1842.
Duties of Bridge Master
To be in constant attendance at the bridge during Flood Tide and 45 minutes afterwards.

To see that the machinery for opening the bridge be kept well oiled and in good working condition.

To open the bridge for all vessels only having fixed or standing masts or sails within 10 minutes after application ... and to close the bridge immediately after the vessel has passed through ...

To see that the switches be replaced and properly fixed after the bridge is lowered and in its place, and remember no excuse will be on any account admitted for the smallest neglect of this duty which may be attended with most frightful consequences.

To superintend and give orders to the persons appointed to wind up the wooden bridge, and to report any neglect of duty or inattention on their part. While unoccupied in the duties above set forth, to render any services for the Interests of the Company which may be required by the Superintendent (Mr Miller).

J. Y. Akerman.

The first bridgemaster, a man named Page, was appointed in January 1839 at a wage of 25s a week.

As the company's profits tended to fall after 1840, the establishment was gradually reduced, the police being the first to go. In May 1842 three conductors were dismissed, and the pay of the remaining nine was increased from £1. 4s 6d to £1. 6s 3d. A month later a lamplighter, an engineman, a fireman, a porter and a cokeman went. By August 1843 the police force had been reduced to six, and one shareholder thought this number excessive, and their embroidered gold collars an extravagance.

There was a tendency on all the early railways to engage and dismiss staff as the occasion demanded, a practice which caused the Board of Trade some concern after a fatal accident on the North Midland Railway in 1843. In a circular letter to all the companies they emphasised the importance of employing adequate staff, and concluded with the following observation:

The experience of the last three years has fully satisfied their Lordships that the comparative exemption which has been lately enjoyed from the alarming accidents which occurred so frequently during the infancy of railway travelling is to be attributed mainly to the gradual formation of establishments of experienced and trustworthy engine drivers and other servants upon all the leading passenger railways, and that it is only by maintaining such establishments that a repetition of such accidents can be effectually prevented.[27]

Chapter 6

Relations with Other Railways

REFERENCE has been made to a number of railways that were associated to some extent with the L&GR in that they were to join it at various points and use its line to London Bridge. Most of the history of the Gravesend extension, in its various guises, has already been traced, but the project actually lingered on for some time after the inquiry of 1837. The Deptford & Gravesend Railway, with George Landmann as engineer, produced plans in March 1838[1] for a line with a separate terminus at London Bridge to the south of that of the L&GR, but the project was shelved. In 1840, however, two Bills for eastward extensions of the Greenwich line came before Parliament. The Central Kentish Railway, stemming from a public meeting held at Canterbury in November 1836, sought powers for a line from Loving Edward's Lane, Deptford, to Deal, with a loop from St Mary Cray to Maidstone, and the Greenwich & Rochester Railway, undeterred by the failure of its predecessors, submitted its plans for a line via Greenwich, Charlton, Erith and Gravesend to Strood.

The Imperial Kent Railway made a brief appearance in the advertisement columns in January 1840 with its plans for a line from Greenwich via Woolwich to Rochester, Margate and Ramsgate. It was the last attempt of George Walter, who had devised a new method of raising the capital; investors were invited to buy the stock outright, by which means the full capital required would be available before construction started, and the bulk of it was to be invested in gilt-edged securities, thus producing interest for distribution until such time as the securities had to be realised to pay for the building of the line.

Yet another line, the London & Chatham Railway, attempted to effect a junction with the L&GR at Deptford in February 1841.

Of the less ambitious projects, the following deserve notice. The Westminster Bridge, Deptford & Greenwich Railway was a development of a scheme of 1835 for a line starting from St Mark's Church, Kennington Common, and sweeping across south London, to join the L&GR at two points and the Croydon Railway at Cold Blow Farm, near New Cross.[2] On applying for an Act in February 1837 the company was found to have produced a fraudulent subscription list,[3] and the application failed, as did efforts to revive the project in 1838 and 1839.

The Grand Surrey Canal Railway advertised its intention of building a railroad along the canal bank to connect the London & Southampton terminus at Nine Elms with the river at Deptford, in October 1835;[4] the scheme lay dormant for nearly ten years, when in July 1845 the SER was asked to construct the section from the Greenwich line to the river, but nothing further is heard of it. The South Metropolitan Railway, later known as the Bermondsey & Lambeth Railway, was virtually an extension of the L&GR from a point just east of London Bridge to a new terminus in Westminster Bridge Road; its plans were published in 1839,[5] and it applied unsuccessfully for an Act in 1840. At the same time, and with no more success, the Joiner Street–Staines Railway sought powers for a line from Staines via Ealing, Hammersmith, Kensington, Chelsea, Clapham, Brixton, Camberwell, Bermondsey, and then parallel with and to the south of the L&GR viaduct, to London Bridge.

The most modest of all these projects was one that originated in Deptford as the Deptford Pier Junction Railway. It was for a line on arches to leave the Greenwich viaduct at Deptford Station and run north to a new pier, to be built on the river, a distance of about half a mile. A temporary pier was erected in 1835 on land given by Gordon & Co, the engineers, and Adam Gordon was a director of the railway company, as were several of the Greenwich Railway board, including Walter, while Landmann was the engineer. This was the only one of the companies mentioned so far to obtain an Act;[6] this it did on 21 June 1836, when a large batch of railway Bills received the Royal Assent, including the South Eastern, Midland Counties and other important lines. After Twells and Walter had severed their connection with the L&GR, the branch line received little encouragement from the new directors, or from the Croydon Railway, which it then planned to join, and the project was finally abandoned in 1839.[7]

For various reasons all these companies failed. Apart from the Gravesend lines, however, their failure probably did not distress the Greenwich directors nearly as much as their success might have embarrassed them; for by 1837 three other companies had obtained Acts, and were eventually to send their trains over the Greenwich line.

The first of these, the London & Croydon Railway, was authorised by its Act of 12 June 1835[8] to build a line from Corbetts Lane on the London & Greenwich, to Croydon via Forest Hill, and to run its trains over the Greenwich viaduct to London Bridge. The South Eastern Railway (generally known as the London & Dover Railway during the first ten years or so) received its Act on 21 June 1836,[9] empowering it to build a line from Croydon via Oxted and Ashford, to Dover, using the Croydon and Greenwich Railways to reach London Bridge. Various amending Acts subsequently altered the route. When the London & Brighton Railway – which had been formed from six separate companies, all of which had been competing for powers to build a line to Brighton – was authorised on 15 July 1837[10] to construct its line from a junction with the Croydon Railway at Norwood, the South Eastern entered into an arrangement with it to share a line between the junction and Redhill.

When the London & Croydon Bill was before Parliament, the Greenwich Company had spent nearly half a million pounds on its line, and the cost had well exceeded this amount when the other companies applied for their Acts. There was no reason to suppose that they could have built separate lines into London more cheaply, and none of them wished to add this sum to their initial cost for a small fraction of their total mileage, hence their desire to use the line already built by the Greenwich Railway through part of London. Not only did they thus save themselves the expense of the most costly section of their route – the cost of the entire London & Croydon being estimated in the Act at only £140,000 – but they avoided the trouble of acquiring land in the metropolis, and consequently, by reducing the number of opponents to their respective Bills, increased their chances of success.

In the year 1839 a dispute began between the Greenwich and Croydon Railways, which in a few years brought to an end the separate existences of both of them. The dispute resolves itself roughly into two phases; the first lasted from 1839 until 1842, and the second from 1842 until it culminated in the London &

Greenwich Railway being taken over on lease by the South Eastern Railway on 1 January 1845.

It is first necessary to go back to 1834, however, when on 14 November the first meeting of the London & Croydon Railway Company was held; the company's intention '... to commence at the present Greenwich Railway about 2 miles from the Borough ...' was entered in the minutes. In December the company approached the Greenwich board on the question of tolls payable for running trains to London Bridge, and the London & Greenwich at that time suggested one half of its own fares.

In September 1835 the London & Greenwich gave a detailed list of the tolls to be paid on a variety of goods, including coal, sugar, grain, cotton and livestock, and on private carriages brought up on the trains, for which 9d was quoted. Meanwhile, the Croydon Company had obtained its Act, and on 30 December 1835 the first toll agreement between the two companies was signed. This was for 3d per passenger, plus £110 a year for additional watchmen, lamps etc to be provided by the London & Greenwich Railway.

The London & Croydon Railway had originally intended joining the Greenwich line at a point just east of the Grand Surrey Canal, no doubt to avoid the trouble of bridging it, but Colonel Landmann suggested Corbetts Lane, about 1¾ miles from London Bridge and west of the canal. On 23 July 1836 the Croydon Railway agreed to meet the wishes of the London & Greenwich engineer, although it would involve the company in additional expense. One of the first sections of the Croydon line to be completed was the short viaduct of thirty-six arches at Corbetts Lane which led to the embankment upon which the line was continued.

The main part of the London & Croydon Railway was built during 1838, and there were differences between the two companies on the question of the purchase of Greenwich Railway land. By April 1839 the Croydon engineers were ready to construct the junction from the new viaduct at Corbetts Lane, but the London & Greenwich refused to allow the section of parapet wall to be pulled down to enable the rails and points to be laid until the outstanding land dispute had been settled. Thereupon, the London & Croydon threatened to petition Parliament to amend a Bill before it to compel the London & Greenwich to co-operate. Work then started, and by 22 April a single line was ready, and the second line nearly laid; on that day a special train ran from Croydon to London Bridge carrying the London & Croydon directors.[11] The junction was eventually completed on 31 May, and the board decided that the opening of the Croydon Railway, provisionally fixed for Wednesday 5 June 1839, '... may be safely advertised'.

By this time the London & Croydon Railway was in deep water, the revised estimate of £195,000 having been exceeded by nearly half-a-million pounds. The company had intended, when it bought the Croydon canal, to drain it and lay its line along the bed, following the curves and gradients of the old canal, thus avoiding the necessity of buying ordinary property. During the arguments on the Brighton Railway Bills of 1836, however, Stephenson had said that such a line would be quite unsuitable for the London & Brighton Railway trains which had to use the Croydon Railway, and in consequence the plans had to be modified at considerable cost.

Labour, materials and locomotives all increased in price during the years when the London & Croydon Railway was under construction, and although this undoubtedly influenced the Croydon Railway in its subsequent dealings with the London & Greenwich on the toll question, it is interesting to note that despite the fact that the Croydon line cost over three times as much to build as was originally estimated, its cost per mile was still only one-third that of the Greenwich.

In March 1839 the London & Greenwich asked the Croydon Railway the weight and power of its engines, and the London & Croydon asked the Greenwich Railway to issue a certificate of their fitness to travel over the viaduct. The matter was referred to Colonel Landmann, who replied that he had no objection to the *Kent*. On 11 May Miller tested the *London* and reported that it was '... a safe and proper engine to traverse the London & Greenwich Railway', and certificates were issued accordingly.

Preparations were made in February 1839 to reverse the running of the L&GR trains so that they ran on the left, and the new arrangements came into effect in April, in good time for the arrival of the Croydon trains on the line. Although only temporary stations existed at this time, extensive modifications had to be carried out after the three years of right-hand running.

The London & Croydon Railway was duly opened on 5 June, but its trains had not been running to London Bridge for quite a fortnight when the first signs that the arrangement might prove to be inconvenient, if not dangerous, began to appear. On 18 June Miller sent the following report to the London & Greenwich directors,

On the arrival of the $\frac{1}{4}$ to 10 up train Mills the driver reported that in coming in he had very nearly met with an accident, he being immediately behind the Croydon train, which was behind time and without signal lights behind, and he had much difficulty in avoiding running into the train.

On 28 June a similar occurrence was reported; the London & Croydon Railway replied that the rails and switches on the London & Greenwich were in such a bad state that the excessive jolting of the trains caused the lamps to be extinguished. This part of the Greenwich railway was still laid on stone sleepers in 1839. The Greenwich services were seriously disorganised on 25 July when a London & Croydon locomotive, travelling too fast over the points outside London Bridge, became derailed.

One of the earliest London & Croydon Railway timetables dated 19 August 1839[12] shows twelve 'Down trains from Tooley Street' daily during the week and nineteen on Sundays. During the week the down trains left at '20 minutes after 8, 9, 10, 12, 2, etc to 9', and on Sundays from '10 minutes before 9' at half-hourly intervals until '20 minutes after 9' pm. There was an interval in the service between 9.50 am and 1.50 pm on Sundays. In each case there was about the same number of up trains.

In October 1839 the London & Croydon rather unwisely altered the times of its trains without reference to the London & Greenwich, and apparently without even bothering to look at the Greenwich timetable, for the new departure times from London Bridge were the same as those of the Greenwich trains. The first intimation the London & Greenwich received was a copy of the printed placard bearing the public announcement of the revised times, which the London & Croydon office sent along for its information, and which it was promptly told to withdraw.

In April and May 1839 the Select Committee on Railway Communications examined witnesses on the subject of the railways using London Bridge station and the Greenwich viaduct, and some interesting comments and suggestions were made to it. Colonel Landmann thought that all the trains of the London & Croydon, London & Brighton, and South Eastern Railways might easily run on a single line, since they would require only three or four minutes to cover the distance between London Bridge and the junction. He did not regard the consequences of a train of one company overtaking or meeting that of another on the viaduct as very serious, adding that '... the crash would not be great if it did occur'. On the question of the speed of the London & Greenwich trains, Landmann said 'The greatest speed is 28 miles an hour', but that 22 mph was normal; they were travelling at their maximum speed as they passed over Corbetts Lane Junction.

Benjamin Cubitt, for the SER, also suggested that the Greenwich trains should use only one line, but that longer trains should be run every half-hour instead of short ones every fifteen minutes. The Greenwich directors stated, however, that a twenty-minute service had been tried for a short time, but that they had been compelled by public demand to revert to the original one. A half-hourly service of longer trains would not meet the case at all, they said, as people would then use the boats: '... it is only the speed which brings persons on the line.'[13]

Cubitt was really of the opinion, however, that London Bridge would never be a satisfactory terminus for the main lines serving an area in an arc extending from Margate to Worthing, and he suggested the following alternatives for the London terminus:

1. A branch leaving the London & Croydon at the Dartmouth Arms, and running via Forest Hill, Nun's Green (Nunhead), Peckham, the Grand Surrey Canal, to a terminus at the Elephant & Castle.

2. A branch to leave the existing line at Addiscombe Road and to run via the Infant Poorhouse, Norwood, and the Half Moon at Herne Hill, to the Elephant & Castle.

Soon after it was opened the London & Croydon Railway had its first experience of dealing with the Croydon fair traffic. At a general meeting on 9 October 1839 the board reported that

... on the second day of that fair 11,209 passengers were conveyed along the line; that the trains were run on that day every twenty minutes from 8 in the morning till 2 on the following morning, and during part of the day every 10 minutes, and that the Greenwich trains were run as usual, every quarter of an hour – making ten trains each way, or twenty trains in the whole passing and repassing each other on these lines within the hour.

The chairman suggested that if the Parliamentary Committee on

Railways could have witnessed the '... facility and utter absence of confusion with which all this was managed ...', it would have had no cause for alarm at the prospect of increased traffic over the London & Greenwich Railway.

It had, however, already become obvious to both companies that, if they took no steps to comply with the wishes of the Select Committee, Parliament might intervene. It was in the interests of both that the Brighton and Dover Railways should use their lines, and it is not surprising, therefore, to find in the minute books of each references to the possibility of widening the Greenwich viaduct as the solution to the problem.

Various suggestions were discussed by the directors and engineers. At a long meeting between the two companies in November the London & Greenwich representatives had a plan to lay a third track on the viaduct. As the Greenwich carriages were only six feet wide, it would have been just possible to run them with about two feet clearance on each side of the train, but the limitation in width would have had to be imposed on the carriages of the other railways for this plan to have succeeded.

The London & Greenwich then offered to give up to either the London & Croydon Railway, or the other three companies jointly, the land required to widen the viaduct if they would pay the cost of building, and to accept a reduced toll of $1\frac{1}{2}d$. In this case the land would have remained the property of the London & Greenwich, but would have been let on a perpetual lease to the Croydon or the joint companies, whichever accepted the offer.

After some deliberation, the London & Croydon made a counter-proposal of leasing the land, building the new viaduct and paying $1d$ toll, or alternatively buying the land, building the viaduct and paying no toll. This proposal was declined by the Greenwich company, and as the London & Croydon would not accept the original offer, both companies promoted Bills at the end of 1839 for powers to widen the railway. The London & Greenwich sought authority to increase the toll to $6d$ to help pay for the work. The two companies also went to Parliament for powers to reconstruct the London Bridge stations.

Of the other railways interested, the London & Brighton acted in harmony with the London & Croydon. The SER on the other hand suggested severing all relations with the London & Greenwich and constructing one of the lines to the Elephant and Castle suggested by Cubitt earlier in the year. The London &

Croydon was not prepared to provide any of the capital required, however, since by doing so it would only deprive itself of the tolls it expected from the other companies' use of its line. As the South Eastern was finding difficulty in raising the money for the sixty-six miles of railway already sanctioned, the proposal did not mature.

One important feature of the situation that had developed between the four companies from the point of view of the Select Committee on Railways, was the excellent illustration it provided of the necessity for some governmental control of the railways. The committee had urged Parliament to consider this in 1839, and it seized the opportunity at the beginning of 1840 to do so again. The affairs of the London & Greenwich Railway were made the subject of its first inquiry of 1840, and its first report of that year was issued on 6 February, two days after it had examined the chairman and deputy chairman of each of the four companies involved in the dispute. It reported that several conferences had resulted in no agreement, whilst in the meantime the arrangements which it had so strongly condemned had produced the accident it feared might occur.

This accident, which took place in thick fog on the morning of Thursday, 30 January 1840, was reported far and wide, and the following facts emerge from the evidence given to the Select Committee on 4 February.[14]

An up train from Croydon, delayed by fog near London, arrived at Corbetts Lane Junction between eight and ten minutes late, and the 10.15am (or 10.30 – no one was quite sure which it was) from Greenwich, which should have followed the Croydon train, passed Corbetts Lane before it, and preceded it to London Bridge. Just outside London Bridge the Greenwich train had stopped '... to put on a rope, so as to let their engine go on one line and the carriages on another'. Meanwhile the Croydon train had passed the Corbetts Lane Junction but the driver was not aware that the Greenwich train was ahead of him; the pointsman at Corbetts Lane, a Greenwich Railway man, usually put up his hand in a particular way to indicate a train ahead, but he thought it unnecessary on this occasion as there was apparently a sufficient interval between the trains. The Croydon train sped on through the fog, and near the place where it always stopped outside London Bridge, came upon the stationary Greenwich carriages from which the engine had now been uncoupled. Although the

Croydon brakesman had all his brakes on, the train could not quite stop in time, and a collision occurred; the Croydon driver jumped off his engine just before the impact. Mr Wilkinson, of the Croydon Railway said:

It was a very slight collision, but the construction of the Greenwich carriages is such, having no buffers, and being joined with inflexible links, that the moment they come into contact with anything pushing them behind, the consequence is the links are driven in ... one carriage is driven on the one side, and the other on the other, and both carriages are sent off the line in opposite directions. That was the case here: one carriage was against the wall and the other was towards the middle of the line.

At this time, and quite unknown to the staff at London Bridge, a second Greenwich train was coming up the line; this was a special, bringing artillerymen to the Tower of London, and had been arranged at very short notice. Hardly had the Croydon passengers been got out of their train when the Greenwich special came in and hit the Croydon train 'with great force', seriously damaging several carriages; none of the Croydon carriages had been affected by the collision of a few minutes before. To quote Wilkinson again: 'Then two other carriages of the new Greenwich train, on coming in, were thrown off the line, in consequence of their faulty construction, for though our carriages were exposed to both those shocks, none of them went off the line.' A few people in the Greenwich trains were slightly injured, but the soldiers appear to have been quite unperturbed by the incident, for '... they kept their places in the train without the least emotion of fear or trepidation,' until ordered out by their commanding officer; by which time they had, no doubt, said all there was to say about the Greenwich Railway.[15]

The boards of the two companies met the next day, and decided that no great blame attached to anyone in particular. This is rather surprising, since the Greenwich Railway had complained to the Croydon only a month before that its trains ran at excessive speed through fog, and that, despite previous complaints, they still took the points outside London Bridge at 25 miles an hour. The outcome was that the driver of the Greenwich special train was dismissed, as it was considered that he had not been sufficiently cautious, since he knew his arrival at London Bridge would be unexpected, and that only one brakesman was available for his train instead of the usual two. He had been in trouble before, and a director described him as '. . . rather a slashing man'. All the usual precautions had been taken by the London & Greenwich, and every man available was on duty along the line. It was revealed at the inquiry that the Greenwich Railway ran about two special trains a year, so they were particularly unfortunate in having to run one on that foggy morning.

A few days after the publication of the report mentioned above, the inquiry into the widening and London Bridge Station Bills opened; this committee sat from February until May 1840. Colonel Landmann was appointed by the London & Greenwich Railway to appear on its behalf, and he said that on his suggestion 75 feet of land had been purchased to allow for the eventual widening of the line, and that the original viaduct was built along the centre of this land. Of the viaduct itself, he said, 'I have made it strong enough for any traffic which may come on it.' He was, however, strongly of the opinion that the widening of the line was not really necessary, but that it was a fad of the Select Committee's which the London & Croydon Railway had seized upon in order to embarrass the Greenwich company.

The London & Croydon Railway's case was most ably presented by Mr Austin, its counsel.[16] He suggested that Parliament had permitted the London & Greenwich to purchase the surplus land in order that the viaduct might be widened when the necessity arose, and that powers for its purchase in order that it might subsequently be sold at an exorbitant price were never contemplated. He scorned the Greenwich company's plea that it was empowered to charge a toll of 9d, and said that if it tried to do so, its own fares would have to be advanced to such an extent that its engines would rumble over the viaduct with trains of empty carriages. The question of Mr Walter's position arose when reference was made to certain statements of his during 1836 and 1837, and it fell to Mr Austin to inform the committee – and the Greenwich Railway's counsel – that Walter had founded the London & Greenwich Railway, and was in fact 'Resident Director' at that time.

Parliament eventually decided in favour of the London & Greenwich Bill, apparently because it was unwilling to permit the rather aggressive Croydon company to deprive the Greenwich of the benefits due to it from being first in the field. It is also possible that the committee was uneasy about the capacity of the Croydon Railway to finance the undertaking.

The Act[17] stipulated that the work be completed in two years, and provided for a penalty of £50 a day to be paid to the London & Croydon Railway – to be divided equally between it and the Brighton and South Eastern Railways – for any period in excess of two years. The use of the new lines was reserved exclusively to the other three railways, and the Greenwich toll was increased to a maximum of 4½d. The Act contained some further provisions which were not directly connected with the widening of the line; no locomotives were to be used between 11am and 1pm on Sundays, Good Friday or Christmas Day, and unoccupied arches were to be fenced 'to prevent nuisances'. The works at London Bridge station formed the subject of another Act passed on the same day.

The company was authorised to raise a sum of £200,000 for the new works, and in November it received several tenders for part of the widening; the lowest, £34,960 was made by Thomas Jackson, and he was awarded the contract. On 9 December eleven further tenders for the remaining work were considered. Of these, McIntosh's was the highest and Little & Sons the lowest at £16,350; this contract went to the latter.

Work started on the new viaduct in January 1841, when the footpaths were totally closed to the public, that to the south to be built upon, and that to the north to be used for the movement of materials. On 17 March Landmann laid the first stone with a silver trowel given by Jackson, the contractor, and into a cavity prepared for the purpose, deposited a collection of coins and an engraved plate of glass recording briefly for posterity the history of the L&GR down to the '... widening of the way from London to the junction with the Croydon Railway. . . . In the Reign of Victoria the First'.[18] Somewhere beneath the wide viaduct the relics presumably lie buried to this day, but exactly where is not recorded. Within a few days of the ceremony 370 men were at work on the new viaduct.

Soon after the widening works were started, an accident occurred, mainly owing to the company's practice of moving materials by passenger train. Miller had given orders for a temporary wooden fence to be put up along the viaduct where the south parapet wall had been demolished, as he anticipated that there would be a considerable amount of trespassing on the scaffolding and the line during the approaching Whitsun holidays. The wood for this purpose was sent to the point where it was needed, between Blue Anchor Road and Corbetts Lane, partly by special engine early in the morning before the regular service started, and partly by passenger trains throughout the day. 'The timber and planks when being carried by the passenger trains, were placed on the hinder platform of the last carriage and were thrown off the carriage upon the line by the brakesman or guard, without the trains being stopped.' It was the duty of a watchman to remove the timber as soon as the train had passed. On 28 May 1841 some of the wood had been dropped on the line by the guard of the 2.15pm train from Greenwich, and the watchman, being elsewhere at the time, had not removed it. When the 2.30pm train approached, the driver, Walker, saw the posts lying across the line 100 yards ahead, and he immediately reversed the engine, telling the fireman at the same moment to apply the engine brake and the conductor of the leading carriage to apply his. The guard at the end of the train was unaware of the obstruction, as he was preparing to throw off a further load of timber from his own train. The train failed to stop in time and the engine and tender passed over a post, but regained the rails afterwards. The first four carriages were derailed, however, alternating to left and right of the line as was usual in these circumstances, but they remained upright and no passengers were injured. The conductor of the first carriage was thrown beneath it and injured, however, whilst a man named Delderfield, a carpenter's labourer engaged in erecting the fence, was so alarmed at the sight of the carriages plunging this way and that, that he leapt off the viaduct in the hope of alighting on the scaffolding, but missed it. Falling to the ground below, he sustained injuries to his back from which he died about three weeks later. The Board of Trade, which by this time had been invested with some authority over the railways, conducted an inquiry, and condemned the practice of moving materials by passenger train. On 19 June the directors gave £10 to the widow of Delderfield, and a week later they gave John Walker the engine-driver £1 reward for his '... care in stopping the engine and preventing an accident on 28th May 1841'. The accident they had in mind was, no doubt, the one that would have ensued had the train gone through the gap in the parapet wall at that point. This John Walker was the man who, as a fireman, had appeared before the Select Committee in June 1836.

The London & Greenwich Railway jealously guarded its right to control the traffic of the other railways when it came upon the viaduct. Following two minor accidents in 1840 the directors issued new regulations, under which they had interpreted their rights rather broadly; the Croydon board wrote to say that '... they must protest against the power assumed by the Greenwich Railway Company to control the traffic of this Company otherwise than may be authorised by Act of Parliament'.

The London & Brighton Railway was rapidly nearing completion as work began on the new viaduct, and three days after the first stone had been laid, a train left London Bridge at 8.10am on 20 March 1841, conveying the directors of that company. It was reported that 'The engine used on this occasion is one of immense power, called the *Merstham*, made by Messrs Sharp & Roberts of Manchester.' A regular service of four trains each way between London Bridge and Haywards Heath began on 12 July 1841; this was increased to seven trains in each direction when the railway was opened throughout to Brighton on 21 September of that year.

As the London & Croydon trains had been absorbed quite easily into the traffic over the viaduct two years previously, so were those of the London & Brighton Railway; these two lines together contributed about 25 per cent of the traffic between London Bridge and Corbetts Lane. After two years working 70,000 trains had passed over Corbetts Lane Junction without accident.[19]

It was decided in July 1841 to lay the rails of the new lines on longitudinal sleepers, as these were considered best 'for fast trains from the South Eastern and London & Brighton Railways'. The London & Croydon line was already laid on this principle, the rails being supported by bearers 50 to 60 feet long, resting in turn upon 9 foot wooden sleepers at intervals of one yard. Learning from past experience, the company had the surface of the new viaduct asphalted as soon as it was built. Many shareholders thought this to be an unnecessary extravagance on the part of the board, and further attempts were made to prove that some of the directors of the railway were also financially interested in the Syssel Asphalt Company which had the contract.

During the later stages of the widening operations sections of the south line were closed and the three companies ran their up and down trains over the single north track. This practice was not so dangerous as it might appear, since the line was quite straight and level, and its elevated nature gave the drivers a very clear view ahead, with little to distract their attention on either side.[20] In any case, no accident appears to have resulted from this single line working.

The new works were inspected by the directors in March 1842, and by 19 April the permanent way on the new viaduct was completed. The original viaduct had been widened by 24ft 6in, making it 49ft 6in in breadth; this widening extended to the fourth arch east of Corbetts Lane, beyond which the Croydon line commenced. The surface of the new viaduct was of concrete, completely covered first by asphalt and then by ballast. A few of the arches had been forced out of shape before the brickwork had properly set, through the weight of gravel piled upon them becoming soaked by rain.

The London & Croydon Railway was informed that the new lines would come into use on 10 May, and that the increased toll of $4\frac{1}{2}d$ would be payable from that date.

General Pasley of the Board of Trade was inspecting the Manchester & Birmingham Railway when the new Greenwich viaduct was due to be opened, and the Board of Trade wrote to the Greenwich directors expressing the hope that Colonel Landmann would take all the necessary precautions in working the new lines pending their inspection.[21] The inspection took place about seven weeks later, and then only because the Croydon board, being dubious about the strength and quality of the new brickwork, had requested it. General Pasley, accompanied by Colonel Landmann and representatives of the other railways, visited the line and reported favourably upon it on 2 July. He mentioned that several of the new arches had settled down, but that many of those in the original viaduct had done so, making it 'undulating in places', but perfectly safe. His report ended with the following observation: 'Colonel Landmann has the merit of being the first to construct a railway on a continued arcade of considerable extent, over low alluvial soil ... the first to adopt a coating of asphalt for his vaults.'

On 26 May 1842 about a fortnight after the new viaduct was brought into use, the South Eastern Railway was opened to Tonbridge, and its trains joined the traffic to London Bridge. Although the Greenwich trains were not permitted to use the rails reserved for the others, a connection between the north line of the new viaduct, and the up line from Greenwich was put in during July 1842.

In 1838, long before the widening of the viaduct was started, it was decided to asphalt the original structure. The work began that year, and was found to be quite successful by the following summer, the arches so treated having dried out during the winter months. The asphalting went on very slowly, as it could be done only during the summer, and a sum was set aside for it each year. By August 1842 the bridges over the streets and several sections over occupied arches had been done, but it was still a long way from being completed, as most of the work had been done at night in order not to interrupt the services. By now, however, the Croydon trains were using the new lines, and it was decided to close one of the Greenwich lines in turn, and press forward with the work; on Sunday evenings the Greenwich trains used the north line of the new viaduct to cope with the up traffic, but at other times they managed with the one line of their own which remained open. The work was suspended again during the winter, but was resumed in April 1843, and was finished during that summer.

The superiority of timber sleepers over stone blocks became very apparent with the opening of the Deptford–Greenwich section, and a decision to relay the original line with heavier rails on wooden sleepers was taken at the end of 1839. The new rails were being delivered by February 1840, and the work started a few months later. By the middle of 1841, however, only the north line on the Deptford–Surrey Canal section had been finished; the stone blocks having been set in concrete, great difficulty was experienced in lifting them. The Croydon Railway had been complaining for some months of the vibration caused to their trains when they passed on to the Greenwich line, and as the matter was now becoming urgent, Miller undertook to relay the London Bridge–Corbetts Lane section at night, without closing either line. Thus the work went on from July 1841 until the relaying was finished the following year.

Although the asphalting of the arches and the relaying of the track went on at the same time, the two contracts were quite separate and the men were usually working on different parts of the line; to add to the confusion, the new viaduct was going up alongside the line, and the drainage system on the original viaduct was being rearranged. The relaying alone cost £25,000, and

a shareholder said that the board was always having the track
torn up for one reason or another.

Except for London Bridge station, the building of which took
some years, the Greenwich Railway was practically completed by
1842, and it might be appropriate here to compare the cost of the
line with that of some of its contemporaries.

Before the first brick of the viaduct had been laid, the company had contracted to spend £134,620; this was increased by a
further £640,000 by 1839. The widening and asphalting of the
viaduct, the relaying of the track, and the provision of stations
evenually brought the total to over one million pounds. A small
part of this came from revenue, but over £993,000 was raised by
shares and loans.

The following figures have been taken from various sources,
and are approximate only:

Railway	Length	Cost per mile	Weekly Receipts
London & Greenwich	3¾ mls	£267,000	£647
London & Blackwall	3½ mls	£184,000	£583
London & Croydon	8¾ mls	£76,000	£241
London & Birmingham	112¼ mls	£53,000	£12,019
London & South Western	76½ mls	£28,000	£5,144
Paisley & Renfrew	3 mls	£10,000	?

These figures are for 1843; the cost of the Greenwich Railway
was eventually exceeded by that of the London & Blackwall.

An American authority[22] writing in 1858, said that the original
cost of the London & Greenwich Railway, at $1,299,651 per mile
was '... forty times the cost of a "first class" Ohio or Illinois
road'. The Greenwich Railway had been the pattern for
'... eleven miles of lofty brick viaducts in the approaches to
termini' in London alone at the time, and for an estimated fifty
miles of viaduct throughout the United Kingdom. Railway construction in London during the remainder of the nineteenth
century has increased the figure for the metropolis to at least
twenty-five miles.

It might be said that both time and money were spent freely
on the Greenwich Railway; the original line was completed at
an average rate of one mile in one-and-a-quarter years.

It now remains to consider the toll question between the three
companies on the one hand, and the Greenwich Railway on the

other, compared with which the disputes over the traffic, the widening of the line and London Bridge station appear almost insignificant.

The Croydon Railway had not been using the Greenwich viaduct for more than a few months when it attempted, unsuccessfully, on 2 May 1840, to get the tolls revised by communicating with the London & Greenwich board through the Joint (Station) Committee.[23] In October 1840 a long correspondence developed following a fresh refusal to reduce the toll, when it was suggested that the tolls be commuted for one year on payment of £4,500. As an alternative, the London & Croydon Railway proposed that the London & Greenwich trains be run to New Cross and to transfer passengers there; or it was willing to allow the Greenwich company's trains to run through to Croydon at the same toll as it considered reasonable for running its own trains to London Bridge, a much shorter distance.

The London & Greenwich Railway declined all these offers, and in the summer of 1841 the London & Croydon adopted the policy of stopping its trains at New Cross, and trying to induce the passengers to complete the journey by bus.

By October 1841 the *Railway Times* reported that the dispute had grown 'very bitter', but during all this time the toll had been only 3d per passenger. When it was increased to 4½d in May 1842 the Croydon Railway immediately complained that its local traffic had practically been killed. The Croydon directors proposed at a company meeting to cease working the line, and to rely solely for their revenue on the tolls paid to them by the South Eastern and London & Brighton Railways. The shareholders agreed, and accordingly, in December 1842 the company asked the London & Brighton, South Eastern, and London & Greenwich companies to work its traffic; all the other railways refused, however, and the board decided to advertise the discontinuance of its traffic from 25 March 1843. The Board of Trade intervened and urged the Croydon Railway not to suspend its traffic, however, and the company agreed to maintain its services pending an inquiry.

About this time the Croydon and South Eastern companies were contemplating the construction of a short branch from the London & Croydon line near Corbetts Lane Junction to a new terminus at the Bricklayers Arms. At first the project was merely a lever to be used against the London & Greenwich in an effort

to persuade that company to reduce its toll, but even the possibility of losing all the traffic of those railways failed to move the
Greenwich directors. In February 1843, the Board of Trade,
having examined the case, agreed with the London & Croydon
Railway on the question of toll commutation, but it could not
induce the London & Greenwich board to accept the principle.
In a final attempt to bring about a settlement Mr Gladstone,
then vice-president of the Board of Trade, met the solicitors
and two directors of the London & Greenwich on Saturday afternoon, 11 March 1843;[24] the toll question and also the Bricklayers
Arms Extension Bill were both discussed at great length, but
even Gladstone failed to convince the Greenwich representatives
that their policy might be ill-advised.

The Bricklayers Arms project, which was a modification of a
plan put forward earlier by the London & Croydon Railway for
a similar line, known as the 'Grange Road Extension', was not
taken seriously by the Greenwich board, who thought that the
other companies had already spent far too much money on the
joint station at London Bridge to abandon that terminus. George
Walter, however, on his own responsibility, planned an extension
of the Greenwich Railway to Croydon, where it was to join the
main line to Redhill for Brighton and Dover, and a year later,
on the passing of the Bricklayers Arms Act, he urged the London
& Greenwich directors to apply for powers to build the competing
line to Croydon.

The companies chiefly concerned unwisely chose to make the
public aware of the dispute over the tolls, although it was probably not their original intention to do so. On 8 December 1840
the London & Croydon Railway issued a thirty-page pamphlet to
its shareholders, in which all the correspondence that had passed
between it and the Greenwich company on the subject up to that
time was published. The Greenwich board soon came into possession of one of these booklets, and the result was that copies of
subsequent letters were sent to the *Railway Times* and other
periodicals for publication, along with the views of the L&GR
on the matter. The year 1842 saw the issue by the London &
Croydon of a four-page leaflet headed *Notice to the Public*;
after opening with the words 'Having been compelled to raise its
fares in consequence of the exaction by the Greenwich Company
of an increased toll . . .', it gave details of the reduced fares it
would otherwise have introduced long since. Abstracts of twenty-

three letters on the toll question, from 6 October 1840 to 30 March 1842, were reprinted as evidence of the company's good faith, and copies were distributed by the hundred from the stations on the Croydon line. On 11 October 1842 the correspondence in full up to that date was published by the Croydon company. Apart from all this, the chairman of the London & Croydon, W. A. Wilkinson, produced a pamphlet purporting to explain the position, in 1841.[25]

The Greenwich directors were quite obdurate in the matter of tolls, however, and the only concession they ever made was to charge toll in one direction only on London & Croydon excursion trains carrying over 150 passengers, in August 1842.

The effect on the public of these attempts by the railways concerned to justify themselves was to produce an attitude of impatience towards both, and it was suggested in 1842 that the South Eastern and London & Brighton Railways should lease both the smaller lines.

Following the failure of the Board of Trade to effect a reconciliation, the SER and London & Croydon went ahead with the Bricklayers Arms scheme, strongly opposed by the London & Greenwich. The Greenwich directors met every day at Ginger's Hotel, and then went to the Commons or the Lords to watch the progress of the Bill. They presented a memorial to the House of Commons regarding the South Eastern company's refusal to carry third-class passengers to London Bridge, and the Croydon Railway's refusal to carry them on any part of their line. The South Eastern turned all the third-class passengers out of the trains at New Cross, and brought the carriages empty to London Bridge, whilst the following fares were charged on the Croydon line:

1st Class between Croydon and New Cross, 1s, plus 1s 3d
between New Cross and London Bridge
2nd Class between Croydon and New Cross, 9d, plus 1s
between New Cross and London Bridge

Protests by board and shareholders alike were ineffectual; during the passage of the Bill the South Eastern Railway raised the question of the substantial traffic in livestock that it was beginning to develop, and argued that no suitable facilities existed at London Bridge for handling these trains, since the station was elevated. It was the inadequacy of London Bridge station that was given in the preamble to the Act as the reason for its existence, the Royal Assent having been obtained on 4 July 1843.[26] The South Eastern Railway was to bear two thirds of the cost of the branch, and was given the option of buying out the London & Croydon.

The line was built on a timber viaduct by Messrs Grissel & Peto, and was opened on 1 May 1844 having taken but a few months to construct. Large passenger and goods stations occupying twenty-six acres were provided at Bricklayers Arms, and the line joined the London & Croydon Railway just south of Corbetts Lane. Although the timber viaduct was replaced in 1849 by an embankment, it was said to have been of great strength. When a goods engine exploded on the viaduct one night in December 1844,[27] it blew a hole in the floor of the structure which took three weeks to repair; on that occasion the Board of Trade inspector commented on the general soundness of construction.

On the advice of Robert Stephenson, the SER decided in November 1844 to establish its locomotive department at Bricklayers Arms, since its withdrawal from the Joint Locomotive Committee was imminent, and notice was accordingly served on the London & Croydon Railway that the South Eastern intended to exercise its right to buy out that company's share in the line.

On the opening of the Bricklayers Arms branch, all the South Eastern trains and half of those of the London & Croydon Railway were diverted from the London & Greenwich. The London & Brighton Railway declined to participate in the scheme and had no financial or other interest in the branch; all its trains continued to use London Bridge station. This company took little part in any of the disputes; indeed, the Brighton and the Greenwich were on very friendly terms with each other during the whole period, a fact often remarked upon in the correspondence between the two boards. A considerable amount of friction existed between the Brighton and Croydon Railways, however. In July 1843 the three toll-paying companies started to pay the amounts due to the Greenwich Railway direct to that company; previously the London & Croydon had collected the tolls and settled with the London & Greenwich.

The passage of the Bricklayers Arms Act caused alarm among the Greenwich shareholders, and they appointed an Investigation Committee in August 1843. When this committee made its report to the board on 24 August it restated at great length the difficulties which confronted the company, all unaware, it would seem, that the board had at least been conscious of the problems facing it for some years, even if it had not found a solution to them. Its recommendations were that the company should offer to sell the new viaduct to the other railways for £240,000 or to let it at a permanent rental of £12,500 a year, but these companies when approached were not interested in the proposal. The committee had also agreed provisionally with the representatives of the other companies on a toll in proportion to the mileage travelled, a concession for which the Croydon Railway had been pressing for years.

The Greenwich Company's general meeting of 29 January 1844 was the longest and stormiest in Herapath's memory, and that gentleman had attended a good many railway meetings in his time. No dividend was paid on ordinary shares, and the preference shareholders received only a reduced amount. It was proposed to make up the dividends from the company's resources, but the directors were advised by counsel that they were not empowered to use the capital for this purpose.

The London & Croydon Railway, which a year earlier had contemplated the abandonment of its traffic altogether, was now expanding southwards to Epsom. Benjamin Cubitt recommended the Croydon board to adopt atmospheric traction for the new Epsom Railway on 13 April 1844, if the atmospheric tracks could be laid over the London & Croydon line either to Bricklayers Arms or London Bridge, preferably the latter. He also proposed that the Croydon should lease the L&GR. Three days later a conference took place between the directors of the two railways, when the London & Croydon board proposed that they should amalgamate and that the Croydon should assume control of the whole concern. The Greenwich directors refused to consider the proposal; neither would they commit their company to accepting the atmospheric trains on its line without further consideration.

In the meantime the L&GR had entered into negotiations with the 'Dover Company', as its board still called the South Eastern, on a proposal by the latter that the shares of the two companies be amalgamated, or alternatively, that it took over the Greenwich line on a perpetual lease. The Greenwich directors seemed to favour a lease, and on 21 May 1844 they asked for £40,000 for the first year, increasing to £45,000 and £50,000 for the second and third years: thereafter, payment on the basis of the number of passengers conveyed over the line was suggested.

Two days later the London & Brighton Railway offered to amalgamate with, purchase, or lease the London & Greenwich; the Greenwich board replied that they welcomed the proposal, but were prevented from entering into negotiations as they were committed to discussions with the SER. It is extremely unlikely that the Brighton directors were unaware of the discussions taking place between the Greenwich and South Eastern Railways since the Brighton board usually included at least one Greenwich director; presumably, therefore, the friendship so often referred to manifested itself in the timely arrival of the Brighton company's proposals to help the South Eastern directors to make up their minds.

The South Eastern did not accept the London & Greenwich proposals as to compensation immediately, however, and the latter threatened the South Eastern in June 1844 that, if its demands were rejected, it would extend its line to North Kent. Joseph Locke was accordingly asked to give his opinion on an eastern extension of the Greenwich Railway, and on 20 July 1844 he reported on various alternative schemes which had been planned. In short, he suggested that the company should proceed, if it could, with a line across Greenwich Park, but if this were not possible, it should abandon the whole idea of a North Kent line.

While the extension of the railway was being considered, the Greenwich company informed the London & Brighton that the negotiations with the South Eastern had broken down, and deputations of the two companies met to discuss the Brighton Railway's proposals. At the end of June the South Eastern was asked what provisions it wished inserted in the agreement to protect its interests, if the Brighton Railway secured the lease.

The South Eastern Railway had in the meantime replied to the Greenwich company's threat by instructing Robert Stephenson to survey a line to North Kent via the Bricklayers Arms, and had invited the London & Croydon to co-operate. It also offered the London & Greenwich £36,000 for the first year, rising to £40,000 a year for the lease. Agreement was finally reached on 28 August; the rent was to be increased to £45,000 a year, and the lease would include land on either side of the viaduct; engines, carriages, stores etc were to be taken over at a separate valuation.

The shareholders decided almost unanimously in favour of

the arrangement; a notable exception was George Walter, who bitterly opposed it. He presented a written protest to the shareholders, which opened with the words: 'I, George Walter, for and on behalf of my children, Charlotte Mary Walter and George E. W. Walter, do protest against the leasing of the London & Greenwich Railway to the South Eastern (Dover) Railway..'[28] He went on to point out that the money for the undertaking was subscribed originally on the assumption that the railway would be the outlet to the south-east, and that now the other lines were built, the company was to be deprived of the toll revenue rightly due to it. It is not difficult to imagine how Walter felt as he saw all possibility of ever regaining control of the railway slip finally away, and he was probably not exaggerating in 1845 when he wrote that he was heartbroken over the business. He honestly believed in the future of the Greenwich company, and genuinely felt that its troubles were solely the result of mismanagement by directors who were not really interested in the railway, whilst he, anxious to devote his whole energy to it, had to stand helplessly by.

Another critic of the arrangement was one R. S. Scrimgeour, who wrote ten letters to the *Morning Post* between 22 August 1844 and 4 January 1845, which were later published in pamphlet form.[29] His argument was not against the leasing of the line, but against what he considered to be the very inadequate rent to be paid by the South Eastern Railway. Most shareholders took the view that a small regular dividend was better than none at all; this was particularly true of the unfortunate holders of ordinary shares – the original proprietors whose money had built the viaduct – for these had received practically nothing beyond the 3 per cent interest paid while the railway was being constructed. These formed a large and hostile group, bitter towards Walter for selling them the shares in the first place, and equally embittered against the directors of later years (who were nearly all preference shareholders on a fairly small scale) for not producing a dividend.

No further difficulty arose over the lease, and at midnight on 31 December 1844 the London & Greenwich Railway ceased to work their line; a week later it was announced that £54,000 would be distributed amongst the shareholders, of which those holding ordinary shares were to receive over £43,000. Part of the money for this purpose came from the sale of the company's engines, carriages, stock and some land.

A farewell party was held at the Ship Torbay Hotel, Greenwich, on 16 January 1845, attended by 150 guests, when a silver cup and snuff-box were presented to Henry Adron, who had for some years been the L&GR Accountant, and who was about to take over the Secretaryship as well. Some 'old and faithful officers' of the company received gratuities shortly afterwards; John Akerman was given £500 and Mr Lawrie, the Collecting Clerk, £125. The clerks received £25 each and the money-takers were allowed to keep their floats of £4 and were given £6 each in addition; various small sums and annuities were paid to certain other employees. When the shareholders agreed to these gratuities at their meeting on 12 February, they also instructed the board to make a gift of £300 to George Walter, whose name had not been put forward by the directors. An injury, caused by a fall in the street, had brought his name into the news at that time, when it was disclosed that he had sustained injuries, from which he had never entirely recovered, by the falling of some scaffolding on the Greenwich Railway in 1835.[30]

The Agreement for the leasing of the line was finally sealed on 11 February 1845, but an Act of Parliament was required and the Bill was only then being prepared; it received the Royal Assent on 21 July, many months after the lease was an accomplished fact. Thus ended the active existence of the London & Greenwich Railway.

Chapter 7

Stations 1836-45

THERE were four stations on the original L&GR, the termini at London Bridge and Greenwich, and the intermediate stations at Spa Road and Deptford. For a few months in 1836 trains ran to Bermondsey Street, just outside London Bridge, but no station existed at this point.

In February 1836 the regular train service started between Spa Road, Bermondsey and Deptford, and Spa Road thus became the first London terminus of the railway, and as such, the first station ever to exist in London. The Commissioners of Pavements considered this to be the most convenient point for persons wishing to reach Westminster Bridge, and they got a clause inserted in the original Act under which the company had to maintain a flight of steps at Spa Road and to stop a train there twice daily, at what times it pleased.

The Spa Road station in 1836 consisted of the wooden staircase on the south side of the viaduct and a small wooden booking office at ground level. A narrow platform to accommodate about six passengers was provided on the viaduct; Colonel Landmann said that when this platform was occupied by intending travellers, any others stood on the steps and waited for the trains. It was not originally intended to provide platforms at the stations, and the carriages were fitted with steps instead; it was found, however, that low platforms were more convenient, but the carriage steps were also retained. The platform at Spa Road could not have been more than one yard wide, and it must have been situated between the tracks. The distance between the outer rail-edge and the parapet wall was 3ft 1in on either side, leaving about 6ft between the inner rails; the carriages overhung 17 inches each side, including the steps, which left 20 inches from the carriage side to the wall and about 3ft clearance in the centre. There were no buildings of any description on the line. The company did not even claim the title of 'station' for Spa Road; in 1840 they described it as 'a stopping place, but no station'. It had, however, been their intention to build one there to the same designs as that at Deptford.

After the London Bridge section had been opened fewer passengers used Spa Road; if the drivers had no request to stop there they went straight through. In March 1838 the directors ordered half a carriage to be reserved for Spa Road on Sundays and holidays, and that trains stop there once hourly throughout the day. They also arranged for a collector to be placed at Blue Anchor Road, nearby, to assist the two at Spa Road by issuing tickets at that point, and allowing the passengers free use of the footpath to the station. By the end of the year, however, so little used was the station that the board decided not to stop trains there in future, and for a long time the place was locked up and deserted.

When the committee was considering the L&GR Widening Bill in March 1840, the question of Spa Road Station came up again, and pressure was brought to bear upon the company to reopen it. It was stated that since the coming of the railway, it had become far more difficult to travel between Bermondsey and Deptford than had been the case before; then there had been coaches, but these had ceased to run in 1836. Since the London & Croydon Company's Bill for widening the Greenwich viaduct was also under consideration by the same committee, the Greenwich Railway thought it wise to agree to restore the service at Spa Road, and plans were made for the steps to be shifted to the north side to permit of the widening of the viaduct to the south. Colonel Landmann also prepared plans for an approach road, although he considered this unnecessary as a 'good turnpike' already existed. The work had to wait for another two years, until the viaduct had been widened.

In June 1842 a tender was accepted from the contractor Jackson for the works at Spa Road, including a waiting room in the arches and a shed over the line, for £450; the new station was opened in October. On 1 February 1843 a man named Birmingham was fatally injured there.[1]

After the new station was brought into use, the train service to Spa Road varied from time to time; Miller was authorised by the directors to stop the trains there as often as he thought necessary. There had previously been no signals at this station, but in August 1843 signal posts and lights were erected. In May 1844 the platforms were extended; less than a year later, however, the whole station was being rebuilt by the SER.

Deptford was the other intermediate point where an 'approach' had to be made to the railway, but all that the company was required to do was to provide and maintain '...a Flight of Steps or an Inclined Plane...'. At Deptford it provided both, and the inclined plane is all that now remains of the original terminus of 1836.

The first station was similar to Spa Road, but more elaborate, since the company's works were situated on an adjoining site and in the arches below the line. The steps leading up to the railway on the south side were of brick and stone; no platforms or buildings existed on the viaduct at first, although a 'large arched shed with a cast-iron roof' was built in 1836. The booking office was at the foot of the steps, and its two large gas lamps provided the only light in that part of Deptford at night, according to a newspaper report of 1839. Originally the viaduct was no wider at Deptford Station than the normal width of twenty-five feet, and the line on to Greenwich changed its direction sharply at this point. Whishaw reported in 1837, however, that the '...angle formed by the viaduct at Deptford High Street is now being altered to a curved line for the safe passage of the locomotives'; this required the widening of the viaduct by about seven feet for fifty yards on each side of the High Street bridge, and this in turn gave a little more space for the station.

By January 1839 the company had provided a waiting room on the up side; a writer confessed that he could not '...commend the architectural beauties of the erection...', but it was a great convenience in winter. A little later comes a reference to passengers who '...kill their spare time, and perhaps themselves too, in the respectable watch-box recently erected for the benefit of Deptford travellers on the top of the arches'.[2] The up and down lines were changed over later in 1839, and passengers from London Bridge arrived on the north side of the line, but an exit was not provided yet as the company intended to build a permanent station at Deptford, and decided to leave any alterations until such time as this work was undertaken. The fact that all the passengers leaving a down train would have to walk across the rails to reach the exit on the south side caused the board no concern, since its passengers had always been accustomed to walk across the line at stations.

The primary purpose of the inclined planes built at Deptford, London Bridge, and later at Greenwich, was to enable private carriages to be brought up and placed upon carriage trucks for conveyance by the trains. The plane at Deptford provided also the only convenient means by which the rolling stock could be raised to the level of the viaduct from the Depot beneath the arches.

These carriage approaches were never used as such, for no private vehicles were ever carried on the trains. It is unlikely that the company even anticipated that any such traffic would arise on the short run between Deptford or Greenwich and London, but when the stations were planned it was expected that the line would soon be extended to Gravesend and Dover.

In April 1839 the clerk to the New Cross Turnpike Trust said in evidence before a select committee:[3] 'I know a vast number of gentlemen who keep carriages, gigs and pleasure horses, who ride up daily to the railroad, take the railroad at Greenwich or Deptford, and pay us no tolls, while they are wearing out the roads.' Their horses were stabled at the stations, and their carriages left there until they returned in the afternoon, in much the same way as commuters now leave cars at suburban stations.

In August 1841 a 'Committee on Buildings for Deptford Station' made its recommendations for rebuilding. George Smith, the architect, was asked to prepare a plan for the station buildings, and Miller was to produce plans for an engine shed, a carriage shed, a coke house and platforms on each side of the line. After considering the merits of a circular engine shed, a rectangular one was decided upon.

The contract for the new station was awarded to Messrs Baker & Sons; of the £6,840 quoted for the work, £4,300 was for the engine shed alone, as several arches had to be widened at the London end of the station to support this structure. The contractors undertook to complete the work by 1 March 1842, and they succeeded despite the short period of less than five months in the middle of the winter.

Reasonably wide platforms were provided at the new station, and these, like the rest of the building, were lit by gas lamps; but the pillars supporting the awnings were very close to the platform edge. The combined coke and carriage house and the engine shed extended beyond the London end of the station on the southern side of the widened viaduct, and a turntable (or 'turnplate' as it was then called) was installed between the coke and engine sheds at the point where the inclined plane joined the main viaduct, by Bramah & Co.

It is unlikely that there were many passengers between Deptford and Greenwich, and the new arrangements made scant provision for them; the principal part of the station was the up side, where a circular turret enclosed the booking office and the stairs up to the platform.

Deptford station was described in 1855 after the up and down lines had again been reversed, as follows:

Deptford Railway Station . . . is a small erection, containing a checktaker's and waiting rooms, with the usual accessories. There are also sidings, a carriage shed, and a goods yard. Its distinguishing feature, from whatever side it is approached, is a circular building, containing the staircase for enabling the 'down passengers' to reach the street . . . a dingy, stuccoed, uninteresting building.

Of the turret itself it was said:

It is not, probably, generally known that the pepper-box entrance to the down platform . . . is modelled after one of the most elegant, exquisitely proportioned edifices bequeathed to us by the Art-loving Athenians, viz:- the Choragic monument of Lysicrates. A more striking example of the utter degradation of the perfection of art by its misapplication could hardly be produced.[4]

Whether or not the efforts of the Greenwich Railway to introduce Classical architecture into Deptford were generally appreciated, their turret endured for eighty-five years, and it is open to question whether its removal in 1927 improved the appearance of the the station, or the High Street, to any marked extent.

The company chose Deptford as the site for its workshops for a number of reasons. It was conveniently situated between the termini, and there was enough spare land there – although this was not a major consideration, since the works occupied only a very small area. This part of the viaduct was the first to be completed, a point of some importance, for had the works been at London Bridge or Greenwich they would not have been available until 1836 or 1838 respectively. Moreover, the inclined plane was essential for transferring the engines and carriages from the viaduct to the works and vice versa. Deptford also had the advantage of being near some engineering firms, notably the works of Penn, the marine steam-engine builder, and Gordon's of Deptford Green. There was also an 'engine manufactury' not far distant, at Blue Anchor Road, the works of B. Donkin & Co where H. R. Palmer had been an apprentice, and the Thames Iron Works.

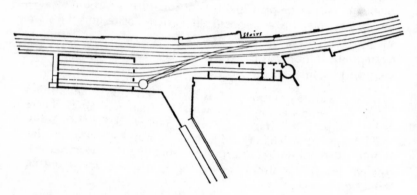

Deptford Station, engine sheds and top of inclined plane, 1845

The Railway Works had their beginnings in a board resolution of 6 December 1834 '... that the Engineer be requested to fit up an arch for the reception of a Locomotive Engine'. This was the arch in which the first engine stood for several months on show, but its exact position is not known. The position occupied by the works, however, is indicated on a plan prepared by the Westminster Bridge & Greenwich Railway as extending to the first two arches on the London side of the station, and the ground in front of them. The smaller arches of the inclined plane were used by the company as stores.

The arches which housed the works were completely open at first, and were guarded by the railway police; in July 1835, however, about the time when the first trials were being made, a hoarding was erected round them; this was the result of the attempts made to damage the locomotives, referred to by Landmann. The workshops were under the direct control of Walter, and here he often worked until 10 o'clock at night during the period when the safety carriages were being constructed. Here also the various modifications to the locomotives were carried out in the early weeks of 1836, viz. the fitting of special brakes and spark-arresters.

At this time William Curtis was trying to interest the company in a method of laying rails on wooden frames, which he claimed to have perfected and used in Mexico in 1834, for he wrote: 'A small length has been laid down in the workshops of the London & Greenwich Railway Company, and has been in use for about eight months without the smallest deterioration up to the present moment.' Although the invention[5] was principally applicable to permanent way laid on embankments, it is possible that it was used at Deptford Works as a temporary track upon which the engines and carriages were moved about the yard and over the inclined plane.

The Railway workshops were chiefly occupied with carriage building during the first year or so of their existence; in March 1836 an observer wrote: 'Some of the arches are used by the Company as workshops. In one the carriage-maker may be seen at work, in another the smith, in another the spring-maker, in another the painter, and in fact all the trades that are necessary to be kept in operation for the purposes of the railway.'

Machinery at the works is first mentioned in July 1836, when a lathe was bought for £45. The Lord Mayor's reference in the following December suggests that there were several machines by that time, and by February 1838 it was necessary to purchase a '...larger engine to replace the small one in the Company's Factory'. There was also a cistern of 'Thames soft water' for the locomotives[6] and a steam-driven pump for raising water from a well.

Despite the hoarding the works were still very open, and it was not until 1838 that the northern entrances to the arches were bricked up. The following year the area enclosed by the viaduct and the inclined plane was fenced off from the High Street. The works were enlarged in 1842 by the addition of five of the eight arches that had been widened to support the new engine shed. This expansion had become necessary following the board's decision to take over its carriage stock which had, until recently, been maintained by a contractor. Some new machinery, including two lathes, a planing machine and a machine drill, had been installed in 1840, and towards the end of 1842 a furnace, the chimney of which stood some twenty feet above the viaduct, was built. After the construction of the engine and carriage sheds, all but the heaviest repair work was carried out therein, and in 1843 a 3-ton crane was erected[7] '... for raising and lowering parts of engines and carriages from the Workshops to the rails'.

The quadrangle enclosed by the inclined plane, which had formed part of the original works, was sold in 1842, and was soon occupied by a Catholic Church and the Mechanics' Institute building. It was at this time that Josiah Stone, formerly employed by Gordon's and who had started business in a workshop on Deptford Green in 1831, became a tenant of the Greenwich Railway, when the first of many expansions of his business led the board to resolve in August 1842 'That the Railway Arches No. 723 ... 726 be let to Mr Stone of Deptford, Coppersmith, at the yearly rent of £50 for the 4 Arches'. These were some of the arches left vacant after the reorganisation of the Railway Works, and a few years later there is another reference to an '... application from Mr J. Stone to be allowed to erect a small engine under one of the Greenwich Railway arches occupied by him, and to rent another'.[8] Within a few years Stone's had spread their activities to all the arches under Deptford Station, including the Railway Workshops, and they remained in occupation of them until 1881, when their factory near North Kent East Junction was opened. It may be appropriate to add here that this firm, which was first established to produce the copper nails for wooden sailing ships, and has for years provided the propellers for the largest steamers afloat, has maintained a close association with railway engineering; from an early date it supplied large quantities of fittings and components, and its axle-driven electric-train lighting system of 1894 is basically that still in world-wide use today. The firm that prospered in four Greenwich Railway arches in 1842 now controls factories in five continents.

Long before the first station was built at Greenwich, a temporary booking office was established there. This was situated at Rose Cottage, which stood in a lane beside the North Pole Tavern in Greenwich Road, and it was opened in 1836. Here passengers would take their tickets and go out through the back door to a footpath that led across a field to the temporary footbridge over the Ravensbourne, to join the railway path to Deptford Station. Although this afforded a pleasant approach to the railway in the summer, it was not the best means of reaching Deptford Station on a dark winter night, for on the path from the cottage to the bridge there was '... but one solitary candle stuck in a horn lanthorn'. The real trouble was not so much the absence of lights as the presence of a pond fifty feet wide and $3\frac{1}{2}$ feet deep in a direct line between the lantern and the footbridge, into which more than a dozen people had been lured by February 1837. The temporary booking office was closed in March 1838, when the arches between Deptford and Greenwich were being built.

In October 1837 the board decided to build the Greenwich terminus at Blue Stile, which was a lane just past the North Pole Tavern, but it discovered that it had insufficient land there, and that the Act did not permit the acquisition of any; on 31 October, therefore, it was resolved to build the station alongside the Prince of Orange Tavern, as originally planned.

Like the other stations the first one at Greenwich was of a temporary nature, and so far as the passengers were concerned, it consisted of little more than the means by which they could reach the trains on the viaduct, or the Greenwich Road therefrom. By July 1838 wooden steps were in position between Church Row and the viaduct, and an inclined plane had been constructed. When the directors inspected the line in December they instructed Miller to install turnstiles near the stairs, and to make other improvements, including the provision of gas lamps on the station and the Ravensbourne bridge.

The points used at Greenwich were patent ones, invented by Charles Fox, engineer to the London & Birmingham Railway. They were rather similar to modern points, of a construction '...whereby the whole of the main line may remain a fixed line'.[9] Previously the company had employed Curtis's switches, but his were of a complicated pattern, and cost £75 each against £30 for those designed by Fox. In a letter to the *Railway Times* on the subject of the replacement of his points, Curtis suggested that the reason was not their unsuitability, but the fact that Miller of the Greenwich Railway was a co-partner in 'Fox & Miller's Switch'. Incidentally the unfortunate Curtis had trouble with the London & Croydon Railway over their switches, which were made by Bramah & Co, and which, he claimed, infringed his patent.

The original line from Deptford ran into Greenwich station on arches, and a few days after it was opened, Miller was instructed to 'make accommodation for the engine men while waiting their turn at the Greenwich Station by fitting up one of the arches, and that he provide an iron ladder to be drawn up at night and secured'.

The temporary station stood back some distance from the Greenwich Road, and to reach it passengers had to cross the vacant land on which the permanent station was to be built; it was described in 1839 as a '...very inconvenient and ragged looking affair'.[10]

Meanwhile the board, with Colonel Landmann's approval, had asked Charles Fox to prepare plans for the stations at London Bridge and Greenwich. These plans were produced in 1839, and in October the contract for Greenwich station was awarded to Baker & Sons, the firm who were later to build Deptford station. By the end of December the building was almost completed, but on the night of 25 February 1840 it came very near to being burnt down. A large coke fire had been left in an office above the Great Room, and the embers had burnt their way through the loose brick hearth, setting fire to the ceiling below. Considerable damage had been caused before the fire was extinguished by the officers on duty, and the opening of the station was delayed until Sunday, 12 April 1840.[11]

On the evening of the opening day one of the company's men almost succeeded in blowing up the station, and himself with it. The gas lamps had all gone out, and the man went down to the room in which the meter was kept to investigate, carrying a lighted candle; the resulting explosion blew out the windows of the new station, and was heard all over Greenwich.[12]

The new Greenwich station was by far the best on the line. It was not on the exact site of the first station, but was a short distance nearer to Greenwich. The *Railway Times*[13] described it thus:

Railway Terminus at Greenwich. – The trains run under a shed of 6oft span, having 12 feet of pavement on each side, forming a promenade 300 feet in length, eleven large windows looking into the London Road, and the same number giving a view towards the Thames. On the roof, at the end of the shed, is a large leaden tank containing 25,000 gallons of water to supply the engines; and above the shed a weather-cock, representing a locomotive engine; the beams and iron stays which sustain the roof of the shed are of prodigious strength, and weigh each four tons; of these beams and stays there are twenty-two in number, weighing together 88 tons, lined inside and out, and covered with slate

1 (*top*) Rough sketch of the piers under construction through Bermondsey,
  1834. The contractor's horse-tramroad can be seen on the right
2 The Railway under construction near the Grand Surrey Canal, 1835

3 A composite representation of the viaduct showing it during construction,
  with a barge-load of stone sleepers in the foreground, and at the same time
  completed, with trains running. Published 14 months before the partial
  opening of the line

4 Caricature of a Greenwich Railway Board Meeting. (*l. to r.*) Dottin, Landmann, Walter, Akerman

5 Before the railway came: Glean Alley, obliterated by the enlargement of London Bridge Station. The railways had, of necessity, to undertake some of the first major slum-clearance projects—at their own expense

6 George Walter (1790–1854) in the uniform of a Lieutenant, Royal Marines, c. 1814

7 (*top left*) Original invitation ticket to the opening ceremony. The date was overprinted 'December 14' when they were distributed

8 One of the first season tickets ever issued. They were not in general use on other railways for some years

9 The scene at London Bridge Station on the opening day as depicted on the title page of a comic song published in December 1836. The principal figures are (*l. to r.*) Akerman, Dottin, Walter, Landmann and the Lord Mayor with, it is believed, his niece

10 Bird's-eye view of the Greenwich Railway from London Bridge. The line did not curve as depicted by the artist

11 The viaduct crossing Neckinger Road (now Abbey Street), Bermondsey. The cast-iron pillars are still in position

12 Viaduct looking towards Deptford from the Grand Surrey Canal, 1840

13 Skew Bridge over the Grand Surrey Canal, c. 1840

14 Arches and viaduct from the towpath of the Grand Surrey Canal, 1836

15 View from near the Marquis of Granby, New Cross Road, 1840; showing the L & GR viaduct, houses built in arches, and the Railway Works surrounded by the fence, with ships in the Surrey Docks in the distance

16 (*bottom*) View of arches from Loving Edward's Lane, Deptford, looking towards London, c. 1840

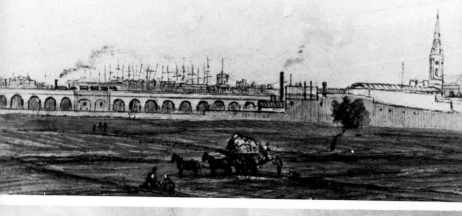

17 The footpath east of Deptford Station, 1840. As Mechanic's Passage, it now connects Deptford High Street and Church Street

18 The first Ravensbourne Bridge at Deptford Creek, 1841

19 View of the viaduct from south of Greenwich, 1836

20 The extension from Greenwich to Maze Hill under construction, c. 1877

21 Spa Road temporary terminus during the period in 1836 when the line was partially open, but still unfinished

22 Viaduct and temporary Station, Spa Road, 1836

23 The first Deptford Station, 1836–42

24 Deptford Station as rebuilt in 1842

25 Houses in viaduct near Deptford Station, 1836. The top of the inclined
plane to ground level is on the right

26 The original Greenwich Station of 1840; first class passengers used the
central door

27 Train shed of the original Greenwich Station, from the banks of the Ravensbourne, 1840

28 A German engraving of Greenwich Station, 1841; a more accurate representation of the station than of the engines

29 (*above*) London Bridge Station, 1836; some buildings have been omitted from the engraving to give a better view of the viaduct

30 London Bridge Station, c. 1837; a more accurate picture of the Company's offices as they actually existed

31 London Bridge Stations, London & Croydon on left, L & GR on right. The entrance in Joiner Street to the Croydon Station is still visible

32 London Bridge Joint Station, 1845

33 London Bridge Station, South Eastern Railway, c. 1853, with the Greenwich Branch Station on the extreme left. Either the artist or the SER had original ideas of spelling place-names!

34 London Bridge Station, SER, from Southwark Cathedral; the building on the left of the Station Approach is the arcade of shops, completed in 1853

35 The single-track Deptford Wharf Branch, LB & SCR, on the original white-painted wooden viaduct, 1848. View looking north, with the London & Greenwich Railway viaduct in the background

36 St Thomas's Hospital in 1862, just before its demolition, showing its close proximity to the stations; SER Station extreme left background, LB & SCR Station and Hotel right

37 (*right*) Locomotive *Walter*, No 6, George Forrester & Co, 1836, as originally built, and showing wooden fender

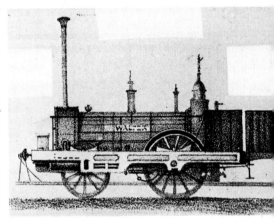

38 Locomotive No 9, R. Stephenson & Co, 1838, was of that firm's standard pattern 6-wheeled engine (2–2–2)

39 (*bottom*) Locomotive No 6, bearing original name *William*, after being fitted with a tender in 1839

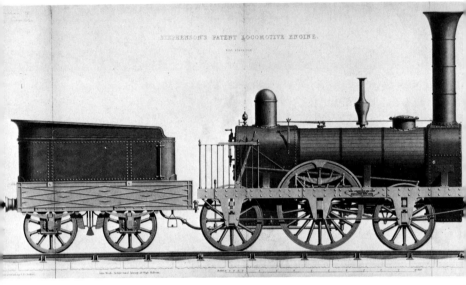

and zinc. A handsomely finished stone staircase, ten ft wide, leads to the waiting rooms, and down about twenty stone steps into a colonnade, through which the passengers pass into the London Road, Greenwich.

Four lines of rails ran into the station, and just beyond it were six sets of points and six crossings. The line ended in a semi-circular recess in which there was a 26ft turntable, or 'traversing frame', designed by Miller, and built by the Haigh Foundry. This was said[14] to be the first device of its kind, and consisted of two cast-iron girders carrying rails, supported by eight small wheels moving on two circular plates. It was moved by a rack and pinion, and could be locked to any one of the four tracks. Its purpose was not to turn the engines round completely; after being uncoupled from an incoming train, an engine would be run on to the traverser, and turned sufficiently to enable it to run off along another line to the crossings, from which point it could back on to its train for the up journey. The water-tank was supported by the walls of the recess, and its leather hose hung down above the tenders of the engines on the traverser.[15]

The buildings which formed the front of the station facing London Street were designed by George Smith. The 'basement' – actually at ground level – consisted mainly of a large hall, the 'Great Room', the booking-offices, and several small waiting rooms; the two first-class waiting rooms were in the south front of the building. Separate stairs for the first and second class passengers led up to more waiting rooms on the viaduct. Soon after the station was opened the '12 feet of pavement' on each side was built up to form granite-faced platforms two feet high, their construction accounting for some of the surplus stone sleepers.

Among other advantages the passengers would enjoy was the reduced chance of having their pockets picked: 'With such ample accommodation the public will be secure from the inconvenience and the brutal misconduct of speculating vagabonds, who have hitherto insulted and robbed respectable individuals when there has been a great influx of visitors.'[16]

Herapath, not very impressed with the new station, said it was badly sited '...at the corner of a public house', and William Curtis, whose own plans for a Greenwich station had been rejected, could discern a few weak points in the building. Although it was '...well adapted for a wet day or for small traffic', the plight of the crowds there at Easter week distressed him: 'It was really shocking to witness the crushing at no less than four distinct points, viz. the outside gates, the pay and turn tables, the entrance door of the waiting room and the exit door of the same.'[17] He added that the basement of the station had been built eighteen inches higher than the level of the viaduct, for architectural effect, and this necessitated three steps down to the

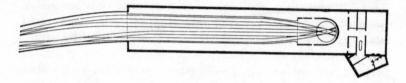

Greenwich Terminus, 1845

platforms from the upper waiting rooms, providing an excellent opportunity for hurrying passengers to trip over; the platforms themselves made entry to the low centre of gravity carriages difficult. Each platform was used alternately, and some confusion was caused by the company's practice of clearing the platform of arriving passengers before allowing those for London Bridge to use it. The passengers were directed to the appropriate platform by a 'swinging gate' – which presumably worked on the same principle as those used for separating sheep – and this was controlled by a policeman.

The buildings had cost a total of £27,871 to erect and equip, a sum which frightened many shareholders, who thought that such lavish expenditure was unwarranted. The directors argued that the station was not too large, as had been suggested, but that it was in fact still too small to handle adequately the traffic at holiday times. In 1841 the courtyard was finished, and iron gates erected at the entrances; the building was finally completed in July 1842, with the painting of the pillars in the booking offices in imitation granite.

The first function to take place in the Great Room was an entertainment in June 1842 for the whole staff of the company, to mark the final completion of the railway, and for which the regular travellers, traders and contractors contributed a large sum.[18]

Thomas Wheatley had secured the contract in 1838 for running a service of buses and flys from the station to Woolwich, Black-heath, etc., and in March 1842 two of the empty arches at Green-wich were fitted up as stables by the company for his horses. By 1843, however, he was running buses to London in competition with the trains, and he was required by the company to vacate the station yard in October, whereupon he chained all his buses and flys across the entrance and '... mustered all his drivers and cads for a fight, whilst the railway authority mustered their con-stables and servants to eject the intruder'.[19] Violence was averted by the timely arrival of lawyers, and about a fortnight later Wheatley agreed to give up the contract for the Woolwich traffic, and to vacate the station yard and stables.

It was found that the second class waiting rooms were little used in 1843, and in August Miller suggested that the approaches be altered in order that they could be let for concerts and public meetings. The board agreed, and authorised him to spend £20 on alterations. Soon afterwards a room was let to the Greenwich Amateur Musical Society for one weekly meeting at £40 a year; the belief that the company provided music at its stations to attract passengers can probably be traced to these performances.

In August 1840 it was reported that a number of unsightly old houses near the station were to be demolished, and replaced by new ones in a line with the terminus. At this time five hundred houses were going up in Greenwich, although there was scarcely a paved footway in the town. The board instructed Miller to build a road from the North Pole to the railway arches in May 1842, as the viaduct was practically inaccessible at this point; this was near the old footpath from Rose Cottage, and was known as Faulkner's Road in 1844. It later became North Pole Lane as far as the arches and Railway Place beyond them to the Ravens-bourne; it is now Norman Road, perpetuating the name of the man across whose osier ground, at this spot, the railway arches were built in 1838.

In choosing Tooley Street for the site of its London terminus, the company brought the railway as near to the City as was then practicable, being separated from it only by the length of London Bridge itself.

Unfortunately for the L&GR, it came up against powerful landowners when it sought to acquire property for its terminus, and not only the purchase of the original land, but that for every subsequent enlargement of the station involved it, or its successors, in trouble, usually with St Thomas's Hospital. The hospital buildings were then, and for the next thirty years, immediately adjacent to the station, on a site that gradually diminished as the railways expanded.

The railway came upon the scene immediately after several improvements had been carried out in the neighbourhood of the present Borough High Street in connection with the new bridge approaches. At this time, about 1830, St Thomas's Hospital had been partly rebuilt and considerably enlarged, and it is perhaps understandable that the governors did not welcome a fresh upheaval outside their very windows for the purpose of building a railway. One of their chief concerns had been to secure for the hospital a certain amount of fresh air by purchasing land around the buildings and laying it out as gardens. This land was threatened by the railway, and the hospital accordingly petitioned Parliament successfully to prevent the company acquiring it.

Another establishment, St Olave's Free Grammar School, was driven to adopting a nomadic existence for many years whilst the railways were fitting themselves into this congested corner of London. Its original buildings, centuries old, were pulled down in 1830 for the Bridge Approach, and a piece of ground in Duke Street was given by the City of London for a new school. Before they had time to build on it, however, the L&GR scheduled this ground for its station approach, and another site was given to the school in Bermondsey Street, Horseleydown, about four hundred yards away, and immediately to the south of the viaduct. The new school was opened in 1835, but in 1849 it was taken by the London, Brighton & South Coast Railway and demolished to provide space for that company's station enlargement. A writer in 1851[20] said that a site had not then been found, and that the school was functioning in a warehouse in Maze Pond; it finally settled down, still in Horseleydown, in 1855.

In view of the difficulty of acquiring the hundreds of small properties needed for the construction of the railway up to London Bridge, work was delayed on this part of the line. After about eighteen months work, however, McIntosh had brought the viaduct within sight of Bermondsey, and on 1 August 1835 the directors called for the plans of the offices and approaches to London Bridge station, based on the designs and elevations of their architect George Smith.

The office block had a frontage of 70ft and an extreme depth of

36ft, but the building had a curious plan as it had to fit into an odd corner between the approach viaduct and St Thomas's Hospital. The booking-office was on the ground floor, nearest the station itself, whilst at the other corner was an 'Exchange'; clerks occupied the rooms at the rear. The largest room in the building, the board room, was on the first floor, and here also were the waiting rooms, secretary's and accountant's rooms, and the 'Accountant's Bed Room'.

The London & Croydon Railway, as early as 1835, did not consider the Greenwich terminus worthy of the name of 'station', for in the first toll agreement of 30 December 1835 it refers to the L&GR's 'Starting Yard'. The station did in fact remain little more than an elevated and enclosed yard for some years. An old print of the station, published in the *Observer* on 30 October 1836 and later reproduced in several other journals, shows it completely devoid of any roof, buffer-stops or platforms. Only the three iron gates which separated it from the approach road, a small ticket-office, a flag, and a temporary awning to accommodate the spectators at the opening ceremony distinguished it from any other part of the line, except of course that the viaduct was 60ft wide from Dean Street to Joiner Street, where the line ended, and had three tracks instead of two. The station extended 400 feet along the viaduct, and the three lines diverged into two a few yards before this point was reached. In 1837 a fourth line was added.

The approach to the railway was by means of an inclined plane continuing the straight line of the viaduct and descending to ground level at Duke Street, a small road connecting Tooley Street with Wellington Street at the foot of London Bridge. This slope was called Dottin Street, after the chairman of the company, and was 50ft wide and 60 yards long, with footpaths on either side.

The railway ran up to, but did not cross, Joiner Street; the arch across this thoroughfare carried the approach road, as it still does today, although now the whole street is beneath arches consequent upon the widening of the line and the extension of the station buildings. From Joiner Street an arcade ran under the railway through seventeen arches, emerging at Dean Street, and the company hoped that it would become a popular market with shops in the arches on each side. This arcade was opened shortly before the railway, but it does not seem to have been a

great success, no doubt owing to the dampness of the place. The
entrance to this arcade can still be seen in Joiner Street, exactly
as planned by Colonel Landmann, although it now forms the
entrance to a warehouse.

Designs for an ornamental arch which was to form the station
entrance were prepared in 1835, and although the company
announced that they were about to build it in August, it was,
in fact, never built. The iron gates, bearing the inscription
'Vires acquirit eundo', constituted the only entrance to the railway for many years.

It was the original intention of the L&GR to build a large
station at London Bridge to accommodate its own trains and
those of all the other railways, and the original estimates of the
London & Croydon Railway were based upon that assumption.
The London & Croydon was informed by the Greenwich Railway,
however, that '...they had expended so much money, that it was
necessary, if we wanted any station at all, that we should provide
it for ourselves', and in April 1836 the Greenwich directors
offered them the ground they required for £18,000, which, they
said, was the cost price. It was agreed that the Croydon Railway

Designs, prepared in 1835, for an ornamental
entrance to the first London Bridge Station;
no such arch was ever built

should take the land at this price when they needed it, and the next year, when the L&GR found itself again heavily indebted to the contractor McIntosh, the directors assigned their claim on the London & Croydon company to him, he in turn agreeing to accept £4,000 and the balance in two years from the Croydon Railway. In the meantime the London & Croydon had obtained an Act empowering it to build a station at London Bridge.[21]

The land bought by the Croydon Railway was on the north side of the Greenwich station, a circumstance which was to lead to future trouble. Akerman, in evidence before the Select Committee of 1839, disclosed that the London & Croydon originally wanted its station on the south side, but the Greenwich Company did not choose to allow them to build it there because they intended to let that ground to the Deptford & Gravesend Railway and its engineer Colonel Landmann had accordingly scheduled all the land required when preparing his plans for Parliament. Akerman also admitted that his company had more power over the Croydon Railway by sending it across to the north side; so long as their station was on that side and the line joined the Greenwich Railway on the south, the trains had to run on the Greenwich viaduct, and the tolls were assured.

Colonel Landmann, however, denied that the London & Croydon was deliberately made to build its station on the north, and Mr Moxon of the Croydon Railway said that it was built there on the suggestion of that company's own engineer.[22] The situation was, of course, that since only two tracks existed on the viaduct when the London & Croydon Station Act was passed, and no widening was then contemplated, the Croydon trains would have had to cross the path of Greenwich trains, even had the station been built on the south side; the only difference would then have been the down Croydon trains would have crossed the up Greenwich line outside London Bridge and have recrossed it at Corbetts Lane, whereas under the arrangement actually made, the down trains crossed only once, but the up trains also crossed once. Since it did not then matter which side the Croydon Railway chose for their station from the operating aspect, it was only a question of which was the more convenient side to acquire the land upon which to build it. The north side was the obvious choice, for the Greenwich Railway had already bought and cleared the ground, and the London & Croydon merely had to purchase it from them, whereas to build a station south of the Greenwich would have required powers for the purchase of land belonging to St Thomas's Hospital, which would have been both troublesome and expensive.

In November 1837 the Croydon board suggested that the railways should take one line each, and run all their trains on it between London Bridge and Corbetts Lane; further, that the two stations at London Bridge should be united, and the positions of the two railways reversed. The Greenwich board replied that it did not deem it expedient that one line only be used for both up and down trains, but it agreed to discuss the exchange of stations. Colonel Landmann approved of the exchange when consulted in December 1837, but a few weeks later the Croydon directors recorded their opinion that the Greenwich board was being obstructive over the scheme. Although the L&GR had the semblance of a station at London Bridge, the Croydon company had not even started to build theirs at that time.

Work on the Croydon station began in 1838, and in April 1839 it was stated that the building would be ready in about three weeks. The following is a contemporary description.[23]

The London Station of the Croydon Railway occupies an area of upwards of an acre in extent, on the northern side of the terminus of the Greenwich Railway; and consists of four ranges of vaulting, with a north and a west front, and supporting a handsome passenger shed or covered way 212 feet in length, 26 feet high and 56 feet in breadth, for the protection of passengers arriving or departing by the trains. Some of the arches are appropriated to the various offices connected with the management of the establishment, comprising a Board Room, Directors' Retiring Room, offices for the Secretary, Registrar and the Accountant, with their respective assistants; and the remainder are to be used as depots for stores and merchandise.

Passing the end of the carriage approach to the Greenwich Railway, we reach the west front, which is an elegant facade of stone in the Roman style of architecture. This leads immediately into a vestibule 60 feet in length, 30 feet in breadth, and 22 feet high, the roof of which rests on a double range of Roman Doric columns, coated, as are the walls of the interior and of the staircases, with a new kind of white cement, capable of a polish equal to that of marble. This is the booking-office of the Croydon Railway; and from it the passengers ascend by a spacious stone staircase on the left to the covered way, where we find ourselves on a level with the Greenwich Railway. The roof of this shed is of timber overlaid with zinc, and is supported on the south upon a range of cast iron columns, the northern side being closed in; and the platform on each side presents a beautiful specimen of the Bastenne bitumen pavement. The vaulting already described, and which has all been covered with bitumen, extends for a considerable space north and east beyond the boundary of the shed, and is intended eventually to sustain such other buildings as the additional traffic, which the Brighton and Dover Railways are expected to bring to this spot, may render requisite. Passengers

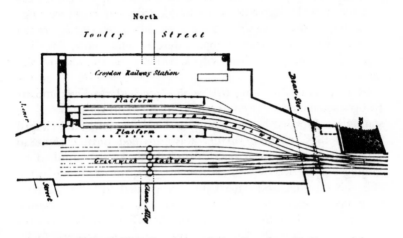

The London Bridge Stations of the London & Greenwich
and London & Croydon Railways, 1839

arriving by the trains depart by a similar staircase to that already noticed, but at the opposite, or south end of the vestibule.

Trains were drawn into the station by tow ropes, and the three tracks under the shed converged into the two Greenwich lines just beyond Dean Street, where stood the water crane between the lines. The trains were signalled by a small lighthouse erected in May 1839 at the same time as the junction was made.

The Croydon Railway, in anticipation of the opening of the South Eastern and Brighton lines within a few years, built a series of arches to provide a raised surface to the level of its own lines to the north of its station. It also bought and demolished most of the houses in Canterbury Square, off Tooley Street, in order to provide an open space in which carriages and carts could stand. An inclined plane led up to the railway from Canterbury Square, and by means of a ten horse-power steam engine, road vehicles were drawn up to the railway. The arches under the railway were laid out for the storage of spare railway carriages, which were also transferred between the viaduct and the ground over the inclined plane; these were shunted into the trains by means of a series of small turntables. Thus, claimed the Croydon Railway, the area of their station was doubled.

The London & Greenwich station remained in practically the same state as when the line was opened, and it appeared austere and unfinished against the London & Croydon building. The lines, trains and passengers were exposed to view, and to the weather, whilst the waiting rooms were in what amounted to a separate building, the office block, situated at the side of the railway.

In February 1835, long before the line had reached London Bridge, a tender had been accepted from McIntosh to cover the station for £105. Although a minute shelter of some kind existed there in 1837, nothing further was provided until early 1840 when the station was covered with tarred canvas, supplied by Edgington's of nearby Duke Street for £27. 10s 0d. It was probably this unusual, and remarkably cheap, method of providing a roof for a London terminus that gave rise to a report that the station was covered by an old sail. Just before the roof was erected it was stated that 'the station at the London end is absolutely impassable, owing to the mud and slush accumulated there.'[24]

In 1838, while its station was still under construction, the Croydon company obtained a second Act [25] authorising it to extend the terminus in order to accommodate the Brighton and South Eastern Railways; another Bill for further powers was presented in 1839.

Early that year the Select Committee on Railway Communications considered the situation at London Bridge, and the possible effect of other railways terminating there. Although assured by Mr Moxon, the chairman of the London & Croydon, that '... the Greenwich discharges more traffic than any other railway in the Kingdom, and there has never been any complaint of want of space', they were not convinced; Edward Bury thought four lines could not use London Bridge with safety, and Robert Stephenson's opinion was that the arrangements on the Greenwich line were positively dangerous. The question of the station now became linked with that of the widening of the line, and with these objects in view, each company promoted its own Bill later in 1839 for the enlargement of the station.

Immediately before the Bills came up for consideration, another Select Committee, that of 1840, investigated the position at London Bridge. It was now suggested that the Greenwich Railway should exchange its station, not for that of the Croydon Railway, but for the vacant space between the '... shed of the Croydon Company and the parapet wall next Tooley Street'. The other three companies agreed that as the existing Greenwich station was sufficient for that railway, all alterations should be done without cost to the Greenwich.

The Parliamentary Committee took three months to consider the Widening and Station Enlargement Bills of the two companies, both of which were taken together; about half of this time was devoted to the station.

From the evidence it is clear that the Greenwich Railway had abandoned the idea of attempting to retain control over the other lines in their use of London Bridge station, but it resisted the efforts of these companies to thrust it into the northern corner of the site. Cubitt was of the opinion that while it was essential for the southern lines to have a terminus at London Bridge, they would eventually need another London terminus as well, but that in any case, the three new lines needed a much larger station than the Greenwich, and that the latter should be 'insulated'. If the Greenwich lines were placed to the north, he added, '... the most active and noisiest part of the station would be farther from the Hospital'. His concern for St Thomas's, or possibly his desire to enlist their support, led him to declare that it was intended to pull down the tall offices of the Greenwich Railway when the London & Croydon acquired the property.

The London & Greenwich office building had offended the hospital ever since it was erected in 1836. Among other curious arguments advanced against its retention, the representatives of St Thomas's maintained that it prevented the free circulation of air owing to its height, with the result that their wards became damp, and even the metal fittings on furniture were caused to rust. The committee found it incredible that the building could cause so much mischief, and on the morning of 7 May 1840, when they visited London Bridge, they inspected the offices also. They then found that the top part of the building was never used; indeed, no floors had ever been constructed in that part of it.

The Greenwich company thereupon offered to pull it down to the level of the viaduct – presumably leaving the ground and first floors – and not to put up any building in future higher than the Croydon station. Some correspondence of 1840 suggests that the hospital authorities were disturbed by the Greenwich Railway's habit of '... pulling down portions of the line and rebuilding same in a different manner, especially at Greenwich and Deptford Stations', and feared that it would do the same at London Bridge – fears that were to prove well-founded.

St Olave's Grammar School was represented at the inquiry by the headmaster. His grievance was that since the railway had undertaken to keep its engines outside the station, (so that the noise and smoke should not cause the hospital any annoyance), they stood outside his school, and the noise of the steam blowing off from the safety-valves made it quite impossible for lessons to be conducted in calm and peaceful conditions.

The Commissioners of Pavements for East Southwark were unremitting in their efforts to thrust upon the company the responsibility and expense of renewing, maintaining and lighting as many streets as possible in the neighbourhood of the viaduct. They suggested that several streets had been spoilt by the railway arches, giving the impression that the company was solely responsible for the appalling conditions in the vicinity of London Bridge Station. At the inquiry they spent hours dealing with each of the many local streets in turn. The commissioners' representative asked if it was possible to find a greater nuisance than Glean Alley in any part of the metropolis, to which Colonel Landmann replied that it was greatly improved since the coming of the railway. 'Improved as it is, is it possible to find a more filthy, disgusting nuisance either used as a carriage or foot way?' 'Within a hundred yards of it,' replied the Colonel, 'I will find a dozen.' 'Tell me any of that size through which a gentleman's carriage ever had to pass.' 'I don't think a gentleman's carriage ever passed through Glean Alley, or ever will,' said Landmann.

The railway had certainly spoiled the district in one sense; some old watercolours exist showing several alleys and lanes near the Maze before the railway was built, and Glean Alley appears to have been quite a picturesque little backwater, with its uneven row of old wooden houses and a number of colourful characters idling away the time nearby.[26] The railway arches must have presented a strange appearance in such surroundings, and they must also have hastened the decay of the district, already at an advanced stage before the railway was thought of.

After many sessions the committee finally decided in favour of the Greenwich company's Bills for widening the line and for providing better station facilities at London Bridge, and both Acts received the Royal Assent on 7 August 1840.[27] The interests of the hospital were safeguarded by several sections in the Station Act; for example, no engine was to approach beyond a point 100 feet east of Joiner Street, except when on the turnplates between Joiner and Dean Streets. Very similar Acts were secured by the Croydon Railway at the same time, authorising it to undertake the work if the Greenwich Railway failed to do so.

On 20 March 1840 the Croydon, Brighton and South Eastern Railways set up a joint committee under the chairmanship of W. A. Wilkinson, for the purpose of co-ordinating their case against the London & Greenwich Bill, and of watching the progress of their own various Bills through Parliament. This committee was only partially successful in the object for which it was formed, and later that year it became the Joint Station Committee. As such, it handled the affairs of the three companies at London Bridge, each of which contributed several thousands of pounds to its funds; it bought land, met building costs, paid the staff, and managed the terminus from its separate offices nearby. Eventually the Joint Station Committee provided its station staff with a distinctive uniform, engaged and dismissed officers and staff, and made rules and regulations for both employees and passengers. It also acted on behalf of the three companies in all negotiations with the L&GR concerning the terminus.

Henry Roberts, the architect engaged by the Croydon Railway, estimated in January 1840 that the cost of widening the station, improving the approach and erecting additional buildings would be £20,000; this was about one-twelfth of what it actually cost. A preliminary plan, dated 8 July 1840 was prepared by Roberts showing how the land at London Bridge was to be distributed. The London & Greenwich were to take the Croydon station and retain about half the area occupied by their own, whilst the southern half of their original station was to pass to the London & Croydon, together with a new surface station on ground to be made available still farther to the south. Actually this plan was modified later, but had it remained intact, the London & Greenwich would have had just about the same area for its station as the Joint Committee had for its three lines.

The final plans for the new station appeared early in 1841. Rastrick, Landmann, Roberts and Smith all had a hand in them, but both the Joint Station Committee and the Greenwich Railway favoured Rastrick's design; indeed, the L&GR wished to adopt it for the principal facade of their own new station, which they then intended to build but never managed to finish. The reason for their failure ever to build a satisfactory London terminus was that, by the time they were in a position to do so, the shareholders objected to the expense, and expressed their determination that London Bridge should never become a 'palace' like the terminus at Greenwich.

The interpretation of the Acts by the parties concerned resulted in incredible complications. Under the station exchange agreement, incorporated in the Act, only the 'surface stations', i.e., the permanent way and buildings on the viaduct were to be exchanged, the arches and land on which they stood remaining the property of the original owners.

Although the Greenwich Railway was liable to pay a penalty of £50 a day to the other railways if its part of the work was not complete by 7 March 1842, it was June 1841 before the plans had been approved, and the contract awarded to Jackson & Co. for the substructure and station approach. Shortly afterwards the land between Joiner Street and the Maze was cleared, during which operation the Railway Hotel at the north end of Joiner Street and the original Greenwich Railway offices disappeared. The average life of a building erected anywhere near London Bridge station in those days seems to have been about five years; the new Joint Station itself was destined to vanish in roughly that time. By January 1842 the Greenwich company had moved to 'temporary' offices at 37 Canterbury Square, and stayed there until after it had ceased to work its line.

On 24 June 1841 the Joint Committee took over the old Croydon station in readiness for the opening of the London & Brighton Railway, and for the time being this became the Joint Station. The committee received a shock five months later when the L&GR intimated that it intended applying for powers to construct a wharf on the river, with a series of arches forming an inclined plane leading down to it. The latter is shown as leaving the original Greenwich station on the north side about

100 feet from the approach road, cutting right through the Croydon station, crossing Tooley Street and ending near the bridge.[28] The project was abandoned a few weeks later.

By the end of 1841 the new arches were in course of erection, and work on the new Joint Station began in 1842 on various parts of the site. Four separate offices were built in Joiner Street for the Station Committee, and the Brighton, Croydon and South Eastern Railways during September of that year, although by the following March the London & Croydon still occupied its old offices at 205 Tooley Street.

In November 1843 the Greenwich company's contractors started to widen Dottin Street, but the work was hampered by the restrictions placed on building over the old burial ground, and was not finally completed until 30 July 1844. As the act stipulated that the arch over Joiner Street was not to be extended – it was 85ft 6in wide in 1840 – the station buildings had to be set back in order to provide an approach along the front.

In the meantime the Joint Committee had drawn up its plans for the permanent station, and in March 1842 the contract for its erection was awarded to Grimsdale & Co. By November the committee had bought most of the remaining Greenwich land, and that company had now decided to buy the old Croydon station, to save the expense of demolishing it and building a new one, for £3,500. The committee bought the last strip of the London & Greenwich station in February 1843, leaving that company with the Croydon station and the land to the north of it, used by the London & Brighton Railway. All the space south of, and including, the original Greenwich station had now been acquired by the Joint Committee, but they were not yet in occupation of it all. The Greenwich Railway was squeezed into a temporary station, about half the width of its original one, close against the Croydon terminus, since it could not occupy the latter until the other railways had vacated it; they, in turn, had to wait the completion of part of their new station before their traffic could be transferred.

Construction started on the new arches to the south, and as the operations spread, it became increasingly difficult to maintain the train services into London Bridge; the total area available was roughly 300 feet by 400 feet. In April 1843 the L&GR gave permission for '... a switchman's sentry box, signal lamp and bell' to be erected near the grammar school, and for the committee to '... extend the ticket platform there, and erect a railing or fence on the parapet wall as a protection to the said platform' – with the usual proviso that it all be removed at the request of the L&GR. These installations were at the extreme south of the station, near the Bermondsey Street bridge.

By the end of May 1843 the new station works were nearly complete, but in the same month the Joint Committee resolved not to extend the terminus, as it had planned to do, in view of the Bricklayers Arms Bill, soon to come before Parliament. In a *Statement of the Case for the Bricklayers Arms Extension*, published at this time, it was stated that the London Bridge station had cost the Joint Committee £250,000 in three years. It was probably the Bricklayers Arms affair that led the Greenwich Railway to adopt an uncompromising policy in its relations with the Joint Committee, with the result that it was still in possession of part of that concern's property some eighteen months later.

The station itself, as distinct from the building in front (which housed the booking offices and waiting rooms and was still unfinished), was similar to that at Brighton. The roofs, which had skylights along each side of the ridges, were supported by three rows of cast-iron fluted columns, supplied by Rastrick's. There were two main platforms, departure on the north and arrival on the south; each was twenty-one feet wide, and was surfaced with Bangor slate paving. On the other side of the tracks which served these principal platforms were isolated, shelf-like platforms, four feet in width, while between these were four tracks used for making up the trains. On the arrival platform was a travelling luggage enclosure, inadequately described as being '... less unsightly than such contrivances usually are'.[29] From the south end of Joiner Street, running up behind the general offices, a new inclined plane for buses and cabs was built, and between this incline and Dean Street was the spare carriage house. A separate bridge carrying one track across Dean Street connected the carriage house with the goods warehouse to the south of the main station; this warehouse was provided with a number of pneumatic cranes. Nearby was a large tank, with a steam engine below, for supplying the station with water. Nearly 5,000 square feet of the valuable space in the station was occupied by the docks for loading and unloading horses and private carriages from the trains. The two tracks coming in from the new south viaduct spread out to six lines in the station, each line being provided with a series

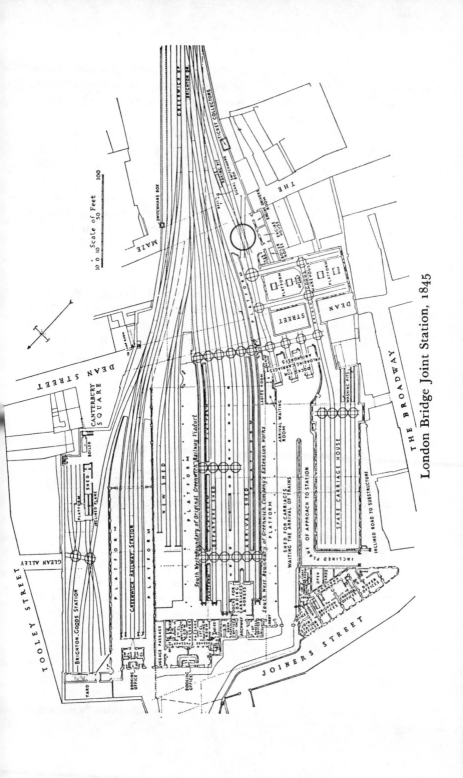

London Bridge Joint Station, 1845

of small turntables for the transfer of carriages from one track to
another. Some of these turntables projected on to the platforms,
and were railed off. The locomotive turntable was situated by
the stationary engine, near St Thomas's Street.

The station buildings running parallel to Joiner Street were
probably the best of any that have occupied the site, although
they were never actually completed – despite the various prints
showing the finished station. They were designed in the Italian
style by Roberts and Smith, for the Joint Committee and the
L&GR respectively; the campanile was the work of Thomas
Turner, the committee's resident architect and engineer.

By the end of 1843 the southern half of the main building, the
campanile, and the archways to the south of it were practically
finished, and at this time the illuminated clock was being fitted
to the turret, having been supplied by a Mr Payne of Bermondsey High Street for £78. It had four five-foot dials, and the Joint
Committee accepted his tender '... on the understanding that all
the dials are to show the time for that amount'. Reference was
made to this distinctive feature of the station in a description
given soon after it was opened.[30] 'The campanile, after the model
of the bell towers placed near some of the churches of Italy,
gives a graceful finish to the whole. The clock it contains is
illuminated at night.' The tower, 71 feet in height from rail
level, was of similar design and proportions to those still to be
seen at Osborne House. Whether Queen Victoria was ever aware
of the resemblance between her new residence and London
Bridge station is not known, but Thomas Cubitt, who designed
the house in 1845, might well have been.

The ground floor of the building consisted mainly of booking
offices, waiting rooms and passages leading to the platforms, while
the various companies had their board rooms on the first floor,
reached by a stone staircase in the tower.[31] The main block was
51 feet in depth, and should have been 128 feet long; almost half
the length – 56 feet, corresponding to the width of the old Croydon station which lay behind it – was set aside for the Greenwich
Railway's booking offices, however, and this part was never built.
Instead, a temporary single-storey building was put up, and this
lasted, with various modifications, until 1851. The stone-faced
gateways south of the tower were the parcels and carriage
entrances to the Joint Station.[32]

The 'strikingly handsome building', as the Joint Station was called, was opened to the public in July 1844, and at this time it was stated to be just under three acres in extent, 1¼ acres of which were covered by the passenger sheds. Eight million bricks had been used in the substructure, not including the arches under the old Greenwich and Croydon stations, and to support the enormous weight on the viaduct, the foundations had been taken down eighteen feet below ground.[33]

When the Greenwich Railway took over its temporary station in April 1843, it also acquired the Croydon booking offices in Joiner Street and the Brighton goods station. The latter continued to be let to the London & Brighton Railway, and the '... front office, next Joiner Street' was let to the South Eastern Company as a booking office.

The trains of the Croydon, Brighton & South Eastern companies used the new station from the end of 1843, and the old Croydon surface station was vacated about this time. The L&GR was not prepared to move out of its temporary station, however, until the matter of £8,300, being the balance due to it on the exchange of stations, was settled. The committee had withheld payment until the Greenwich company had accepted responsibility for the soundness of the new arches which had to bear the weight of the large Joint Station, but on Cubitt's advice the committee agreed to waive its claim for this undertaking. The L&GR was still in no hurry to vacate its temporary station, and Miller insisted on the modification of the Croydon station to suit the requirements of his company before he would advise the board to transfer the traffic.

After several alterations had been made, the building of the party wall between the old Greenwich and Croydon stations in March 1844 compelled the Greenwich Railway at last to move into the latter. A signal post for the Greenwich line was erected by Stevens & Co in May, and repairs to the Dean Street arch by the Joint Committee enabled the Greenwich Railway to occupy the Croydon station completely about the middle of June.

A minute of the Joint Committee dated 30 October 1844 states that the Greenwich company was still in occupation of its original station, as well as the Croydon one, and that it was to vacate it within seven days in order that the Joint Station could be finished. About this time the Greenwich board managed to persuade the Joint Station Committee that it was responsible for the cost of providing the temporary station, and for the alterations to the former Croydon Station. After obtaining a certificate to the effect that the L&GR had no further claims against it, the committee paid the contractor's account, and secured possession of its property about the middle of November 1844. The agreement for the exchange of stations, prepared in September 1844, was still circulating among the railways concerned the following February, as one by one they affixed their seals to it.

The old temporary station of the Greenwich Railway was incorporated in the Joint Station in 1845, and a plan of that year shows it with three tracks under a 'New shed'.

Chapter 8

Signalling

I N the early days of the Greenwich Railway the signalling of the line was entrusted entirely to the policemen, a practice common to most of the early railways. At first the police made their signals to the engine drivers with painted batons, hand-flags and, by night, lamps; some code of signals evolved, which was perfectly intelligible to the men concerned, but which was not officially recorded. The earliest reference to any form of fixed signal is in March 1837 when, following a fatal accident, the company adopted the practice of hoisting a white flag at each end of the line to warn passengers and staff of the approach of a train.

Neither head nor tail lamps were carried by the trains for the first two years, and it was not until the lighting of the viaduct was discontinued in April 1838 that the board made an order that all trains should carry '... two lights in front and one light behind ...'; the headlamps were later abolished in order that the Greenwich trains could be distinguished from those of the Croydon Railway, although it is surprising that some more satisfactory means of identification did not suggest itself.

The coming of the London & Croydon Railway demanded rather more elaborate arrangements for signalling, particularly at the junctions of Corbetts Lane and London Bridge. In July 1838 the Croydon company decided to erect a large gas lamp at Corbetts Lane, and a little later came the suggestion of having a 'lighthouse' there. In May 1839 permission was obtained from the L&GR for the construction of a second lighthouse at the end of the line, opposite the Hop Warehouse just outside London Bridge Station. Both were built at the expense of the Croydon Company, under an agreement with the Greenwich.

The Corbetts Lane lighthouse has been referred to as the first signal box ever to be built, although it would more accurately be described as a signal with accommodation for the two men who worked it, and it was quite independent of the points, which were operated from the ground by a switchman. It was octagonal in shape, and contained two powerful parabolic reflectors; the illumination was by gas lantern. A flight of steps was built against the viaduct at this point to provide access to the line for the signalmen.

Mr Akerman referred to the Corbetts Lane lighthouse in evidence before the Select Committee on Railways in May 1839; he said '... there is a watchtower lighted, and two persons, who can see an immense distance, stationed at the point of junction.' These men were referred to as 'Conductors', and received a higher rate of pay for their special responsibility. The lights were said to be visible two miles away;[1] indeed, Gibbs of the London & Croydon Railway claimed that they were actually visible at a distance of three or four miles, and that they could be seen plainly at a quarter of a mile 'in a most severe fog'. This rather extravagant claim (made on oath), suggests that he had something to do with the design of the apparatus.

About the time of the appearance of the lighthouses the first fixed mechanical signals were installed. Their purpose was to signal the junctions during the daylight, and they, like the lighthouses, were erected by the Croydon company but operated by Greenwich Railway staff. These signals consisted of an iron rod, attached to the top of which was an iron plate at a height of about fifteen feet; a lever at the bottom of the rod permitted it to be turned through 90°, to bring the plate either parallel with the rails, and invisible to the engine drivers, or broadside on to them.

Signalling regulations were drawn up by the two companies early in 1839, and the following section refers to the line between London Bridge and Corbetts Lane:[2]

Junction at Corbetts Lane

Lighthouse for Signals at Night.

At all times when the switches are in proper position for the Greenwich traffic a white light will be shown from the Light House on all sides.
When the switches are in position for working the Croydon line, then a red light will be shown on all sides.

Day Time.

A circular disc or plate, painted of red orange colour, and revolving on a pivot, will be turned edgeways, so as not to be visible when the switches are in position for the Greenwich traffic.

When the switches are in position for the Croydon traffic, the disc will be turned so as to be seen in full both on the Greenwich and Croydon lines at the same moment.

Marks by which to distinguish the Greenwich from the Croydon trains at night.

The Croydon engines will carry a double white light in front.
The Greenwich engines not to carry any light in front.
Both Greenwich and Croydon trains to carry a red light attached to the last carriage.

Croydon trains leaving London by day.

The conductor will sit on the first carriage, and display a red ball at the end of a rod, which he will hold out on the right-hand side.

Two switchmen will be employed at the junction, to work and attend to the switches.

Enginemen on the Croydon Railway to be instructed to slacken speed at all times when approaching switches, in sufficient time to stop the train with the tender brake, if the switch signals are not made.

Entrance to London Station at night.

When the switches are in position for the Greenwich traffic, a white light will be displayed at the switches, throwing a strong glare of light down the Greenwich line.

When the switches are in position for the Croydon traffic, the white light will be changed to red. The Croydon engines may be distinguished from the Greenwich by carrying a double white light forward.

By day.

When the switches are in position for the Greenwich line, an orange red disc or plate will be turned edgeways so as not to be visible.

When the switches are in position for the Croydon traffic, the disc or plate will be turned so as to be fully visible either way.

The Croydon train may be distinguished by the conductor exhibiting a red ball at the end of a rod on the right-hand side.

Owing to its situation near the river the railway was often

troubled by fog. Akerman, describing the precautions taken, said the speed of the trains was checked and each carriage carried a lamp. Policemen were stationed at short intervals along the line so that each could communicate with the one on either side ('Our staff is very abundant, and our men are of the best description'). When the fog was too dense for the lamps on the train to be seen, the men relied upon the whistle and noise of the engine.

Normally visibility between Deptford and New Cross was sufficiently good in those days for engine drivers at one point to see the trains at the other. This had, on occasion, led to trains racing to Corbetts Lane, a practice condemned by the committee on the Widening Bill, and eventually countered by the London & Greenwich Railway. By May 1842 posts had been erected at points half a mile distant to the east of Corbetts Lane on both lines, and as the drivers passed these points, they whistled; the switchman at Corbetts Lane Junction thereupon set the points in favour of the first train he heard, and signalled the other to stop with his flag, until the first had passed the junction and reached a point 400 yards along the viaduct. In fog, the London & Croydon engines had to whistle twice.

An article on the L&GR engines written in 1841[3] refers to the whistles which by that time had been fitted as part of the signalling arrangements with the Croydon line: 'To prevent danger a small apparatus is attached to the locomotives to announce their approach to a station by a whistling or screeching noise caused by the rushing of steam through an open valve, and heard at considerable distance.'

In July 1841 Sir Frederick Smith of the Board of Trade, in the course of a report on the London & Brighton Railway,[4] and the running of their trains over the viaduct, then about to commence, referred to '... a red flag being used as a signal of *safety*, contrary to the almost invariable rule upon other railways'. The position on the Greenwich line, however, was that the same red and white signals meant one thing to a Greenwich engine driver, and exactly the opposite to a driver from the Croydon line.

The original Croydon lighthouse at Corbetts Lane did not have a very long life. One of the first steps taken by the L&GR on the widening of the line was the erection, on Miller's advice, of a 'parabolic signal light' of its own on the north side of the viaduct. No description of this signal has survived, but it could not have been very elaborate, for it was supplied by Stephens &

Sons for only £11. 7s 6d in October 1840; a second one from the same firm was ordered in February 1841. These new signals were erected about the middle of 1841, and in September the L&GR instructed the Croydon Railway to remove their original one as it would '... interrupt the signals which the Greenwich Railway have substituted on the opposite side of the line'. The London & Croydon agreed to remove it on the understanding that if it was ever required again in the future, the Greenwich Railway must pay for its restoration, but the Greenwich board would accept no conditions as it considered the removal of the signal 'essential to the safety of the line'.

In January 1841 the Greenwich Railway notified the Croydon that in future a speed limit was to be observed on the line, and that London & Croydon trains '... would not be allowed to approach nearer than 400 yards to any train in advance'. The letter was accompanied by a printed code of signals.

John Entwhistle represented the L&GR at the Conference of Railway Directors held in Birmingham in January 1841 to consider what action should be taken on the proposed Bill for the Better Regulation of Railways;[5] here he mentioned the company's rule book, *Duties of Men, Rules and Regulations for Conductors, Platelayers, Enginemen, Firemen, Foreman of Locomotive Department*, approved by the board on 22 December 1840. He also appeared before the Select Committee on the Prevention of Accidents on 26 March 1841, when he spoke against the proposal to give discretionary powers to the Board of Trade to make general regulations for the safe working of the railways, on the grounds that each company required different rules to meet its special responsibilities. As a case in point, he mentioned the practice adopted on the L&GR in foggy weather, of having about twenty men stationed near the junctions; although perfectly satisfactory on the Greenwich Railway, where the weekly receipts were about £250 per mile, it would be out of the question on some of the long lines where the weekly receipts per mile were less than £20. He argued that all railways could safely be relied upon to make and enforce appropriate regulations for themselves, and with regard to the Greenwich Railway, he pointed out that, despite its impoverished condition, it had never economised at the expense of safety.

Colonel Landmann's ideas on the subject of signalling are worth noting. In 1839[6] he suggested what was, in effect, a distant signal; this was to be placed a quarter of a mile from Corbetts Lane junction to warn drivers of any danger in good time. He added '... there are many other ways: by placing the Waterloo Cracker on the rails, which would necessarily be broken by the wheels; that would give an explosion that would warn that engine immediately of the danger ahead'. (Some five years later, on 18 April 1844, General Pasley suggested that the Board of Trade recommend to the railway companies '... the adoption of a new Danger Signal by means of gunpowder'. He referred to the recent introduction of detonators on the London & Birmingham Railway by '... Mr Cowper, son of the King's College Professor of that name'.) Landmann's other suggestions for signalling Corbetts Lane Junction in foggy weather included the beating of a drum, the tolling of a bell, and the blowing of a whistle at the junction itself. A further idea of his was that all trains should carry signal-rockets; in the event of a breakdown the rockets were to be sent up from the disabled train as a warning to other drivers, and to stop further trains being sent off if possible. So far as is known none of these suggestions were ever tried on the Greenwich Railway, although Gregory allowed Cowper to experiment with his fog signals on the Croydon line in 1841.

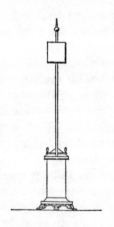

Hand-operated
board signal, 1839

Chapter 9

Locomotives

THE novelty of the Greenwich Railway viaduct so occupied the attention of contemporary journalists that none of them paused to describe in any detail the locomotives that were to run over it; neither did the hundreds, perhaps thousands, of people who paid their threepences to see the first London & Greenwich engine while it was on exhibition before the line was opened. Consequently this engine, the first to work regularly in London, disappeared with its sisters over a century ago, leaving hardly a trace.

Colonel Landmann was convinced of the superiority of steam power over any other form of traction from the inception of the railway, and the Act of May 1833 recognises that steam locomotives will be employed by making the usual provisions concerning them. Section 171 stipulates that the engines must not burn coal, and makes the company liable to a penalty of £5 for each infringement of the Act; it continues 'every such engine shall be fed or supplied with fire only by good Coke or Charcoal, or by other fuel which shall not cause or emit any smoke.' The use of horses for drawing trains, or for any other purpose on the railway, was prohibited.

On 29 March 1834, just as work on the viaduct was starting, Landmann was instructed by the board to advertise for '... locomotive engines, stone and iron', and the following appeared in several papers a few days later:

LONDON & GREENWICH RAILWAY.
Incorporated 1833.

THE DIRECTORS of the COMPANY being desirous to avail themselves of such improvements as may have been made in the construction of Loco-motive Engines for Railways, they invite the manufacturers of such Engines to forward to this Office for their consideration any proposition, with all particulars, for supplying the same. The Directors anticipate that four Engines of ten, and two of fifteen-horse power, will be best suited for their work at the commencement of their operations.

GEORGE WALTER
Secretary to the Board.

Office, 26 Cornhill, April 2, 1834.

Some response to the advertisements had been received by 10 May, when the Committee of Works recommended

... that the Engineer do proceed to Manchester and other places in order to inspect such as may be considered improvements in the general principle of the Loco-motive Engine as soon as he can be conveniently spared from the Works, and that one of 15 Horse Power be ordered of Mr Wm Marshall, to be prepared in seasonable time.

In early July Landmann and a director, Mr Beeby, visited among other places Manchester, Liverpool, Birmingham and Derby, but they seem to have spent most of their time on the Liverpool & Manchester Railway where they were more likely to have an opportunity of observing a passenger railway in operation than anywhere else in the country in 1834. They would have seen engines of the Planet and Mercury classes at work, alongside the new Stephenson 2–2–2, *Patentee*. Perhaps the fact that the latter was not working very well at the time confirmed Landmann in his belief that four-wheeled engines were preferable to six-wheeled.

In June the London agent of the Horseley Iron Company of Tipton, Staffs, had tendered to construct four locomotives; this firm built a few early railway engines, but no order was placed by the L&GR. Among others who approached the company were a Mr Blackman, who in May 1834 offered to act as engineer and to supply locomotives, and a Mr Ward who, in the same month '... laid before the Board a plan for a Locomotive Railway'; on 28 June the directors considered '... Mr Ward's plan for using Manual Labour instead of steam on the railway', and decided that since the invention was not in use on any other line, '... they could not ascertain the merits of the project.'[1]

The report of Colonel Landmann and William Beeby was read at the board meeting of 26 July 1834, and it was recommended '... that 2 engines of 12 inch diameter in the cylinders be ordered of Mr Berry [sic] of Liverpool, two also of Mr Stephenson and one more of Mr Marshall'. The two engines from Bury & Co were ordered in October and the directors evidently expected them to be supplied from stock, for on 6 December they wrote 'requesting him to complete the order given some time since for two Loco-motive Engines'. By the following June they had still not arrived, and the company asked what state they were in, and when they might expect to receive them. In actual fact they never did receive them; Edward Bury's locomotives were in great demand at this period, and he seems to have kept all his customers waiting.[2] Neither were the two engines ordered from Stephenson ever delivered; he too was overwhelmed with work, and had to decline further orders. As a result, most of the engines that eventually ran on the L&GR were built by firms little known in the field of locomotive engineering.

The first engine to be delivered was one ordered of Marshall & Sons on 10 May 1834. The makers probably relied on canal transport and sent the locomotive in a partially dismantled condition, as was the practice of the neighbouring Horseley Iron Co.[3] *The Public Ledger* of 23 February 1835 announced '... we find the first locomotive-engine is arrived from the manufacturers in the country, and is now erecting on the works at Corbetts Lane, Bermondsey.' This engine was named *Royal William*, and after being exhibited in one of the arches, it made trial runs in June 1835, as soon as some track had been laid, and the Deptford inclined plane completed. It was the only locomotive on the railway at that time, and it was the first to haul a train in London. It cannot be claimed that it was the first ever to work in London; this distinction belongs to Richard Trevithick's *Catch me who Can* of a generation before.

The *Royal William* was apparently entirely satisfactory, for on 20 June 1835 the company ordered two further engines similar to it from Marshall; this makes a total of four ordered from the firm, and the last was delivered in time for the opening of the railway in December 1836.[4]

The Marshall engines seem to have been practically identical originally, and to have approximated to the Planet type of the Liverpool & Manchester Railway. They had 5 foot driving

Drawing, probably partly conjectural,
of Engine No 1, *Royal William*, Marshall & Sons, 1835

wheels, 3 foot leading wheels, 11in by 18in cylinders and weighed
$9\frac{1}{2}$ tons. The only contemporary illustration that has come to
light is one of a pair that once hung in the offices of the L&GR.
Marshall was paid £2,950 by bills of exchange over a period, and
probably some smaller amount in cash which was not recorded,
indicating that the locomotives cost £750–£800 each. The *Royal
William* was probably the engine involved in the accident at
Spa Road on 7 March 1836; when asked during the inquest,
'What is the value of the engine?', the driver replied 'About
£800.' What this had to do with the accident is not very clear,
unless the court was contemplating placing a deodand on the
locomotive – a practice fairly common in those days – as being
indirectly the cause of a death. The other three engines built by
Marshall were named *Royal Adelaide, Dottin* and *Twells*.

William Marshall & Sons were established at Lea Brook,
Tipton, Staffs, by 1834 as coal and iron masters,[5] and there was
some connection between them and the firm of Marshall &
Rodgers of the Britannia Foundry, Derby, and Liverpool. The
latter supplied railway equipment of various kinds, but not loco

motives, to several of the early companies, and were among the railway contractors who subscribed to Robert Stephenson's testimonial in November 1839. William Marshall, who financed the concerns, was not himself an engineer, but a partner in the banking firm of Barber & Marshall of Walsall; this firm was associated with the bankers, Spooner, Attwood & Co., and thus with John Twells of the L&GR board of directors. Marshall's sons William and John ran the engineering works and Herbert's Park Colliery, Darlaston, Staffs. The locomotive building department was in the hands of Joseph Mills, another of the early locomotive engineers of whom little is known. He had once been with the Horseley Iron Company, and by 1842, after the bankruptcy and death of William Marshall,[6] he was in business on his own account at the Eagle Steam Factory, Great Bridge, Wednesbury as a steam engine manufacturer, millwright and locomotive engineer. The firm he founded survived until the 1930s, and in 1905 he was referred to as having built '... the first four locomotive engines for the London & Greenwich line ...'.[7]

Shortly after the *Royal William* started its trials, a second engine, of unorthodox pattern, constructed to the designs of Lord Dundonald (better known as Lord Cochrane), made its appearance on the line. He had spent some years in trying to perfect a rotary steam engine (best described as a primitive form of steam turbine), early models of which had been used to drive a circular saw and a steamboat on the Thames.[8] The locomotive engineers Sharp, Roberts & Co of Manchester and the directors of the Liverpool & Manchester Railway were interested in the invention, and its possible application to railway locomotives, and they came to London to see it in January 1834. It was probably the model fitted to the steamboat that they saw, as this was undergoing trials on the Thames at the time – until it blew up when the engineer started racing against another boat.

By September 1834 Dundonald was ready to make trials of his engine on a locomotive, and after long correspondence, the Liverpool & Manchester Railway agreed to lend him the *Rocket*, by then withdrawn from service, and to pay up to £30 towards the cost of converting it. In late October trials were held, but opinions as to its performance varied; George Stephenson, who was convinced it would not work, and did not attend the trials, said it was incapable of moving a train of empty carriages.[9] Shortly afterwards the apparatus was removed from the *Rocket* and sent to London, and it is at this point that the L&GR became involved.[10] Walter and Landmann both knew the details, not only of the rotary engine, but of numerous other improvements '...applicable to locomotive steam engines which are to travel on iron railways', and also to carriages, all the subject of a patent application,[11] and on their recommendation the board, on 8 December 1834, arranged with Lord Dundonald to have two pairs of rotary engines made, at their own expense, for locomotive or other purposes, on payment to him of one farthing in acknowledgement of his rights as the inventor.

A locomotive driven by rotary engines arrived on the railway in June 1835, and was examined by James Walker who reported '...none of the modifications yet attempted have been found to work well owing to the nicety of workmanship required'. He suggested that the engines should be made by Seaward of Limehouse, but that the rest of the locomotive should be constructed by '...engine makers in the locomotive engine line (as Mr Bury of Liverpool)'. However, its first steam trials took place on 24 June in the presence of Landmann, Walter, several directors and the Earl of Dundonald, all of whom were said to have been 'highly gratified' with its performance. The next day the board accepted the engine on terms suggested by Walker – the payment of a premium of £100 for each one built – and arranged to have another one constructed on the same principle. In September George Walter undertook to manage the patent for 25 per cent, and contributed £160 towards the cost of obtaining it; by this time Lord Dundonald had spent about £4,000 in developing the rotary engine.

The first locomotive was probably a makeshift prototype incorporating some of Dundonald's other improvements. The boiler was only a few inches clear of the track and two long horizontal wooden beams, the ends of which were curved, ran underneath the boiler and tender to act as a sledge in the event of derailment. The locomotive had only two wheels to secure the maximum adhesion with lightness, the whole machine being nicely balanced on its axis. The wheels were driven by the two rotary engines mounted on the axle between them; each comprised a fixed cylindrical chamber through the centre of which the driving axle passed, and vanes attached to the axle were driven round by high pressure steam which entered and escaped from the cylinder by valves. Among other refinements, the loco-

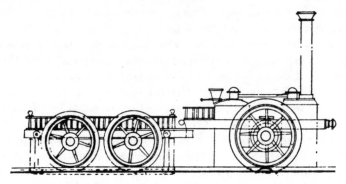

The Earl of Dundonald's rotary locomotives, 1835 and 1836;
probably the only 2-wheeled railway engines ever constructed

motive was to be charged with boiling water at stations, and
heated firebricks were to replace the normal firebox. The
inventor's intention was to dispense with engine drivers,
'... whose attendance in revolving engines is not required'.

The following comment was made by W. B. Adams[12] soon after
the appearance of the locomotive on the Greenwich line:

Even with four-wheeled engines, the difficulty of getting sufficient
adhesion is considerable; and this led the Earl of Dundonald to
patent a method of working two-wheeled engines, connecting
the engine with its tender by a similar contrivance to that used
in the army for connecting a gun-carriage with its tumbril. But
the contrivances the Earl has resorted to are so extremely clumsy
and inartificial that they do not mend the matter.

The engine appears to have worked well at first, but gradually
to have developed defects leading to its final breakdown towards
the end of 1835; one writer states that the steam pipe twisted and
fractured when the steam was turned on, while another refers to
a tradition that when steam was applied the wheels remained
stationary, and that the locomotive itself revolved around the
rotor.[13] Although its behaviour could hardly have been so bizarre,
its construction was such that, with the weight of a train behind
it there would have been a decided tendency for the front end
to rise and the rear to be thrust down upon the tender coupling
when starting.

Another locomotive was built under the Earl's supervision by John Hague incorporating rotary engines made by Seaward & Co; promised for early 1836, it did not eventually reach the railway until November, by which time a bitter dispute over patent rights in brakes and carriages had arisen between Lord Dundonald and the company. One day towards the end of November Simon Fenwick, the Locomotive Superintendent, towed it out for trials, but could not get it beyond the first set of points as the boiler was hung so low that it fouled the track. Fenwick said that it could never have been used in its original form, and Landmann reported that it was '... unfit for this, or any other railway made in the usual manner'. In fact, a specially constructed track with a deep trench or pit between the rails was required for it, and this had been outlined in the patent specification. Towed back to Deptford Works, it was laid aside until October 1838, when the board ordered it to be broken up.

Lord Dundonald abandoned all further attempts to apply his rotary engine to railway locomotives, but several were tried for other purposes. Some were built by Bramah & Robinson of Pimlico, and Timothy Bramah reported on them in 1837 to the Academie des Sciences, Paris.[14] American engineers were familiar with them, and in one of their reports the marine model was described as being '... not larger than two Cheshire cheeses'.[15]

In the course of a letter on Liverpool & Manchester Railway engines, Robert Stannard said 'The *Venus* was sent up to open the Greenwich line after the failure of one built by Lord Dundonald'. The *Venus* was built in 1831 by Stephenson, and was out of service by 1835 awaiting a new firebox; it disappears from the records after this time, so was presumably repaired and sent up on loan or hire. Stannard was an engineer on the Hull & Barnsley Railway, who had in his youth witnessed the building and early years of the Liverpool & Manchester Railway; his father had been the contractor for the section of that line across Chat Moss.[16]

In 1836 the company purchased two locomotives from George Forrester & Co of Liverpool; the first appears in a list of accounts passed for payment:

28 May 1836 George Forrester & Co (Victoria Engine and waste) £1010. 10s 0d.
The second engine, originally *William*, arrived just before the

opening of the line in December, and was renamed *Walter* to avoid confusion with the *Royal William*; at this time Forresters named their engines before they left their works. These were the first tank engines to run in England, and were similar to one supplied by the firm to the Dublin & Kingstown Railway earlier in 1836.[17] Whishaw[18] thought the *Victoria* sufficiently unusual to warrant the following note: 'On the Greenwich Railway there is an engine built by Messrs Forrester of Liverpool, having the water-tank beneath the boiler; the receptacle for coke also forms part of this ponderous machine.'

Of a type known later as well-tank engines, they had 11in by 18in horizontal outside cylinders, 5 foot diameter driving wheels and 4 foot leading wheels. Both pairs of wheels had outside bearings, the cranks being keyed on to the driving axle outside the bearings. This produced a certain amount of unsteadiness, although this was said not to have mattered very much on the slow Greenwich line. The boilers had 82 tubes, and the fireboxes were unusually large for that period. These engines weighed 13 tons, and were of greater power than Marshall's.

Early in 1837, trials were held between the *Royal William* and the *Walter* to ascertain the effect of wind resistance on the speed of locomotives. With a strong north-west wind blowing across the line at 30° both engines made several runs in each direction; the *Walter* was less affected, being more powerful and presenting a smaller surface area from the absence of a tender.[19]

On 8 March 1836 William Curtis, an engineer lately returned from Mexico,[20] met Walter for the first time at Deptford Works and demonstrated his locomotive brake which, he claimed, would have prevented the accident at Spa Road the previous day. It was described as a pair of 'cycloidal cams' fitted to the engine frame behind the driving wheels. Normally they were an inch above the rails, but when screwed down the eccentric flanged segments touched the rails, were turned a few inches by the momentum of the engine and lifted the driving wheels an inch clear of the rails; a weight of seven tons was thus transferred to the cams, to bring the engine to a halt by friction. Curtis stated that an engine so fitted, travelling at full speed with a train, had pulled up in forty yards without stopping the wheels.[21] The brake, made by Gordon & Co, was adopted immediately, and was attached to new engines as they arrived, but appears to have been removed from the locomotives by 1839, for then the only references to brakes concern those on the tenders. The latter could not have had much braking power on the small tenders of the Greenwich Railway, and when an accident occurred at Spa Road on 1 February 1843, the driver reversed the engine to stop the train, a method widely practised in those days, although one on which engineers differed in their opinions as to its efficacy. All agreed, however, that the practice was objectionable in that it was bad for the rails and the engines.

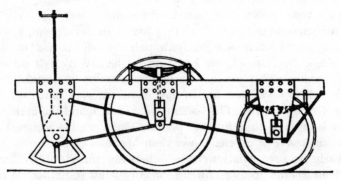

Curtis' sledge-brake or cycloidal cam,
fitted to the engines in 1836

Another of Curtis's inventions carried by the L&GR engines for a while was a complicated spark-arrester.[22] This contraption was fitted to the top of the engine chimney and consisted of a concave plate supported by brackets a few inches above the chimney-top, which deflected the steam, smoke, sparks and cinders downwards. Just below the chimney-top was a small circular open water trough, into which the sparks and cinders fell, and were extinguished, while the smoke and steam escaped into the air. The trough was kept filled by a thin pipe running up the side of the chimney and connected to a pump, excess water overflowing into the chimney. This apparatus was soon replaced by simple and effective wire guards fitted over the chimney-tops.

The Greenwich engines were fitted with yet another of Curtis's devices, his improved ashpan. This was made watertight, and it collected water which filtered through the firebox. As the hot ashes fell into it they were extinguished, and at the same time the water vapour rising from the ashpan passed up into the fire-box to assist combustion therein. They were hinged at the front, and some had a wheel-release, whilst those fitted to the Forrester engines were held by a chain attached to the footplate. On arriving over a pit, the driver released the ashpan, which swung down and emptied itself.

It was stated in 1835[23] that the company intended to adopt some method of slipping and taking on carriages without stopping the trains. Curtis was then experimenting with devices for this purpose, but how far these trials went on the Greenwich line is not known; the practice subsequently adopted of slipping the whole train from the locomotive may have been a modification of his system.

There is no evidence that Curtis's various inventions were ever used, or even tried, on other railways. He offered the Liverpool & Manchester his brake in April 1836, but they were not interested. He seems to have had a fairly free hand on the L&GR, however, of which company he was at one time a shareholder.

The parallel wooden sledge-beams suggested by Lord Dundonald were fitted to all the early engines. The original design was modified and the wheels were actually enclosed by a frame, the front and rear components of which supported the locomotive in the event of axle-breakage, whilst the side members provided a fender to protect it from damage caused by striking the parapet wall when derailed.

In 1836 the L&GR came near to being the first railway company to construct its own engines, in their case, through a subsidiary concern similar to the Railway Gas Company. An old prospectus survives of the 'Locomotive-Engine & Railway Carriage Company', formed by Captain R. Page, George Landmann and George Walter, all of the Greenwich Railway, with William Curtis as the engineer.[24] The capital was to be £200,000, and it was proposed to erect works in or near London; the document opens with the following paragraph:

The necessity of immediately forming a Company for supplying the railways now constructing and already in want of Locomotive Engines and Carriages is a well known fact. The existing Manufactories are fully engaged and refuse to take further orders; and without the aid of new Establishments the tenth part of the Engines at present required in this country alone could not be obtained.

In May 1836 it was claimed that the company had the option of several sites near London for its works, but the project was abandoned shortly afterwards. In 1837 Walter said, 'It was connected with the Greenwich Railway Company, which required a great many engines';[25] considerable numbers would have been needed for the Gravesend and Dover extensions, then contemplated, rather than for the L&GR itself.

At the opening in December 1836 there were six engines in service, and the *Railway Magazine* reported that '... several of the engines bore the names of gentlemen who have distinguished themselves in the prosecution of the work, as Walter, Twells, Dottin, etc'. They were not numbered at this time, but numbers were allotted in 1837, when locomotives by the same maker were grouped together; thus *Royal William*, *Royal Adelaide*, *Dottin* and *Twells*, built by Marshall became Nos. 1–4, and *Victoria* and *Walter*, by Forrester, Nos. 5 and 6. For a period the engines retained their names, and two new ones were given names and numbers, but all the names had been removed by 1840.[26] Some contemporary water-colours show them as painted green, but in others they are black.

During the summer of 1837 a locomotive shortage seems to have developed, and it was as much as the engineers could do to keep the company's six engines running. The amount of overtime worked at Deptford caused the board some concern, and in November they ordered it to be discontinued except in emergencies, and that the engineers be employed on locomotives only, and not on carriages. In April it had been rumoured that two engines had blown up, killing fourteen persons. The company's assertion that 'No engine blew up during the Easter Week' seems to imply that one had exploded at some time, although the incident could not have been very serious.[27]

Just before his resignation in July 1837 Walter ordered locomotives from Gordons of Deptford,[28] Summers, Grove & Day of Southampton and John Hague of the Thames Iron Works, without informing the board. In September Gordon & Co offered the company an engine, and protested when the offer was declined. However, no further steps were taken, either by Gordons or the company.

In December 1837 one of the new directors, Major Thornhill,

inspected the workshops and the engines under repair. By this
time the condition of the locomotives was causing the board
grave concern, and led them to take some desperate steps to
remedy the situation. It was said 'that on taking office they found
nearly all the engines either disabled or in bad order', and on
23 February 1838 the directors Yates and Hodges '... agreed to
place the engines and Engine Department in a proper state'.

In December 1837 Forrester was asked how soon he could
supply two locomotives and tenders, but no order resulted. About
the same time Yates, Hodges and Thornhill, with an engineer
named Dickson, visited the works of Braithwaite, Milner & Co
in Bath Place, off the New Road (now Euston Road) to see the
engines under construction there. They were interested in one
with 11 inch cylinders, weighing 8 tons, which was to be ready
in ten days, and for which the makers asked £1,300. It was
ordered, and finally accepted after a further examination, on 12
January 1838, to become No. 7, *Greenwich*, on the L&GR.

When the engineer Theodore West read a paper on locomotives
before the Cleveland Institute of Engineers in 1886[29] he observed
that many of the details he gave then were based on his notes
and recollections of the earliest days of railways, which, if not
soon recorded, would be lost. Included in the illustrations was a
drawing of the L&GR Braithwaite engine, supplied to him by
another eminent engineer, E. A. Cowper, who was serving his
apprenticeship at Braithwaite's when the engine was built.[30]
The drawing shows an outside cylinder four-wheeled engine, with

Engine No. 7, *Greenwich*, Braithwaite & Co, 1838

an intermediate rocking shaft to transmit the motion to the driving wheels, an arrangement designed to promote steadiness in four-wheeled locomotives.

The *Greenwich* had been in service for less than three weeks when it came near to being reduced to scrap; Walter states that the '... Engine man jumped off the engine when taking a train to Deptford, and but for the exertions of the fireman, all the passengers, engine and carriages would have gone over the end of the railway into High Street [Deptford] and dashed to pieces.' On 6 February, after the pumps froze and several tubes had burst, the locomotive was taken out of service, but it was working again ten days later, for then '... the axle of Messrs Braithwaite's engine broke; subsequently the stays, tubes, chimney etc. gave way, and the engine was removed from the line.'[31] It was then returned to the makers, who seem to have repaired it very promptly, probably because they had not yet been paid for it, and the company accepted it back again.

The first quarter of 1838 was a particularly bad period for the locomotive department. Walter wrote that on 10 January, during a spell of severe frost, '...through not keeping proper men to attend the fires of the engines at night the pumps were frozen, and on starting the next morning the pump levers and many valves of the engines were broken, and several trains lost their turn...'[32] The next day engine No. 5 ran off the line, and the day after that the tender of No. 1 was smashed. A few days later the newspapers reported that the '... Greenwich Railway has got rid of its frost-bitten engines...', and that the service was then normal. On 15 March No. 6 engine '... ran off at a crossing but fortunately struck upon the Guide Rail and regained the train...', whilst on 25 March '... through the carelessness of an engineer improperly appointed, who jumped off the engine, it ran against another, and considerable damage was done to No. 1 engine.'

Walter attributed the trouble to the reduction in staff at that period, and particularly to the replacement of '... Simon Fenwick, the Engineer I hired from the Liverpool & Manchester Railway'. He continued:

The Engines which I had ordered of Messrs Gordon & Co and Messrs Summers & Co for the purpose of keeping up a proper supply having been thrown upon the manufacturers' hands, two new ones were with the utmost difficulty obtained; these with the six old Engines ... in the course of a few weeks, were put into excellent condition under the direction of Mr Yates and the new Superintendent Mr Hayton...

In a copy of Walter's pamphlet,[33] once the property of J. Y. Akerman, the secretary, the following comment is written against the above paragraph:

The credit of this is due to Mr Ward the Engineer and Simon Fenwick, and most certainly not to Mr Hayton, who did not know the difference between a low pressure and a high pressure engine when he came on the Works.

In February and March 1838 the company tried unsuccessfully to obtain locomotive power by contract, approaching Edward Bury first, and then Fairbairn, Lloyd, and Gordon & Co. In the meantime it was decided to install a more powerful engine at Deptford Works to facilitate the heavy repair work going on there.

About this time another new engine came upon the L&GR; it was purchased during the early months of 1838 from the firm of Twells & Co of Birmingham, engineers and 'manufacturers of Dr Church's Patent steam engine boiler'. The proprietor, Philip M. Twells was related to John Twells, former deputy chairman of the railway and to Philip Twells, one of the MPs for the City of London and a member of the bank, Spooner, Attwood & Co. Dr William Church lived in Birmingham, and was a prolific inventor; many of his patents from 1818 until 1835 related to steam engines of various kinds, the later ones mainly to locomotives.[34] From his connection with the builders it seems likely that he had something to do with the design of the locomotive built for the L&GR, but to what extent it has not been possible to determine. Twells & Co do not appear to have been very successful in the field of locomotive building, no other examples of their work having been traced. The Twells engine had 5ft 6in driving wheels, horizontal cylinders, weighed 10 tons and cost £1,270; it went into service in April 1838 as No. 8, *Thames*.

In August 1838 G. M. Miller was appointed engineer to the company and on 14 September he '...reported that Mr Stephenson had a new engine which he would spare the Company at £1,570, although made to order...'; it was decided to purchase this engine and a week later the specification arrived. It was for a standard 2-2-2 tender locomotive, with 12in by 18in cylinders and of 13 tons total weight; the price, including tender, duplicate wheels and numerous other spare parts, was now £1,940.[35] On Miller's advice it was ordered immediately, and a cheque sent to R. Stephenson & Co; on receiving advice that the engine was about to be shipped by the makers, the company insured it for £2,000, and it was in service by 19 October.

In September John Hague had intimated that he was about to deliver the locomotive he claimed was ordered by the former directors, but Miller considered it quite unfit for the line, and as no trace of the original order could be found, the company would not accept it.

Miller, on 9 March 1839, gave the board a detailed report on the locomotives, of which there were then nine. The original six had all been thoroughly overhauled, some in the company's workshops, others, where almost complete rebuilding was necessary, by Penn's of Deptford, and one, No. 4, by Braithwaite. Penn charged about £200 to fit new frames, cylinders, pistons and crank axle to No. 2, re-turn the wheels and replace other worn parts, and he was later to rebuild other engines for the company. Apart from No. 4, all the engines were in excellent condition, the two Forrester locomotives being described as nearly equal to new; these had been converted from tank to tender engines when under repair just previously. The Stephenson engine was practically new, and much of the report is devoted to its merits. Miller considered the *Greenwich* and *Thames*, purchased the previous year, as 'totally unfit for this line', and recommended that they be sold as soon as possible.

An inquiry for surplus locomotives had already been made by the Clarence Railway, a line principally concerned with coal traffic in County Durham, and they were offered *Greenwich* and *Thames* for £650 and £600 respectively, but an engineer's report suggested that they were of insufficient power, and the offer was declined. On being reduced by £100 each, the *Greenwich* was accepted, and it arrived on the Clarence Railway on 18 May 1839 to become their locomotive No. 11, retaining its old name. This company was unwilling to pay more than £350 for the *Thames*, a figure that Miller strongly recommended the L&GR to accept on the grounds that the engine was nearly useless, and when at work consumed far more fuel than any other; the company thereupon drew a bill for the £350 which the Clarence Railway accepted, together with the engine, in September 1839. It became

No. 12 to its new owners, and was hired to Mr Walton, the contractor for the passenger trains, in April 1840. It was said that his '...locomotive engines and coaches are very good',[36] but by what standards they were judged is uncertain, for the trains took 1 hour 20 minutes to cover the 19½ miles of line open to passengers. When the Clarence Railway was leased to the Stockton & Hartlepool in 1844, the two ex-Greenwich Railway engines were still in service, and the *Greenwich* survived at least until May 1857, when it was sent, with *Sir Robert Peel*, to R. Coulthard & Co, who made an allowance of £475 for the two old engines against the cost of a new one in a part-exchange transaction.[37]

The original board of directors, on 17 June 1837, decided to purchase a locomotive from Summers, Groves & Day, the firm having offered one then in their factory for £1,050; it was described as having been built on Stephenson's plan. In July Simon Fenwick, then employed by the L&GR but later to become superintendent of locomotives on the Croydon Railway, was sent to inspect it, but it had been sold elsewhere in the meantime, and the firm then undertook to build and deliver another one in five months for £1,270.

Some eighteen months later the company was still making inquiries as to its progress, and threatening to rescind the contract, but it was not until 5 March 1839 that the locomotive was completed; Miller was given a copy of the contract and specification, and sent off to Southampton that same night to inspect the engine. In his report a few days later he said,

...it worked to my entire satisfaction, and I consider it to be a well-made engine, and at the price of £1,270 I should recommend that it be ordered up immediately, but I must observe that it is not the sort of engine I should now recommend your Board to have made for the Railway inasmuch as many improvements have been introduced since the order for this engine was first given.

The locomotive was delivered soon afterwards, and paid for on 25 May. It became No. 7, replacing Braithwaite's engine, but it was not named.

The specification of this engine has been preserved:

Specification of a locomotive engine and tender similar in principle to engines of the same diameter of cylinder and length of stroke of Robert Stephenson.

Cylinders. Two cylinders placed in the usual manner inside the smoke box with the view of working a double throw cranked axle in the driving wheels, the cylinders to be 11 inches in diameter with 16 inch stroke, and fitted with metallic pistons.

Boiler. The boiler to be cylindrical, 3 feet diameter and 8 feet long, and to contain not less than 80 best brass tubes each $1\frac{5}{8}$ inches diameter.

Firebox. To be of copper and of proportionate dimensions to the boiler.

Wheels. The driving wheels to be 5 feet diameter, made of wrought iron, except the naves, which are to be of cast iron: the fore wheels of the engine to be 3 feet in diameter.

Frame. The frame of the engine to be of wood supported by an internal and external plate bolted securely to it.

Tender. The tender to be of the same form and plan as those now used upon the London & Greenwich Railway, and in keeping with the engine, and to contain not less than 600 gallons of water.

The mechanical execution of the said engine to be of the first description and all materials to be of the very best quality. Payment to be made in cash after one week's trial of the engine upon the Railway.

Summers, Groves & Day is another of those concerns whose early history is obscure, since the firm's own records of its activities in the 1830s have long since vanished. Nathaniel Ogle,[38] a steam road carriage pioneer, was a partner in 1832 and the firm built at least one of these vehicles which ran between Southampton and Birmingham, but the rapid development of railways drove these carriages off the roads before they had been properly developed. The firm then turned the resources of its works, already equipped for the construction of steam-driven vehicles, to the manufacture of railway locomotives and marine engines. They probably built only four or five locomotives in all; their first seems to have been the *Jefferson*, sent to the United States in 1837,[39] and this was undoubtedly the engine originally offered to the Greenwich Railway in that year. At least two were built for the London & Southampton Railway, and several of that company's engines were repaired by the firm.

The new engine had only four wheels, but within two months of its arrival Miller ordered a third pair from the makers and converted it to six-wheeler; it was thus the first of several engines to be modified in this way. The old Marshall engine No. 3 had additional wheels fitted in 1840, followed by No. 5, one of Forrester's machines, in January 1841. In February 1842 it was decided to convert the remaining four when they came into the works for repair, and trailing wheels were eventually fitted to Nos. 1 and 2; the other two, Nos. 4 and 6 by Marshall and Forrester respectively, were never modified.

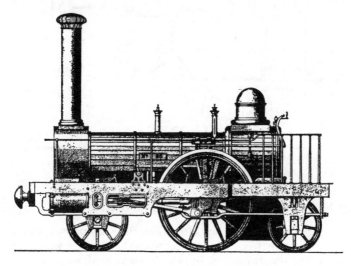

A Forrester 6-wheeled (2—2—2) locomotive of 1839; No. 5, *Victoria*, was of similar appearance after the addition of trailing wheels in 1841

The last engine ever bought by the L&GR was built by Hawthorn & Co of Newcastle. It was decided late in 1839 that a new engine would be required before the following Easter, and Hawthorn had sent an estimate for one at £1,751 16s 3d, for delivery in February 1840; on Miller's recommendation it was ordered, and it was in service by 28 April, on which date the account was settled. It was of the firm's standard 2-2-2 pattern, and appears to have been one of a batch originally intended for the Great North of England Railway;[40] it was given the number 8, left blank by the sale of Twells' engine.

Miller's policy of employing heavier engines on the railway evoked immediate criticism and, as soon as Stephenson's engine appeared, John Herapath expressed concern for the safety of the viaduct. Observing in the *Railway Magazine* of December 1838

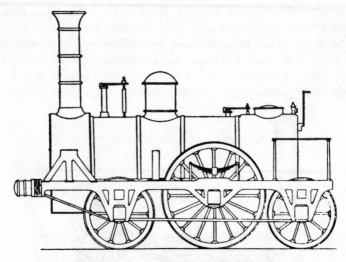

Engine No. 8, Hawthorn & Co., 1840

that he had recently visited the line, he continued:

...we were struck with an alteration the Company appears to be making in their engines. Heretofore the engines were of 8 to 10 tons; the one, however, by which we were drawn, we should think was from 12 to 14 or 15 tons. What can have induced this unfortunate alteration? No such Goliath can be wanted for the loads they have to carry . . . it appears highly improvident to rattle such heavy engines over the arches.

Herapath's views were shared by Landmann and Walter, both of whom appear to have had less confidence in the strength of the viaduct they had done so much to raise, than had Miller. Walter argued that the large engines were capable of taking twelve carriages, but since they pulled only six, and those but half full, smaller locomotives would be more economical; further, the large engine took two minutes to accelerate. Landmann was equally nervous about the London & Croydon locomotives which were beginning to appear at this time and tried to impose a maximum weight of $12\frac{1}{2}$ tons. C. H. Gregory used six-wheeled engines exclusively on the Croydon Railway and most of those eventually employed by the Brighton and South Eastern Railways were of the 2-2-2 variety. Gregory preferred them on grounds of safety, apart from any other consideration, and in his manual for engine drivers he wrote: [41] 'The breaking of an axle in a four-wheeled engine is an accident which is almost of necessity attended with the overturn of the engine. In a six-wheeled engine it requires the stoppage of the train until assistance arrives.' Nevertheless, his directors, probably at the insistence of Landmann, ordered fenders to be provided for all their engines in November 1839, of a similar design to those fitted to the L&GR engines, where they were retained until at least 1841.

When Miller had put the locomotives into a state of efficiency he spent some time in carrying out various experiments at Deptford Works; he refers to tests on carriage springs, the effects of rust on engine and carriage ironwork, and of carriage panels being exposed to the weather to measure the effect on the paintwork. There are fewer references to broken axles in the later years; this resulted from the employment of the improved axles made from about 1838 by the Patent Shaft & Axletree Company of Wednesbury This firm's products were in general use by 1843, and they claimed in March of that year that none of the 25,000 axles made had been reported as having failed in use. [42]

The use of engines by officers of the company for their personal transport appears to have been a fairly common practice, and on one such occasion in July 1842 Akerman, the Secretary, after missing his train, the 9.45am from Deptford, rode up on a light engine provided for him. When the train he should have caught stopped suddenly, his engine ran into the back of it, shaking up several passengers, and he gave the board an undertaking to drop the practice of using engines for this purpose in future.

From November 1842 the company paid a monthly bonus to engine crews who could reduce the quantity of coke used; for the consumption of only 16lb per mile the driver received 5s and the fireman 2s 6d, and for a reduction to 15lb, the rates were 12s and 6s respectively. In March 1844 the company had a contract with the Deptford Coke Co for the supply of twenty-five to thirty tons of North Country coke a week at 24s a ton, delivered in sacks.

Back in 1839 a member of a Select Committee[43] had asked if there should not '...be one person having the entire control of all the engines working on the line?', in the interests of safety. The Greenwich and Croydon railways never made any such arrangement, but on 26 March 1842 the Croydon and South Eastern lines formed a Joint Locomotive Committee, and pooled all their engines and rolling stock; they were joined by the London & Brighton Railway in March 1844. The arrangement was actually more for economy than safety.

G. M. Miller resigned in June 1844, and the following testimonial to his service appears in the board minutes of 30 July:

Mr Miller, the Superintendent of the Locomotives, having resigned the Office of Engineer to the Company which he has filled for the last six years, and being about to leave England, the Directors have great pleasure in bearing this testimony to the zeal, talents and industry he has constantly shown in the fulfilment of the various Duties of his Office, and to record the fact that a traffic conveying 1,596,366 persons per annum, should have been conducted under his arrangement and superintendence without accident or casualty.

He was presented with a 'handsome silver snuff box, value 15 gn', to which the workmen contributed. Miller went to Jamaica to construct a railway on which Joseph Locke was consulting engineer, and he completed the work in two years. On his return he was appointed Engineer to the Great Southern & Western Railway of Ireland, where he died, aged 50, on 4 January 1864 after contracting pneumonia from riding on an engine.[44]

When Miller left the L&GR the lease to the SER was pending, and no engineer was appointed in his place. The foreman of the Locomotive Department, Wakefield, had his wages increased by 7s per week, and it seems likely that from this time a certain amount of maintenance was carried out for the Greenwich Railway by the Joint Locomotive Committee, who certainly had some dealings with the L&GR locomotives.

The SER, desperate for engines and dissatisfied with the Joint Committee, had decided to withdraw from it, and had ordered thirty locomotives on its own account by October 1844. At this time it asked the L&GR to release to it the two most powerful engines, Stephenson's and Hawthorn's, which it would acquire in a few weeks anyway. The Greenwich company agreed, and after being valued by Mr Gooch, engineer to the London & South Western Railway, Nos. 8 and 9 left the Greenwich line.

The locomotives were eventually valued by Gooch at £16,471, this figure including also the plant and machinery at Deptford Works. Jeffrey, the carriage builder, and Bridges, carriage superintendent to the Joint Committee valued the carriages at £7,137. The amount actually paid by the SER was £22,808, a difference of £800, probably explained by the sale of engine No. 4 referred to later.

It appears that eight of the nine L&GR engines went to the SER, and they all worked for a number of years in some capacity on that line. They kept their old numbers until 1 March 1848, when those that had survived as locomotives were renumbered into the main locomotive stock.

The old No. 1 (*Royal William* of 1835) became SER 127 and was extensively rebuilt in 1849, after having been out of service for two years; it was broken up in 1863. No. 2 (*Royal Adelaide* of 1836), after rebuilding in 1847, became No. 128 and worked as a locomotive until 1863; it then worked as a stationary engine at Canterbury until broken up in 1871. No. 129 was the former No. 3 (*Dottin* of 1836) which after being rebuilt in 1848, was finally scrapped in 1864. Nos. 8 and 9 became 131 and 132 respectively; the first (Hawthorn 1840) was rebuilt in 1849 and lasted until 1859, while No. 132 (Stephenson 1838) worked as a locomotive until 1860, and then as a stationary engine at Reading until broken up four years later.

The old Forrester engine, No. 5 (*Victoria* of 1836) was used as a pumping engine at Bricklayers Arms from December 1845 and was eventually sold for scrap to C. Tomkins of Reading for £110 in March 1857. Its sister engine, No. 6 (*Walter* of 1836) became a stationary engine at Redhill Repair Shed in January 1846, was shifted to the sandpits at Gomshall in 1853, and was ultimately sold with No. 5 for scrap. The Summers, Groves & Day engine, No. 7, was used as a sand-drying boiler at Bricklayers Arms from March 1846; its tender went to Tonbridge for use as a water tank. Its remains were sold for £88 as scrap in 1856.[45]

The old Marshall engine No. 4 (*Twells* of 1836) seems to have ended its days in interesting, but very tragic circumstances. At the beginning of 1845 the two old wooden bomb-ships *Erebus* and *Terror* were being prepared for Sir John Franklin's Arctic Expedition, when Sir Edward Parry, the Comptroller of the Steam Department of the Navy sent for drawings of the ships '... to enable him to judge of the practicability of fitting small auxiliary engines and screw propellers'. It was decided to install the engines, and the work was entrusted to Maudslay, Sons & Field in mid-February; the expedition was due to depart in May. The Admiralty agreed that secondhand engines would suffice if made thoroughly efficient, and Maudslays purchased two old railway locomotives for the purpose. Their first trials off Woolwich showed that some adjustments were required, and on 8 May the Admiralty ordered '...another trial of the steam machinery of the *Erebus* and *Terror* as soon as the alterations now in hand by Messrs Maudslay have been completed'.[46] The vessels then went to Greenhithe where further trials were held on 16 May, and a description of the departure of the expedition on the nineteenth ended with the following reference to the *Erebus*: 'The screw propeller is worked by an engine of 25 horse power, which formerly ran upon the Greenwich Railway.'[47]

The engine for the *Terror* appears to have come from the London & Birmingham Railway, and it is from a letter written by Lieutenant John Irving RN of that ship to his sister that we know how the locomotives were adapted:[48]

H.M.S. Terror
Greenhithe,
May 16th 1845.

My Dear Katie,
...We tried our screws and went *four* miles an hour. Our engine once ran somewhat faster on the Birmingham line. It is placed athwart ships in our afterhold, and merely has its axle extended aft, so as to become the shaft of the screw. It has a funnel the same size and height as it had on the railway, and makes the same dreadful puffings and screamings, and will astonish the Esquimaux not a little. We can carry 12 days coal for it; but it will never be used when we can make any progress at all by other means.

Each ship carried an engineer, three stokers and a copy of Gregory's book on locomotives; but whether the engines were ever used is not known, and what eventually became of the ships has also remained a mystery.[49] Abandoned in April 1848 by the survivors of the expedition, themselves soon to perish, the two ships are believed to have sunk in Arctic waters off King William Land, Northern Canada; so at least the remnants of one Greenwich Railway engine may well exist today beneath the ice of the north-west passage.

As a postscript to the locomotive history of the L&GR brief consideration might be given to three systems which, in their time, were regarded as possible substitutes for locomotives.

Diagrammatic sketch of *Erebus* by Lieut. John Irving RN, showing converted locomotive in position

The company had been approached in 1839 by Clegg, the Patentee of one of the atmospheric systems then enjoying a short vogue. He sought permission to lay down his apparatus on the L&GR but Landmann and Miller would not permit this; Landmann, however, saw possibilities in the invention, and Clegg was given permission to conduct trials on the railway's vacant ground between the Grand Surrey Canal and Corbetts Lane on the condition that, if the experiments were successful, he would install his system on the Greenwich Railway at the lowest price and accept £500 per mile for the patent rights. Nothing came of the negotiations, however, and in view of the experiences of the Croydon and South Devon Railways with Clegg & Samuda's atmospheric trains, the L&GR was perhaps fortunate in not being too closely associated with the early experiments; these were usually very successful, and the company might well have been tempted to adopt the system, with consequences it could ill afford.

The building of the London and Blackwall Railway led to some attempts to persuade the L&GR to employ stationary engines and rope haulage for its trains. The Blackwall Railway had been compelled to adopt this form of power because of the supposed danger from locomotives causing fires in the congested area through which it ran. One advocate of stationary engines referred to the successful ones at Euston Square, and the committee on the widening bill of 1840 considered inserting a clause making their use compulsory between Spa Road and London Bridge. This immediately involved the Croydon, Brighton and South Eastern Railways, whose trains would also have had to be worked into London Bridge by the same method, and it was probably because of this that the proposal was defeated.

The company was presented with a plan by Thomas Motley in January 1843 of working its traffic by horses '... as all railways did but a few years ago'. Briefly it involved selling all the locomotives, and with the proceeds buying 84 to 100 horses for £5,000, replacing the drivers and firemen with twenty grooms, and macadamising the track between the rails; each horse could then take one or two of the new large carriages. Miller was asked to report on the scheme and on 4 July he expressed the opinion '... that it would not be practicable on the Greenwich line', although whether he took six months to reach that conclusion or did not take the scheme seriously in the first place is not clear.[50] Its adoption would, in any case, have required a new Act to permit the use of horses, and the presence of the other companies' steam trains on the adjacent tracks might conceivably have disturbed the creatures.

Chapter 10

Carriages

COLONEL Landmann and Mr Beeby, when making their tour of the railway centres of the north in the summer of 1834, gave their attention to the question of carriages as well as to that of locomotives, and they noted the methods employed in coach building by those with a few years experience in such matters. The first result of their recommendations was a board resolution of 26 July 1834:

That four coaches, complete with three bodies, each body two seats, each seat to accommodate four persons, the backs to be stuffed, the extreme breadth of all projections not to exceed eight feet and in all other respects similar to those making for the Dublin & Kingstown Railway be ordered of Messrs. Beeston & Melling of Manchester, who are requested to send a specification thereof, with price, including delivery to London.

The carriages ordered of Beeston & Melling were first class, and within a short time a further order had been given to Robert Jeffrey, of City Road, London, for two more coaches of the same class. In each case only coach bodies were supplied, and the underframes and wheels were fitted to them at Deptford. Jeffrey's coach bodies were delivered in May or June 1835 and cost £190 each; the company was apparently very satisfied with them, for a further twenty at £150 each were ordered in July, probably second class. Beeston & Melling's began to arrive in London during September; these also cost £190 with an additional £27 13s 0d for freight. At one of the locomotive trials in October 1835 a train of eight carriages is mentioned, this probably being the total possessed by the company at that time.

Jeffrey's two railway carriages, the first to make their appearance in London, were described in the *Herald* of 1 August 1835 as

...triple coach bodies, something like a diligence, without the
clumsiness; they are very strongly and neatly built, and, accommodating eight persons in each body, carry altogether twenty-
four persons. They are mounted on metal frames with powerful
springs, and being coloured and varnished as carefully as any
other species of coach, have no inelegant appearance.

According to another report they were '...similar to those used
on the Liverpool & Manchester Railway, but are more com-
modious and more adapted for the ease and comfort of the
passengers'.

The technique of railway carriage construction had not progressed very far in those days, and the Greenwich Railway
directors still thought of first class carriages in terms of stage
coach bodies mounted upon iron frames. Their manufacture was
largely in the hands of road-coach builders, and as late as 1842
the trade directories contained such entries as 'Railway Carriage
Makers:— see Coach & Harness Makers'.

William Bridges Adams, in his comprehensive book on coach
building, devoted one chapter to railway carriages;[1] writing only
seven years after the opening of the Liverpool & Manchester
Railway, and within a few months of that of the London & Greenwich, he said:

The engineers accustomed to stationary machines had much to
learn in locomotion, and laughed to scorn the practical carriage
builders. The carriage builders, on the contrary, thought it
presumption in the engineers to interfere with their trade; and
the result has been that they have separated the branches of the
art:– the carriage builder for railroads has become a mere
wooden box maker; and the engineer has gone through a part
of the process of getting at what will do, by consecutively finding
out what will not do.

A reference to '...the passenger carriages of the most approved
kind, now used on the Greenwich Rail-road...' suggests that
these were probably among the best vehicles in existence when
new.

The early trial runs and free trips over the line were made
by the first class carriages; one of the accounts of the trials held
on 22 October 1835 refers to the carriages as not being '...in

omnibus style, with the passengers sitting at the sides, but each carriage is a three-bodies coach...'. The omnibus type subsequently adopted by the Greenwich Railway for its second class coaches seems to have been fairly well known to the writer at that time, and not to have been very popular.

All the first class carriages were divided into three compartments, and appear to have been of a more or less uniform pattern. They were upholstered and fitted with horsehair cushions. The second class, however, were of various designs, some having compartments, and others '... are without the divisions, having seats all round except where the doors intervene'.² Some of the latter type also had a double row of seats, back to back, along the centre. None of the original second class carriages were upholstered, and all were open at the sides.

Both first and second class carriages were 14ft 6in long and had an inside width of 6ft; they weighed about 2¾ tons. Most of the vehicles had an open platform at each end, covered with a guard sheet or tarpaulin. The original purpose of these platforms appears to have been for the conveyance of goods, for in 1834 it was estimated that small parcels, pigs, fish, fruit etc., carried on 'the enclosed platforms' (and also by separate goods trains), would produce an income of £70 per day. The frequent passenger trains on the Greenwich Railway would have provided an excellent service for suitable goods, had the traffic been forthcoming; since it was not, these platforms were used for passengers' luggage and, when the trains were crowded, for the passengers themselves. A few carriages had an elevated seat, reached by steps, for the brakesman, but in most cases he rode on the end platform. The second class carriages held twenty-four passengers inside; four more could be taken on each platform. Some carriages were fitted with sets of three collapsible footsteps. None of the earliest carriages had any buffers, and they were all coupled with chains. There is no evidence that any of them had lamps, and the passengers presumably relied upon the lights along the viaduct when travelling by night.

It is believed that the carriages were painted yellow, but whether any or all of them were this colour cannot be stated with any certainty since the records do not mention the colours used for engines or carriages. It was possibly the company's intention in 1832 to paint its first class carriages yellow for the lower panels and black for the upper ones, and to use blue for the open second class carriages; a coloured print exists showing the trains in these colours.[3] A rather obscure French book has the following footnote to a chapter on locomotives: 'Vires acquirit eundo. Devise des voitures du chemin de Greenwich.'[4] As the writer accurately describes the English railways of 1840, it seems that the company's motto appeared somewhere on the carriages.

The company's first train of eight carriages did not last very long, for on 12 November 1835, during one of the trials it met with disaster from axle failure. The directors somehow managed to suppress news of the accident at the time, although it crept into the columns of *John Bull*, and it was not until 30 May 1842 that George Walter, in the course of a letter to the Minister of Public Works, admitted that it was anything but trifling: 'The high carriages then in use, on an accident occurring (being attached to each other by chains) dashed over each other, and were broken to pieces and upset, by which many passengers were injured...'

The board was thoroughly alarmed by this accident, although it might have been much more serious had the train fallen from the viaduct, a possibility which always haunted them; as it happened, no passenger was killed or fatally injured. George Walter at once sought means to reduce the danger of accidents, and appears to have been persuaded by Lord Dundonald that it was all a question of lowering the centre of gravity of the carriages, which would not only make them safer, but would reduce the effects of cross-winds on the exposed viaduct. Walter accordingly wrote to Robert Jeffrey '...pray make the carriages to Lord Dundonald's plan', and after lengthy consultations with the Earl, Jeffrey produced four rough models of low centre of gravity carriages, none of which were wholly satisfactory.

At this time an engineer, Robert Pollock, who was also the London agent of the Horseley Iron Co, was employed at Deptford Works to superintend the assembling of the carriage bodies, frames and wheels, all of which had been made by separate firms. Most of the wheels were supplied by John Hague, but some came from Penn's of Deptford; they were spoked wheels of wrought iron, three feet in diameter, and a driver described them as being identical with those in use on the Liverpool & Manchester Railway. The frames came from Marshall & Sons, the locomotive builders, and sufficient were on hand to complete all the carriages on order.

In the meantime the railway had been partially opened, and the accident at Spa Road in March 1836 gave new impetus to the search for safety devices. The day after the accident Walter ordered Pollock to construct a new carriage frame on the low centre of gravity principle without delay, but in the first instance the modification was effected by removing the body from the undercarriage and turning the latter upside down. Wooden blocks were then fitted to the chassis and the body mounted on these, bringing the carriage floor 25 inches above the rails. The wheels, now protruding through the floor, had metal guards fitted over them. At the same time, strong oak beams in the form of a frame were fixed to the iron carriage frame at a distance of four inches above rail level, to act as a sledge in case of derailment.

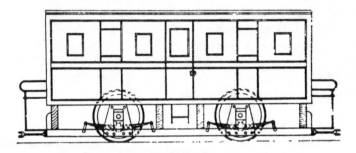

Low centre of gravity carriage with inverted frames,
end platforms and rigid bar couplings, 1836

The idea of inverting the carriage frames was Walter's, and it had the merit of economy since the frames already in stock could be used.

It was at this time that William Curtis became associated with the L&GR and he was temporarily engaged at a salary to superintend the conversion of the carriages and the modification of the locomotives. The first train of five new carriages went into service on Easter Monday 1836, and on 30 April the *Mechanic's Magazine* contained the following report:

The newly invented brake for stopping the train of carriages at a moments notice, was exhibited to Mr Rennie and several scientific gentlemen on Saturday last, 23rd April, as well as the

carriages fitting upon Lord Dundonald's principle, with which
they expressed themselves perfectly satisfied as to the impossibility
of accident, or their upsetting.

On 15 June Curtis wrote to the same journal, referring to the
safety carriages '...invented and constructed by me for the
London & Greenwich Railway Company. A train of six of these
are now upon the line; and the whole establishment of the
carriages of the Company are in course of being altered to the
same plan'.

The six carriages of the train referred to were coupled to each
other by a flat solid iron bar; this also served as a central buffer
and eliminated '...the disagreeable shocks incidental to the
mode of connexion by chains'. Normal buffers were fitted to the
end carriages, which were coupled to the engine. It was at first
thought that a locomotive would be unable to start a train
coupled in this way, since it would not be possible for it to take
up one carriage at a time; it was discovered, however, that the
engines had more power than they had been given credit for, and
moved the trains quite easily. The modified coaches were made
up into permanent trains of six or seven units.

Early in May 1836 Lord Dundonald discovered that each of
the new carriages bore a metal plate stating that Curtis was the
inventor, and that the trains were becoming known as 'Mr
Curtis's trains'; after some correspondence with the company, his
solicitors wrote claiming that the safety carriages were an infringement of his patent, and towards the end of the year he started an
action against the company, Walter and Curtis. In December
two of the directors agreed to indemnify Robert Jeffrey against
any legal expenses he might incur in the suit then pending, but
soon afterwards Lord Dundonald withdrew his claim. From the
drawing in the patent specification[5] it is clear that his carriages
bore little resemblance to those on the L&GR, for his were fitted
with four guide wheels each, while the weight of the carriages
was borne by large flanged wheels arranged between them on
the articulated principle, three pairs of wheels to two coaches.
As Walter had pointed out, the guide wheels or rollers would
have made it impossible for the trains to negotiate points and
crossings, and would in any case have defeated the principle of
stopping the trains in emergencies by preventing the fenders or
sledges from coming into operation.

William Curtis, on the other hand, persisted in his claim, and he set forth details of the safety carriage in his book of inventions. It was stated to have been used successfully on the L&GR – and it was almost certainly peculiar to that line at the time, since no other is mentioned. An illustration of a model for export to the U.S.A. was given, this being a double-deck carriage in effect, two of the five compartments (those above the wheels) being about 2ft 6in higher than the others. It is supposed to have been tried on the Boston & Providence Railroad, and returned to England as unsuitable.

The principle of low centre of gravity vehicles was said by Colonel Landmann to have been derived from H. R. Palmer's suspended railway of the early 1820s, and Simon Fenwick mentions that, while employed as an engineer on the Liverpool & Manchester Railway from 1828 to 1834, he had seen several trains a day which came on to that line from the Bolton Junction Railway[6] made up of low-hung carriages of a design quite different from the normal coaches of the Liverpool & Manchester.

In July 1836, a third firm, Messrs I. & T. Wheatley, started supplying carriages at £170 each. This was the firm of 'Coach Masters', of Park Place, Kennington Cross, who eventually ran road coaches in competition with the Greenwich Railway.

The third class carriages were built by the company in its Deptford workshops during 1836. They were, in effect, trucks with a roof supported by posts at each corner, and open all round, in which the passengers stood; called 'Stanipedes', Stand-up carriages or omnibuses by passengers and the company alike, they were intended to carry twenty-four passengers, and were of the very simplest construction.

At its formal opening in December 1836 the railway possessed forty-four carriages –

... of various constructions, some being close omnibuses ... others ... open at the sides, but close at each end ... and others open all round ... The object of this arrangement is obviously to create a proper classification ...

Among other fancy carriages which have been constructed is one in the form of a Roman galley, which will be brought into use on the opening day, and which will, no doubt, have an extraordinary appearance as it floats as it were in mid-air.[7]

Herapath had previously referred to this carriage as an engine in the *Railway Magazine* of April 1836, where he wrote:

Great curiosity was excited in the City on Saturday 5th March, on the passing along Cornhill of the frame of an engine now constructing for the London & Greenwich Railway. This frame is formed on the model of an ancient Roman galley, and when running along the line will present no bad idea of one of these vessels of war.

Ordered by Walter, and built by Robert Jeffrey in February 1836 to the designs of the Earl of Dundonald, its original purpose was to encase an engine presumably the rotary locomotive then being built. There were probably four or five of the 'fancy carriages' at the opening of the railway, but they appear to have been altered in the company's works afterwards to coaches of normal design, since they are never heard of again. The idea was undoubtedly borrowed from the Liverpool & Manchester Railway, where a number were used at the opening.

Late in 1838 the board was considering the employment of a contractor to supply and repair its coaching stock, and on 11 December a tender was accepted from Joseph Wright, who was eventually to build and repair most of the carriages on the London & Birmingham Railway. The Greenwich carriages were by this time in a very bad state, although the company had spent over £18,000 on them since 1835. The contract stipulated '... the sale to him of the Company's carriages on the Railway for £4,439, and for his supply of carriages for three years at 3½d for every eight passengers passing along the line ...'[8] Wright paid for the carriages by bills of exchange over two-and-three-quarter years, and the amount he received was the same as the passenger duty, i.e. one-eighth of a penny per mile, an amount probably decided upon to simplify accounting. As in the case of the tax, there was no distinction between the classes of carriage. Under the terms of the agreement Wright repaired or replaced the carriages when necessary, and they remained his property.

Joseph Wright was an indirect public benefactor since his determination that his carriages should receive more considerate treatment than the company afforded its patrons resulted in the inclusion of a clause in the contract binding the railway to '... erect sheds at the stations, for their protection, which are also much wanted for the accommodation of passengers'.

At a general meeting in September 1839 the directors stated that the safety carriages were unpopular with the public, who disliked their ugliness, and that they were being replaced by normal coaches; these were supplied by the contractor Wright.

Mr Walter said of the old carriages,[9] '... nearly 8,000,000 of passengers have been carried in safety, although innumerable accidents have occurred, such as running off the rails at the crossings, and the breaking of axles of both engines and carriages.' These minor accidents were of such frequent occurrence as not to warrant mention in the board's minutes, and consequently records of but a few have survived; the following details, which are necessarily incomplete, will give some indication of their nature:

1838	'... a wheel of a carriage was dashed to atoms whilst the train was at full speed; the frame dropped upon the rails ... the carriage was dragged more than three-quarters of a mile.'
17 June 1839	Near Deptford; both axles of a large open carriage in the middle of a train broke: '... not a single spoke left in the wheels'. This carriage was dragged for over a mile without injury to the eight passengers in it.
21 Aug. 1839	Carriage axle broke; dragged across the Corbetts Lane Junction without further disaster or disturbance to the two passengers within.
15 Sep. 1839	Axle of brake-carriage fractured. The carriage, with eight passengers, pulled over a mile on its sledges.
25 Dec. 1840	Two axles broke whilst train running at full speed.
12 Jan. 1841	Accident to afternoon train, caused by broken carriage axle.
16 Jan. 1841	Carriage axle broke while train running.
19 Jan. 1841	At about 9.30pm, train thrown off line by broken rail.
20 Jan. 1841	Train derailed at London Bridge owing to negligence of pointsman.

To quote Walter again: 'The sledge has always acted most efficiently, even for half a mile at a time, before the engine has been stopped, the passengers in the broken carriage scarcely knowing of the accident, except from the dropping of the sledge

upon the rail.' It would seem, therefore, that the London &
Greenwich carriages ran almost as well on their frames as they did
on their wheels.

The decision to abolish the stone sleepers, together with the
improvements in the manufacture of axles, made the continued
use of the safety carriages unnecessary, and despite all the arguments of Walter and Curtis, they began to disappear from the
line after Joseph Wright took over the carriage department. The
task of replacing them was made more difficult because the new
carriages could not be run in the same trains as the old ones, and
it was not until a complete new train was ready to take its place
that an old one could be withdrawn.

Booth's patent coupling was adopted in July 1839, the company paying the inventor £50 for the whole period of the patent.
Invented by Henry Booth of Liverpool in 1836, this was the
forerunner of the familiar screw-coupling still in use. It was
probably fitted in the first instance only to the new carriages
supplied by Wright, for these were the only ones with buffers.
The provision of normal buffers on the safety carriages was still
considered superfluous with the bar couplings. The *West Kent
Guardian*, reporting the double collision at London Bridge in
January 1840, strongly recommended the railway '... to have
proper fender protectors to the carriages, as well as to line and
stuff the inside of all the close carriages, and cushion the seats,
which at all events might lessen the severity of the bumps consequent upon an accident'.

Wright had supplied three new first-class carriages during 1839,
and in July he was asked to fit all the coaches with window
springs and extra door fastenings. His second-class carriages were
reported to be 'noisy and uneasy', however, and he was sum-
moned before the board to answer for them in June of that year.

During 1839 the London & Greenwich carriages went farther
afield, travelling over the recently opened Croydon Railway when
a carriage shortage developed on that line, and thereby earning
Wright three shillings each for the whole journey of 21 miles.
In the next few years the Greenwich and Croydon Railways
regularly lent each other carriages to cope with the traffic
arising from the fairs which they served.[10]

Early in 1840 the old third-class open carriages, which had
been withdrawn in 1837, were reintroduced, adding to the already
large variety of stock to be seen at that time on the Greenwich

line. The safety carriages were then losing what popularity they might have had, since the provision of platforms at Greenwich Station made it difficult to enter or leave them, the floor and footboard being considerably below platform level.

The adoption of wooden wheels for the carriages was suggested in December 1840, following the accident on Christmas Day. The breaking of the axles on this occasion was attributed to the concussion set up by the wheels travelling at high speed, and striking against points that had been improperly set; frosty weather was also partly blamed. There is no record that the suggestion ever received serious consideration, and it is not unlikely that the company had come to regard the fracture of wheels and axles as a minor hazard. The train concerned was of low-built carriages, and the passengers were uninjured; the belief had possibly grown up by 1840 that they were more or less immune from danger whilst in those trains.

The board appointed a Carriage Committee early in 1841, and one of its first recommendations was that the types of carriage be reduced to two, '... the one fitted up like the present first-class carriage, the other an open stand-up carriage, but covered with a roof ...'. In April the committee was in consultation with Wright on the question of new carriages, but the matter was left in abeyance until the company could gauge the effect of some new steam boats, then going into service, on the Greenwich traffic. Two months later, however, the need for new vehicles had become desperate, and Wright agreed to provide ten new ones of a composite type.

At this time, June 1841, Herapath

... inspected several of the much-abused Second Class carriages, which have been described as so uncomfortable, and in so filthy a state as to be unfit to be used. We can only say that as far as our inspection went, they appear to be far cleaner and more comfortable than the Second Class carriages on many of the great lines. They have wide and comfortable seats, are closed at the sides, have glass windows, and are inferior to the First Class carriages only in not having cushioned seats and backs.

The oldest carriages on the Greenwich line had been in service for only five-and-a-half years at this time, although they probably looked older owing to constant exposure to the weather; they were left about in the open until 1842, when the first carriage

sheds were provided. In September 1841 the company itself recog-
nised that at least two of its old carriages had had their day so
far as passengers were concerned, and they were brought back
from Wright to be converted to timber trucks for use in the
widening of the line.

In June 1840 three waggons were bought from Beattie of
Liverpool, and a further seven were ordered in February 1841;
these were for the ballast to be used in relaying the line, and they
cost £68. 10s 0d each. Before the final batch were delivered, however, Miller discovered that he could buy ballast waggons for £15
each from Hoof, a contractor to the Croydon and Brighton Railways, and the second order to Beattie was reduced to three.[11]
Beattie's waggons, six in all, were used in 1841 as third-class
passenger carriages, and are the ones referred to by George
Walter, although he does not appear to have known what their
original purpose was. Despite frequent complaints of the difficulty of boarding them, and of the danger of travelling in them,
the directors contended that there was '... no reasonable justifica-
tion for the murmur. If the people would insist on travelling at
so cheap a rate, it was only reasonable that they should pay the
penalty in a certain amount of discomfort.'

By December 1841 four of the new composite carriages built
by Wright had been placed in service; they were described by J. Y.
Akerman a few weeks later as follows: [12]

The carriages on this Railway are similar to those of the Blackwall, the second class passengers occupying the end divisions and
the first class the middle. The end divisions hold about 20 second
class passengers, and are 7 feet wide by 5 feet long, and 7 feet
from the floor to the roof. They are without seats.
The two first class divisions are 7 feet wide by 5 feet long, and
hold 8 passengers.
All the above carriages are provided with under springs, draw
springs, and buffing apparatus, and are mounted on six wheels.

The year 1842 saw the expiration of Wright's original contract,
and on Miller's advice it was not renewed. The carriage department was placed under Miller's control, and in his report to the
board of 1 February he said that the expense of this department
from the opening of the line until 1838 had induced him to advise
the employment of an outside contractor. He continued:

... but experience has shown that this excessive expenditure may be attributed to the circumstance of the 56 carriages then on the line being of sizes and construction differing from each other, there being no uniformity in the lengths and diameter of the axles, thus rendering it impossible to change them from one carriage to another, which is indispensably necessary in repairing a stock of Railway Carriages. These old carriages are now nearly worn out, and are about to be replaced by others of a different construction.

The total carriage stock was to be reduced to one-third, since each train would consist of only two new carriages instead of six old ones; it was contemplated that eventually only composite carriages would be in service, all exactly alike in size and construction. The improved state of Deptford works would ensure that repairs could be carried out quickly and economically.

'Wright himself had not been anxious to renew the contract on the same terms, and during the negotiations between him and the company in January 1842, he had suggested revised terms which were unacceptable to the board. He was at this time heavily engaged in building carriages for the Brighton and South Eastern Railways, among others, at his works in Fetter Lane, Grays Inn Road, Clerkenwell, and Regents Park, and it is not unlikely that he took on the Greenwich contract in the first place to gain experience in this field; it was probably not a very profitable venture financially.

The carriage stock was valued by Robert Jeffrey and Mr N. Worsdell[13] on 29 January, and a fortnight later the company bought the carriages back from Wright for £5,609, paying by four bills of exchange over 2½ years.

While the carriage contract was under discussion, the directors ordered that four of the open trucks, supplied by Beattie, be covered; the remaining two, which were stored at London Bridge, were covered in April. In each case a canvas awning was provided. It was becoming increasingly clear to many of the shareholders that the railway had to rely upon its third-class passengers for its revenue, and they urged the board in February 1842 to be more considerate to those who could pay no more than the lowest fare. The practice of making them '... stand like cattle in open trucks to be gazed upon as they travelled along the viaduct . . .' was condemned. It was said that these open 'stand-up' carriages were quite unknown in France, Belgium or Germany, or upon the trunk lines in England. In actual fact they were only in general use on local lines by 1842; the London & Black-wall Railway used them, as did the Croydon, and they ran on the Shoreham branch of the London & Brighton. Other railways employed open carriages, but fitted them with seats for long journeys.

The directors still argued that if they made the third-class carriages more comfortable, they would merely attract the passengers who could afford to pay for better accommodation, but as it was estimated that the average number of first-class passengers to a train was two, this could hardly have mattered. However, nothing had been done to improve the lot of the third-class passengers some sixteen months later, for at a special general meeting held on 15 August 1843, the suggestion was put forward that, if it was quite impossible to provide seats in the open carriages, they should at least be fitted with iron rails to which the passengers could cling for support.

The appearance of new carriages on the line emphasised the dilapidated condition of the old ones still running; a minute of 7 June 1842 refers to complaints of their '... linings being moth-eaten and much out of repair'. It was decided at this board meeting to convert two of Wright's new second-class carriages, which were fitted with spring buffers and seats, to first-class, '... whereby the ordinary traffic would be worked by new carriages'. The company was anxious to replace its old stock as quickly as possible in order that it could increase the fares, a step it dared not take yet in view of the upopularity of its trains as expressed almost every week in letters to the press. As the new carriages were not ready, Miller arranged to borrow six second-class from the Joint Locomotive Committee of the Croydon and Dover Railways in September, and a further six, also second-class, were hired for three months from the North Midland Railway in October at £15 per month each, the L&GR paying all the expenses of transfer. By 11 October Miller had '... secured the six carriages required to enable the company to work the line at the increased fares', and notice boards were ordered to be prepared accordingly.

On 18 October 1842 Miller reported that four new carriages and four new carriage bodies were still required, and tenders for their construction were invited. The orders for these carriages went to S. Adams and A. McVey respectively.

S. Adams was the brother of William Bridges Adams, to whom

a patent had been granted in December 1840 for 'improvements in railway carriages'. In May 1839 a description of his 'Verte-brated train-carriages for Railways' had appeared in the *Mechanic's Magazine*; this carriage embodied some of the ideas set forth in his book of 1837, and was apparently quite a success at its trials the same month on the London & Birmingham Railway. The vehicle had a frame of light stays instead of the usual heavy iron undercarriage, and the compartments consisted of four separate bodies, arranged in groups of two, supported by a central longitudinal bar, described as a 'spine'. The carriage had a slight flexibility in the centre, where a gap of a few inches was left between the two sets of bodies, and it ran on four wheels. These carriages were fitted with Adams's patent bow-spring coupling, a device in the form of an archer's bow, fixed across the end of the carriage with the 'string' outermost, which also served as a central spring buffer. These 'bow-springs' were also fitted to carriages constructed by other builders, and they enjoyed a vogue for a few years; between 1838 and 1842 some 322 carriages had been fitted with them. Of the South Eastern Railway's seventy-two carriages, twenty-five were on Adams's plan, and they were also to be seen at Hamburg and elsewhere on the continent.

The eight new carriages were of the first- and second-class composite type; McVey had supplied bodies only at £128 each, but Adams's were complete at £299, except for axle-boxes. This item had, apparently, been omitted from the specification, for Miller intended making them at Deptford; it was found, how-ever, that they could be purchased from Fox, Henderson & Co for £1. 19s 0d a set of four, and a set for each of the eight carriages was ordered. McVey's carriages were completed at Deptford, where a number of old carriages had recently been repaired and placed in reserve for emergency use. Apart from the fact that both the types were fitted with lockers, nothing further is known about them. There is a reference in *Herapath* in June 1843 to the new large carriages capable of taking eighty passengers, and this is about the time when the eight coaches mentioned above would have appeared

Another carriage shortage developed in the summer of 1843, when the company wished to restore the third class, but had not the necessary vehicles available. Several were borrowed from other lines, and Miller put in hand the construction of new ones within a few days of the board's decision. A report of 4 April 1844 stated that 'The Directors of the Greenwich Railway have just had completed a new set of carriages for third class passengers. They are furnished with seats.' On 23 April 1844 Miller recommended the purchase of four third-class open carriage bodies, and a week later Robert Jeffrey's tender for £63 each was accepted These were the last carriages to be bought by the London & Greenwich Railway.

It was stated some years ago that an 'Improved eight-wheel jointed carriage' was introduced on the line in 1844, and what purports to be an illustration of it shows a four-compartment vehicle, apparently running on two four-wheeled bogies.[14] Carriages of this description, forty feet in length, were introduced by the South Eastern Railway in 1849, but their use was restricted to the North Kent line. Built by W. B. Adams, they were identical with those which had been running for three years on the North Woolwich line. There is, however, no evidence that carriages of this design were in existence in 1844, or that the London & Greenwich Railway had, in fact, any eight-wheeled carriages.

There was, perhaps, no short stretch of line in the country that could have presented so rich a variety of carriages as could the Greenwich viaduct in the early 1840s; the Greenwich Railway alone had by this time a large collection of different types, which were augmented from time to time by the North Midland vehicles, quite apart from the other railways which used the line. The trains must have been quite colourful, too, as different colours were used by the various companies to distinguish their carriages. Unfortunately, research has disclosed little concerning the colours used; in only one case, that of the London & Croydon Railway, do the minute books refer to the painting of the carriages. Here it is stated that the board resolved on 16 July 1838 that '... passenger carriages be coloured blue, the shade to be approved by the Board', and in the following February that the first-class carriages should carry the City Arms on their centre panels, and the letters 'L & C' '... on the panels of the ends'.

Three weeks after the South Eastern Railway took over the Greenwich line, Messrs Jeffreys and Bridges, the carriage builder, and the carriage superintendent of the Joint Committee respectively, valued the carriages at £7,137. 5s 4d, and it was approximately at this sum that the South Eastern bought them. How many there were at this time, or what eventually became of them is not known; presumably they continued to work over the Greenwich Branch as long as they could reasonably be kept in service, and were then gradually replaced by ordinary South Eastern coaches.

Chapter 11

1845 and After

FOR the last 125 years the old L&GR has formed a vital part of the south-eastern approach to London by the SER and its successors, and it is against this background that its subsequent history must be considered.

The London & Greenwich Railway Company from 1 January 1845, until it was eventually wound up on 3 January 1923, existed solely for the purpose of receiving the annual rent for its property, and distributing it as a dividend. Provision was made in the leasing agreement, but not in the Act,[1] for the London & Greenwich to have taken over the line again had the payments ever failed, although such a course would have been hardly practicable. In May 1845 its office was moved from the London Terminus to 10, Coleman Street; the new offices consisted of two rooms and a strong room, and the old headquarters at 37, Canterbury Square were taken over by the London & Brighton Railway.

The leasing of the Greenwich Railway had given the South Eastern almost complete control of the vital section of line between London Bridge and Corbetts Lane, whilst at the terminus it was in possession of the Greenwich Company's station; it also had a one third share in the Joint Station. It was bound by the agreements which the Greenwich Company had previously entered into concerning the use of the lines on the widened viaduct, and its use of the Joint Station was subject to the approval of the Joint Station Committee. The tolls previously payable to the Greenwich were now due to the South Eastern.

The South Eastern had attempted to lease the locomotive lines of the Croydon Railway in 1844, after the agreement with the Greenwich Railway had been made, but the Croydon Company would not accept the terms offered; a certain amount of friction between the two companies followed.

In 1845 the SER obtained an Act[2] for the widening of the Greenwich viaduct on the north side to carry one additional line; since this was intended to make one of the other lines available for conversion to the atmospheric principle by the London & Croydon, this company also obtained powers to widen the viaduct if the South Eastern failed to do so.[3] The line was not widened under either of these Acts, however, as a financial panic had arisen which prevented the raising of the necessary capital, and the powers lapsed.

The London & Croydon amalgamated with the London & Brighton to form the London, Brighton & South Coast Railway in June 1846, and the atmospheric system was abandoned shortly afterwards; it never reached the Greenwich viaduct, stopping short at New Cross. At a conference between the South Eastern and London, Brighton & South Coast Railways held on 12 November 1847, it was agreed that both companies should run trains free of tolls between Croydon and London Bridge, and that the Brighton Company should have the use of the line originally intended for the atmospheric trains. The South Eastern seems to have had the better bargain, since it gained the free use of two Brighton lines for $7\frac{1}{2}$ miles between Corbetts Lane and Croydon, against the Brighton's free use of three South Eastern lines for $1\frac{3}{4}$ miles between Corbetts Lane and London Bridge. This agreement, eventually signed on 10 July 1848, took effect from 13 November 1847, and was to assume considerable importance later in the relations between the two companies. For the year ended 31 January 1848, the last year in which tolls were payable for the use of the Greenwich Railway, the South Eastern received £8,596.

Meanwhile the LB&SCR was constructing its Thames Junction Branch under powers originally applied for by the London & Croydon.[4] This line, later known as the Deptford Wharf branch, was $1\frac{1}{4}$ miles long, and ran from a siding at New Cross to the river, passing under the Greenwich viaduct about a quarter of a mile west of the Surrey Canal bridge; it was not connected with the Greenwich line, and was always used for goods traffic only. Most of its single track was on a low embankment, part of which was composed of mud from the dock excavations, but near the

Greenwich viaduct it ran on a white-painted wooden trestle viaduct for some 635 yards.

The Act for the North Kent Railway was passed in 1846,[5] and
it now became imperative for the South Eastern to widen the
viaduct to a point just beyond the Surrey Canal; accordingly
another Act for this purpose was obtained in 1847,[6] giving
powers for the construction of two additional lines on the north
side. Still another Act[7] of the same year gave the South Eastern
Railway powers to build a junction line between the Greenwich
viaduct and the Bricklayers Arms branch, connecting these lines
for the first time, by a spur which ran under the Brighton main
line to join the branch at '... the new turnpike road (formerly
Corbetts Lane and Galley Wall)...'.

With the construction of the Bricklayers Arms spur and the
Deptford Wharf branch, there was intense activity in the neighbourhood of the Greenwich viaduct; in addition, the viaduct
itself was being widened during 1848 and 1849, and the North
Kent line was under construction down to Gravesend. At this
time also, (the summer of 1849), the Bricklayers Arms wooden
viaduct was being replaced by the present embankment. All these
works were completed within a few months of each other, and the
lines were opened on the following dates:

Deptford Wharf Branch (LB&SCR)	2 July 1849
North Kent Line (SER)	30 July 1849
Bricklayers Arms Junction line (SER)	1 September 1849
New lines on viaduct (SER)	24 February 1850

On 30 July 1849 a section of the North Kent Railway from
North Kent East Junction to Charlton was opened, and for the
next few months the two Greenwich lines between London
Bridge and the junction, just west of Deptford, carried all the
additional traffic. At the same time the work of widening the
viaduct was proceeding, and early in 1850, had been completed.
On 24 February 1850, when the new lines were brought into
use, the six lines available were rearranged as follows:[8]

No. (from north)
1.	New line	Greenwich up
2.	New line	Greenwich & North Kent down
3.	Old Greenwich down	North Kent & Dover up
4.	Old Greenwich up	South Eastern & Brighton down

5. S.E., Brighton, &

   Croydon down South Eastern & Brighton up

6. S.E., Brighton, &

   Croydon up Croydon up

This arrangement gave the South Eastern Railway three up lines and two down, and during the years ahead the concentration of the increasingly heavy traffic from London on these two tracks led to serious congestion; this in turn resulted in constant delays to trains, and in the South Eastern Railway acquiring a reputation for unpunctuality. The company was in the position, however, of being the virtual owners of six tracks, but it had the exclusive use of only three of them.

With the rearrangement of the tracks, the Greenwich lines were once again reversed, and although, as will be seen later, the South Eastern Railway attempted for years to restore the branch to normal left-hand running, it was nearly fifty-two years before it was able to do so. In 1850 it did not matter on which side the Greenwich trains ran, and the arrangement made then was the best possible one. With only three lines at its disposal for the Greenwich and North Kent trains, it was better to have two up lines, since there was more likelihood of up trains accumulating between North Kent East Junction and London Bridge than there was of down traffic being held up on this section. Apart from delays caused by shunting at the Bricklayers Arms Junction, down trains had a straight run to the North Kent East Junction, where they either ran on to Greenwich, or diverged on to the North Kent line. By keeping the up Greenwich trains on the north line, they did not interfere with the other traffic; the arrangement also allowed the down Greenwich trains to be run without the risk of their fouling the up North Kent line.

While the South Eastern had been widening the Greenwich viaduct, the Brighton had been doing the same from Corbetts Lane onwards, and by 1849 an additional track was laid. In 1845 it was suddenly discovered that the London Bridge Joint Station was inadequate, and on 5 March 1845 William Cubitt presented plans to the station committee for extensions estimated to cost £110,000. These extensions were to be undertaken in conjunction with the original plan for widening the viaduct.

During the same year the Board of Trade made a report on railway termini,[9] and in 1846 the Royal Commission on Railway

Termini in the Metropolis issued a long report based on the evidence of many leading engineers.[10] Much of the document was taken up by the problem of London Bridge, where the situation was rapidly becoming acute owing to the completion of distant South Eastern lines, and the failure of the alternative terminus at Bricklayers Arms to afford much relief as regards passenger traffic. The South Eastern pressed for approval of the original plan to extend the North Kent Railway to Waterloo to join the London & South Western Railway, and provide a connection with the northern lines for its hop trains. It was stated that the hops came up from Kent '... in enormous trains, 40 to 50 waggons in a train', and that they all had to be unloaded and taken across London by road.

A number of other plans had been put forward, including the extension of the lines to a new station in Union Street, Borough. Another was to extend the Bricklayers Arms branch to Waterloo, with a great Central Terminus south of the Waterloo and Hungerford bridges; this reached the stage of an application to Parliament but it failed owing to an error in the survey.

Robert Stephenson suggested the lengthening of London Bridge station as being preferable to building any new terminus; he said 'Every railway station that has yet been made has been found to be insufficient in that respect, in towns especially.'

Some trifling alterations were made to London Bridge – including the widening and lengthening of the Greenwich platforms. Also in June 1846 notices were served on the London & Brighton Railway to vacate property they occupied in Dean Street and Canterbury Square, as this was required for widening the viaduct. A little later the South Eastern gave notice that it required the Brighton goods station.

In 1846 the Joint Station handled 129 trains each week for the London & Brighton Railway, 270 for the Croydon, and 104 for the South Eastern, a total of 503; 112 men were employed there, including 31 porters. About 800 trains a week were handled at the tiny Greenwich station by a staff probably not much exceeding a dozen men.

About this time the South Eastern became dissatisfied with the administration of the Joint Station, and suggested that it be enlarged and divided between the two companies. The reason for this proposal was that, on the amalgamation of the Brighton and Croydon Railways, the new company had twice as many representatives on the Joint Committee as had the South Eastern. It was decided, therefore, to replace the Joint Station by two separate buildings, and both companies obtained Acts for this purpose in July 1847; the Brighton Company's Act condemned the new St Olave's Grammar School to another move. In November 1847 arrangements were made for the Brighton Railway to have a site for a goods station adjoining Bricklayers Arms at Willow Walk; this was opened in 1849 when the company vacated their London Bridge depot.

In August 1849 the LB&SCR took over the goods warehouse and empty carriage shed of the Joint Station, both on the south side, and the South Eastern converted the former Brighton goods station on the north side to a passenger station for the Greenwich line. The temporary single storey building in front of the old Croydon shed was extended northwards to the Tooley Street edge of the viaduct to provide booking offices for the Greenwich branch, and the former Greenwich booking office and station, (the original Croydon shed), became the North Kent terminus.

The temporary station consisted principally of booking offices, and so far as it went, it occupied the same site as the permanent station was to occupy. The Greenwich terminus was set back fifty-five yards from the front of the North Kent station, and thus about half the area of the old Brighton goods station became the Greenwich station approach. The far end of the station was extended across Canterbury Square and the site of the old Hop Warehouse, to the Maze.

The Joint Station was demolished during 1850, the clock and clock-tower being removed by the South Eastern Railway in July. The actual division of the station became effective at 10pm on

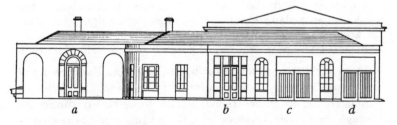

South Eastern Railway temporary station, London Bridge, 1849-51: (a) Greenwich Booking Office; (b) North Kent Booking Office; (c) Carriage Entrance; (d) Way Out

1 August 1850, and construction of the permanent South Eastern station, which was designed by Samuel Beazley, began almost immediately.

The new station was a three-storied block, with waiting and refreshment rooms, booking offices etc. arranged on the ground floor and enclosing the end of the station. The Greenwich terminus, on the north side and lying back, was no longer a separate building, although the interior of the station was still divided into three distinct compartments, Greenwich, North Kent and Dover. A separate three-storied building was erected along the north side of the approach road at the same time; it was 150 feet long and 60 feet in height. The ground floor, which was in Tooley Street, formed a row of ordinary shops whilst the first floor consisted of an arcade. The Greenwich station was hidden by this arcade, and does not, therefore, appear in any of the contemporary prints of the London Bridge stations. A pencil sketch of the South Eastern terminus exists, however, in which a corner of the Greenwich station is shown lying back some distance from the front of the main buildings, with slender, graceful chimneys rising several feet above the roof.[11]

The appearance of new stations at London Bridge was no longer remarkable by 1851, and the following is one of the few contemporary accounts of the opening.[12]

The London Bridge Railway Termini. –January 3rd was the day appointed for the completion and opening of the permanent termini at London Bridge, of both the South Eastern and Brighton Railways, and which for several months past have been in progress of erection. It will, however, be three weeks or a month before they are completed. A new and elegant device, not hitherto adopted in the construction of railway stations has been adopted, that of roofing both stations with sheet glass, which gives to the whole range of platform, of some 300 feet long, a light and cheerful appearance. The flagged pavement to approach the North Kent and Greenwich Railway is covered with a light glass roof.

The LB&SCR terminus, completed just before the opening of the Great Exhibition, was soon found to be inadequate. When, a year later, the Brighton company came to be closely connected, through some of its directors, with the scheme to shift the Crystal Palace to Sydenham, on the Brighton line, it became obvious that better accommodation would be required at London Bridge. Consequently in 1853 the station of 1850 was pulled down and

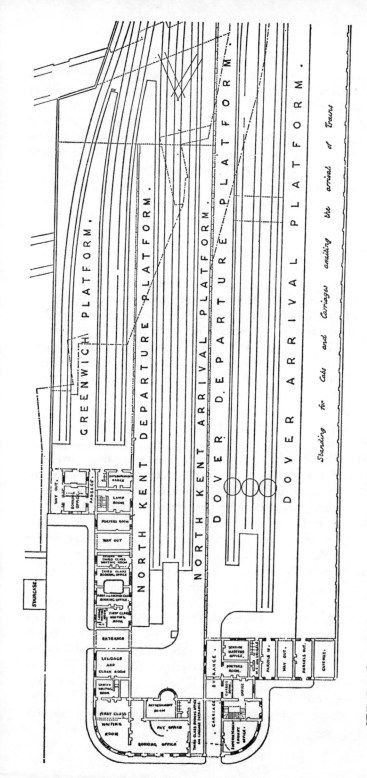

SER London Bridge Station 1851; modified 1863 and 1901, station buildings demolished 1971 (Scale 20ft: 1in)

replaced by a new one; this in turn was enlarged in 1866 when the viaduct was widened for the third time to carry the traffic of the South London line. There have been no radical alterations since this time – apart from the disappearance of the large hotel from the corner of Joiner and St Thomas's Streets, where it stood from 1861 until it was destroyed by bombing – and the station of 1866 remains substantially the same today.

In August 1853 the SER obtained another Act[13] for the further enlargement of London Bridge station on the north side, although the alterations were not very extensive; the provision of stone steps from a point in Tooley Street between Glean Alley and Joiner Street to the railway was included.

In an article on London Bridge station in the *Illustrated London News* of 24 July 1858, it was stated that great confusion existed as to the ownership of shares and property within the group of lines terminating there, since by that time no fewer than 137 separate acts of parliament had been passed in connection with these lines. 'As the whole series grew out of, or stuck themselves on to the little original Greenwich line, the various Boards from time to time accomplished a succession of fusions, amalgamations, extensions, purchases and leases, whose final result defies the keenest perception of the most deeply interested proprietors.' By the middle fifties, £100,000 had been spent on London Bridge station by the SER alone.

There was little change in the working of the line – even the practice of towing the trains into London Bridge persisted for many years – and many of the former Greenwich Railway staff were retained.[14] By 1852 there were forty-nine men employed on the branch, including one policeman, but excluding drivers, firemen and other train staff; of these, probably eighteen were originally employed by the London & Greenwich.

The Greenwich carriages seem to have fallen short of the standards expected by 1846, for in June of that year a correspondent wrote to *The Times* asking why eight people, 'particularly ladies', should be forced into 'their low and narrow first-class carriages, when on other lines of the same size, the number is limited to six'. The Greenwich branch was one of the places where the older South Eastern carriages spent their declining years, although in October 1853 six new covered third-class carriages were ordered for the line.

The custom of smoking in the Greenwich trains did not survive long under the SER; a minute of 19 June 1845 records that 'Complaints having been made that the practice of smoking had been allowed to be introduced upon the Greenwich Branch, the Superintendent was directed to take the necessary steps to put an end to this practice as has been done upon the other South Eastern lines and all other Railways.'

From 1845 until 1863 the train service was almost the same as in the days of the L&GR. In May 1847 the Greenwich trains ran from 6am until 10.15pm on weekdays, and from 6am until 11pm on Sundays, but with an interval from 10.45 to 1.15 during church services. The fares on the 'Parliamentary Trains' which left London Bridge at 6.15am and Greenwich at 6am, were: London Bridge to Spa Road, 1d; London Bridge to Deptford, 3d; London Bridge to Greenwich, 3d; Spa Road to Deptford, 2d; Spa Road to Greenwich, 2d; Deptford to Greenwich, 1d. The free carriage of parcels was discontinued in May 1845.

Mr Akerman remained as the manager of the Greenwich Branch until he was transferred to the Gravesend & Rochester Railway on 6 October 1846; on 21 September 1847 he received notice that his services were no longer required by the SER. In 1848 he became secretary to the Society of Antiquaries, and seems to have had nothing further to do with railways from this time until his death in 1873.

George Walter and Colonel Landmann both died in 1854, within three days of each other, Walter at Leigh, Essex on 24 August and Landmann at Shacklewell, near Hackney, on the 27th. Landmann had completed two volumes of his memoirs, but they did not reach the period of his association with the L&GR.[15] In 1844 George Walter had become manager of the Patent Kamptulicon & Elastic Pavement Co of Lombard St and Greenwich Road; this was probably connected with a composition of cork and rubber invented by him, which '... when placed inside iron men-of-war, will effectually close the holes made by cannon-shot, as proved at Woolwich'.[16] He married twice and had twelve children; two of the houses in Greenwich once occupied by the family still stand. On his death, in not very prosperous circumstances, some of his sons emigrated to Australia, and his descendants live there at the present time.

For a few years the South Eastern maintained the footpaths alongside the line, but the second stage in the widening of the viaduct disposed of the northern path, as that of 1842 had the southern one. The paths after 1850 existed only between the Surrey Canal and Greenwich, and they became neglected, and in wet weather, impassable. The company allowed the public free use of what remained of them, although the short section across the Ravensbourne Bridge was still subject to a toll in 1901.

In the 1850s the arches at each end of the viaduct were usually occupied, but in the centre, between Blue Anchor Road and the Surrey Canal they were empty. The land here had not been completely built over, and a few market gardens and meadows still existed. Although the footpaths had gone from this section, it was still possible to follow the line of the railway by walking beneath the viaduct through the small connecting arches in the piers. Mr A. R. Bennett, writing of the viaduct as he remembered it in the 1850s, lonely and deserted at night, remarks on the fact that no one had ever thought of it as a suitable place for committing a murder. It would appear that someone had done so about ten years before, however, for on 26 April 1842 the Greenwich Railway police found the body of a murdered boy in Arch No. 176.

From July 1845 the Greenwich branch locomotives were taken over by the new Bricklayers Arms locomotive depot and no further repairs were undertaken at Deptford. At this period the Joint Locomotive Committee of the Brighton, Croydon & Dover Railways had just distributed the joint stock of engines between the three companies, but the South Eastern already had some of its own, apart from the Greenwich stock. Repairs to the main line locomotives were carried out at New Cross, and the South Eastern continued to use certain shops there during 1846, while the Ashford works were being constructed.

The 'Engine Stables', as the South Eastern called the shed at Deptford, remained in use for the few locomotives used in working the Greenwich trains, and the Deptford Repair Shops were used for the construction of goods trucks, fifty of which were built there in 1845-6 at a cost of £92 each. By July 1851 all new construction had been transferred to the carriage and waggon department at Ashford, and the Deptford shops were used for repairs only.

On 25 May 1850 the board received a report on the delays which occurred on the Greenwich branch, from which it appears that the trouble was mainly caused at Greenwich, where the engines could not be filled with water quickly enough to get away

again on time. Nearly two years later the position had not
improved very much, and the board ordered that the trains perform the journey in twelve minutes. The delays on the Greenwich
line, however, were negligible compared with those on the North
Kent, when that line was first opened. Gravesend in those days
was an important holiday resort for Londoners – hence the
anxiety of the London & Greenwich Railway to reach it – and the
first trains to serve the town in the summer of 1849 were terribly
overcrowded. A passenger complained that the 8.15pm up train
on 5 August took five minutes short of three hours to cover the
twenty miles, and that the engine, being unequal to the task of
pulling twenty-seven carriages crowded with passengers, stopped
for thirty-five minutes in a tunnel, much to the distress of the
travellers in the open carriages. These were not only choked by
the smoke and steam from the engine, deafened by its whistle
and drenched by the water falling from the tunnel roof, but were
apprehensive lest the next up train, long overdue, should run
into them.

The South Eastern was one of the first railways to adopt the
electric telegraph, and on 15 January 1852 the installation of the
system on the Greenwich line was authorised. By the following
August the work was completed, the cables having been laid
along the viaduct in wooden troughs. For some years two distinct
systems were employed on the SER; that of the Railway Electric
Signals Company was used on the Greenwich and North Kent
lines, and the railway's own system operated over the main lines.
Thus the three tracks on the north side of the viaduct were
worked separately from the next three tracks, and 'joint wires'
were laid from London Bridge to the junction. The old octagonal
lighthouse at Corbetts Lane is shown on a plan of the line prepared in 1853; but whether it remained until the Corbetts Lane
signal box was built in 1874 is not certain.

The important Surrey Canal and North Kent East junctions
were only 270 yards apart, and the arrangements in force there
in 1855 are described in a Board of Trade report that followed an
accident at the latter.[17] It was stated that the North Kent line
commenced '... with a pair of self-acting facing points on the
down line, weighted to stand open for the Greenwich down line,
worked from an elevated signalman's box, placed opposite to the
point'. The Bricklayers Arms branch also started from self-acting
facing points, weighted in favour of the main line. Here there

was another signal box reached by six steps, controlling two semaphore posts, one for the Greenwich and North Kent line, and the other for Bricklayers Arms.

A curious accident occurred on 7 December 1855 at this point. A pilot engine, returning on the down Greenwich line after a day's duty at London Bridge, crossed to the down North Kent and then reversed on to the up North Kent in order to reach the Bricklayers Arms line. After stopping at North Kent East junction to deliver a sack of coal to the signalman there, the driver went on to Surrey Canal junction to deliver a sack of coal to the signalman there. This signalman set the points for the Bricklayers Arms line, and then wedged them in that position by putting a block of wood in the groove in which the lever moved. He then helped take the sack of coal from the engine, after which the engine went off up the Bricklayers Arms line. A North Kent up train followed almost immediately, and, the signalman having forgotten to remove the wedge from the lever, the engine and leading carriages were diverted to the Bricklayers Arms line. At this moment the man panicked, and moving the wedge, allowed the weighted points to change under the moving train, half of which was now over the points. The rear part was derailed, and only saved from falling into a market garden below by the parapet wall.

At the inquiry it was stated that the signalman had been employed for twenty years on the Greenwich and South Eastern Railways, and thus must have been one of the first employees of the former company. He was, at the time of the report, awaiting trial. The company stated that its signalmen received about £1. 5s 0d per week, which was a better rate of pay than on other railways for that type of work, and that it was very perturbed at the number of cases of negligence brought to its notice. A summary of such cases for the month of October 1855 shows that twenty-six of the company's servants were fined, three suspended, three sent to prison for one month, and one sentenced to imprisonment with hard labour for one month. In all these cases, it was pointed out, the company's rules had been disobeyed, the passengers exposed to danger, and the railway involved in heavy claims for compensation.

The signalmen at North Kent East and Surrey Canal junctions worked for eleven hours when on day duty, and thirteen hours on night duty; by a kind of private arrangement they were able to have two Sundays off in four by working for eight and eighteen hours on the other two.

An accident that might easily have been a major disaster occurred on 30 October 1856. Down trains still entered Greenwich station by alternate platforms, and on leaving, were diverted to the up line by self-acting points. These points were watched by a man named William Wheeler, who had been a Greenwich Railway pointsman for twenty years, but on that night he failed to notice that the 9.05pm up train, which started on the down line, did not cross to the up track through some fault in the points, but continued towards Deptford on the wrong line. The night was dark, and the driver noticed nothing amiss until the train crossed the Ravensbourne Bridge, and he saw a down train approaching on the same line. He shouted to the fireman to apply the brake, but regrettably the fireman was no longer with him. Having seen the down train an instant before, and believing '... a collision was inevitable ... he took a desperate leap for life ...' clear off the engine, over the parapet wall and into a street below where he lay injured. The collision occurred near Deptford station, and thirty-six passengers were injured, together with both drivers, guards, and the fireman of the down train. The up train was driven by John Watson, who had had eighteen years experience on the line; he said the consequences would have been serious but for the fact that he was travelling slowly as it was not worth getting up speed for the short distance between Greenwich and Deptford.[18]

A regulation appeared in 1857 against racing on the viaduct between trains on the main line and those on the Croydon, North Kent and Greenwich lines. The practice, which began back in 1842, seems to have been well established by this time, however, for in July 1851 correspondence appeared in *The Times* on the subject of races between the Croydon, Epsom, Brighton and Dover trains. The writers were, of course, too preoccupied with the safety aspect to leave any record of results or times for the contests.

The six tracks over the viaduct were becoming inadequate for the increasing traffic in the 1850s, and with the opening of the Lewisham–Beckenham section of the Mid-Kent Railway on 1 January 1857, the pressure on two of the Greenwich and North Kent lines was increased still further. In the meantime the LB&SCR had opened its Crystal Palace line (1854), and all the

down trains on this service, together with the down Croydon
local and all the long distance South Eastern and Brighton trains
travelled over the one down joint main line (No. 4); up Crystal
Palace trains ran on the Croydon line (No. 6).

The South Eastern Railway rule book of 1857 contains the
following special regulations for the working of the Greenwich
branch:

218 Each train will be worked by one guard, who will ride on
the brake at the *rear* of the train.
219 The Greenwich Branch guards are under the control of the
London Bridge Station Master.
220 The Greenwich engines will take coke at London and water
at Greenwich.
221 When a North Kent or Mid Kent, and a Greenwich train,
are timed to leave London at the same time, the *North Kent* or
Mid Kent train must always start first.
222 Tickets are collected at Spa Road and Deptford, viz. Spa
Road for *Up* trains and at Deptford for *Down* trains.

The headlights for Greenwich trains are given in this book as
'two white lights, one on each buffer beam' – presumably one on
each side of the buffer beam.

In July 1858 the number of South Eastern trains using the
viaduct in the down direction was given as: Greenwich, 49;
North Kent, 29; Dover and Margate, 15; Beckenham etc (Mid
Kent), 11. There was about an equal number of up trains, and in
addition, there were 63 Brighton trains each way, making a total
of nearly 340 trains a day, excluding excursions and specials.

By 1857 a number of signal posts carrying double and single
semaphore arms towered above the viaduct. Those at London
Bridge and Surrey Canal junction have been mentioned: at North
Kent East junction a double semaphore was erected on the stage
of the switchman's box, whilst at Spa Road a single post carried
the 'arm and light . . . for the Main Line and Croydon down, and
Main Line up' at the top, and a lower arm and light for Croydon
and Crystal Palace up trains.

Since the early 1840s the railway companies using London
Bridge station had been endeavouring to extend the line to a
terminus in the West End of London, and plans for a station at
Charing Cross, on the site of the present terminus, but about
twice the size, originated in 1845, about the time of the South
Eastern company's application for powers to extend the Brick-

layers Arms branch to Waterloo. This 'Charing Cross Station and Railway' was to have constructed a line across the Thames to join the London & South Western Railway near Waterloo, but no direct connection with the South Eastern was envisaged, because other lines linking various parts of the London & Greenwich with Waterloo had already been projected. However, like many other schemes of the Railway Mania period, the original Charing Cross line came to nothing, and twelve years elapsed before the scheme was revived.

In 1857 a Parliamentary Committee recommended the extension of the SER westwards, and the next year a pamphlet by Samuel Smiles, then secretary, was published entitled *A Statement in support of the proposed London Bridge & Charing Cross Railway*. This gave the figures for passengers who used London Bridge in 1857 as over $13\frac{1}{2}$ millions; 7 millions of these used the South Eastern station.

A company was incorporated to build the line by an Act of 8 August 1859,[19] and the South Eastern was to provide £300,000 of the capital, and work the traffic; at Waterloo Junction the new line was to connect with the London & South Western Railway.

The line was planned to pass to the south of Southwark Cathedral, involving a severe curve west of London Bridge; this in turn necessitated taking the railway over a corner of the grounds of St Thomas's Hospital. The hospital still occupied most of the land between Duke Street, St Thomas's Street, Borough High Street and Joiner Street; views of the front of the hospital in 1849 and 1858 show respectively the top of the Joint Station campanile and the Brighton Station building in the background behind railings separating the properties. The hospital authorities opposed the Charing Cross Extension Bill, and got a clause inserted compelling the company to purchase the whole of its property if required to do so. This the company did, and the hospital vacated the site completely soon afterwards.[20]

The Charing Cross Railway Company obtained another Act on 28 June 1861[21] for a second bridge across the Thames to a City terminus at Cannon Street. The extension to Charing Cross was opened on 11 January 1864, and the Cannon Street section on 1 September 1866, some two years after the subsidiary company had been absorbed by the South Eastern Railway.

The effect of the western extension on the Greenwich branch was twofold; in the first place its trains ran on to the new termini, and secondly the Greenwich terminus at London Bridge was swept away to make room for the new lines; with it went the northern wing of the South Eastern station and the arcade on the station approach. The new lines had to be built at a higher level than the 22ft of the old Greenwich viaduct in order to clear the Borough High Street, and consequently they were raised on a gradient of 1 in 100 from a point just to the east of the station. All traces of the original London & Croydon station on the viaduct went with the Greenwich Branch station, but the stone facade of the booking offices on the corner of Tooley and Joiner Streets remains to the present day, although hidden behind some public conveniences.

Apart from some minor alterations, the present station is very much as the reconstruction of the 1860s left it. In Joiner Street the several widenings of the station approach can be plainly seen from the differing styles of brickwork, and here are the only visible relics of the original Greenwich station – the two rusticated arches, one of which was the entrance to the arcade of shops under the railway, and the small dome-shaped recess in the roof of the arch which probably at one time held a lantern.

As soon as the Charing Cross extension was opened some four hundred trains a day were thrown on to its lines, and within a very short time the railway had captured most of the bus traffic between Greenwich and the West End of London.[22]

The intermediate stations on the Greenwich viaduct had a somewhat chequered history in the century following the leasing of the line. Spa Road station, which had been reopened in 1842, was the first to be rebuilt; in March 1845 the SER abolished the stairway on the north side of the viaduct, and constructed an internal stair approach from the arch in West Street (now Rouel Road) next to the one occupied by the booking office. The two Greenwich tracks were made to diverge slightly, and an island platform 10 feet wide was built between them, upon which was provided a small shelter with its roof 12 feet above rail level, and projecting about 8 inches bringing it level with the carriage sides. A passenger was killed here on 1 April 1850 while riding to Greenwich in a third-class open carriage '. . . of somewhat different construction from those in general use, being formerly a covered carriage, but the roof having rotted, was removed, while the framing of the sides and ends was allowed to remain'. For some reason the man had climbed up the framing, and hit his head on the projecting roof of the station. The Board of Trade suggested that '... considering the unruly class of passengers that are conveyed during Fair Time at Greenwich, every reasonable precaution should be taken to put it out of their power to injure themselves', adding the recommendation that all such carriages should have the sides and ends cut down to correspond with the third-class carriages then in general use.[23]

About 1850 a small ticket-collector's shelter was erected on the platform at Spa Road, and it became the practice to stop the up trains there for ticket collection to save time and confusion at London Bridge; this system continued until the opening of the Charing Cross extension. At the same period a North Kent ticket platform was in use just outside London Bridge station, situated between the North Kent up line, and a shunting siding which separated it from the down main line at this point.

In 1867 Spa Road station was again rebuilt, on a new site about 200 yards east of the original.

A new station called Commercial Dock was opened on 1 May 1856; situated at Corbetts Lane Junction, it consisted of a single, narrow island platform, curved on the south side to allow for the divergence of the down line. No provision was made for North Kent trains to use the station since no platform was provided for the NK line. A narrow path from the arch which formed the entrance, muddy and unlighted at night, ran past the arches to Rotherhithe New Road, itself little more than a cart track bounded by ditches at that time. The chief purpose of the station seems to have been to serve the St Helena Tavern and Pleasure Gardens, although in 1858 there was a scheme afoot for connecting the station with the London & Blackwall Railway across the river – by what means is not clear – and also with the Brighton line.[24]

The station was advertised in 1860 as serving Rotherhithe, Hatcham and Peckham, but it was very little used. By 1865 Peckham had a station of its own on the London, Chatham & Dover Railway, and the South London line giving direct access to London Bridge was nearing completion. As the traffic did not warrant the stopping of trains on the busy down line any longer, Commercial Dock Station was closed on 31 December 1866.

As a result of a public meeting in March 1878[25] the people of Rotherhithe petitioned the South Eastern Railway to reopen the old Commercial Dock Station to meet changed conditions

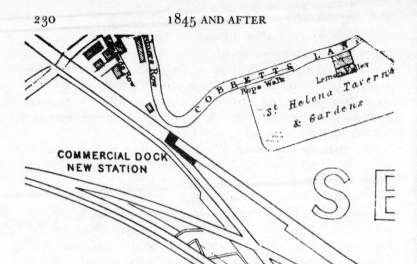

Commercial Dock Station, SER, 1856. Said to have been used principally by visitors to the St Helena Tea Gardens rather than to the Docks

in the district. The company was not anxious to comply, but after about ten years agitation, a Bill was promoted in 1888 for powers to make a junction between the North Kent and Bricklayers Arms lines, and the Brighton Company's up Croydon line, and at the same time to widen the viaduct and build a station at Rotherhithe Road (formerly Corbetts Lane). The Bill was opposed by the Brighton Railway on the grounds that there was no public necessity for a station; and if there had been, then the old one could be reopened at any time. Another fourteen years passed before a station was again provided.

When the SER took over the line the re-fuelling of the engines was transferred to London Bridge, and the Coke House at Deptford was converted to a second engine shed; situated between the two sheds was a turntable at the point where the inclined plane joined the main viaduct, and a line of rails led from the turntable down the slope. On the opening of the Charing Cross extension the refuelling arrangements were transferred back to Deptford, and a wooden stage was erected on the northern parapet wall, from which men used to tip the coke from baskets into the tenders or bunkers of engines waiting there; the small eastern engine shed reverted to its original use as a coke store at this time.

About 1876, in preparation for the extension of the line to Charlton, the platforms were lengthened across the High Street Bridge by 16 yards; the new sections were only 4 feet wide, however, and were considered dangerous by the Board of Trade. It was intended to demolish the engine sheds and remove the locomotives to Charlton in order to improve Deptford Station on the opening of the new line.

One of the first considerations of the South Eastern Railway on leasing the Greenwich line was the possibility of extending the railway through Greenwich Park and on to Woolwich and Charlton. Accordingly, the old Greenwich and Gravesend scheme was revived, but it did not get very far. The Board of Trade published reports and correspondence on the supposed effects of a railway through the park covering a period of eleven years, and occupying ninety pages of print, accompanied by about twenty coloured maps and plans.[26] These papers traced the whole history, in outline, of the attempts to cross the apparently sacred lawns of Greenwich, from the early experiments of Colonel Landmann in 1835, down to an elaborate series of twelve conducted by Robert Stephenson on the London & Birmingham Railway, to ascertain the amount of vibration caused by trains in the Chalk Farm and Kensal Green Tunnels. A representative of the Greenwich Observatory also sent in data he had collected from experiments at Dublin, where, it was stated, the railway ran over similar soil formations to those at Greenwich.

From all these reports it is clear that the main opposition to the railway did not come from the Observatory in 1846, any more than it had ten years before, but from the Admiralty, and the vicar and churchwardens of Greenwich. The latter, in May 1845, had successfully opposed a Bill to move Greenwich Station 430 yards to the east (which would have brought it to the edge of the park), on the grounds that this was only the first part of the main plan to cut through the park itself, to be launched by the company when the time seemed propitious. Stephenson's scheme for a tunnel through the park had a promising start in Parliament, but was defeated in May 1846 after a meeting on the subject had been held at the Admiralty.

The project for a direct North Kent line having thus failed, the circuitous route via Lewisham was adopted. Again in 1852 the board considered preparing a Bill to extend the line from Greenwich, but presumably the opposition was still as strong, for no progress was made. The next move was made in June 1858, when a deputation of residents from Greenwich and Woolwich sought to persuade the company to provide direct communication between these places. By 1860 plans had been prepared by the interested parties, and laid before the railway. The directors stated that they could not entertain the proposal, however, and by October 1863 the local residents (whose earlier hostility to the railway had helped to defeat previous attempts to build the direct Gravesend line) were talking of an approach to Parliament for a line to connect the North Kent Railway at Woolwich with the London, Chatham & Dover Railway's '. . . branch to Greenwich, when completed'. The LC&DR branch to Greenwich Park, contemplated in 1863, did not materialise for another twenty-five years, but the threat of connecting the two systems seems to have been sufficient to convince the SER that it had better forestall any such arrangement by building the line itself. The company accordingly obtained an Act in 1865, the House of Commons Committee at last having agreed to a line indicated by Sir George Airy, the Astronomer Royal.

The railway was in no hurry to construct the line, and in February 1870 it stated its objections to the route for which powers had been granted, on the grounds that only about three minutes journey time would be saved between London and Charlton, and even that would be doubtful if the Astronomer Royal exercised his power to stop the trains. By 1872 the railway had another line planned across the park, on the north side of London Street – '. . . at such a distance from the Observatory as to remove all cause for alarm', Sir George Airy wrote in his diary, adding 'I trust that the contest, which has now lasted thirty-seven years, is now terminated.'[27]

A section of the new line between Charlton and Maze Hill was opened on 1 January 1873, and work on the Greenwich and Maze Hill section, which included the tunnel, was well advanced by 3 June 1875 when the company gave the Board of Trade one month's notice of its intention to open the line from Church Street, Greenwich, for public traffic. This was a single line running on from the original Greenwich Station round a sharp curve and down a steep gradient to the tunnel mouth, an arrangement at which Colonel Hutchinson demurred. The gradient must have been uncommonly steep, since the original station at Greenwich was built on arches and the line had to descend to a tunnel less than a quarter of a mile away.[28]

During the next twelve months the gradient was eased and the curve reduced by demolishing the forty-three arches between Norman Road (near the Ravensbourne Bridge) and the end of the line, and replacing this section of the viaduct by an embankment which ran down to ground level opposite the station. This embankment curved slightly to the north, and consequently the lines no longer ran through the station; moreover, the station had been built for a line some twenty feet higher than the new one. It was, therefore, decided to replace it, but in the meantime, the company invited the Board of Trade to inspect the new works with a view to the line being opened for traffic.

Colonel Hutchinson's report of 18 July 1876 mentions the unfinished state of the line – it was still single track for 500 yards – and other points upon which he was not satisfied. The company was required to close a road level crossing close to the east end of Greenwich station, and to give several other undertakings, which, it declared in August, it was not prepared to do; the Board of Trade was informed that the opening would be deferred until all the works were complete, despite the public agitation for a service to begin.

The report of July 1876 refers to Greenwich station, '... which ... is to be entirely removed, a new one having been (partially as yet) constructed close to its site'. In November work was started on temporary platforms, and on 11 January 1877 the traffic was transferred to them.

It has been stated that the original station was carefully dismantled and re-erected on the new site, but this was not the case. There was a certain similarity between the two buildings, and some of the Portland stone from the old station was re-dressed and used in the new one, but no attempt was made to preserve the original building. The new station was even larger than the one that had been the terminus of the line, and it stands today in its courtyard, which once was filled with hansom cabs, in almost exactly the same state as when it was opened in 1878. The spacious waiting rooms, with their large fireplaces and corniced ceilings, are now used for other purposes. The canopy which once extended the whole length of the station frontage has now been cut down, to provide shelter over the entrance only, and the iron gates and railings of the forecourt disappeared during the war.

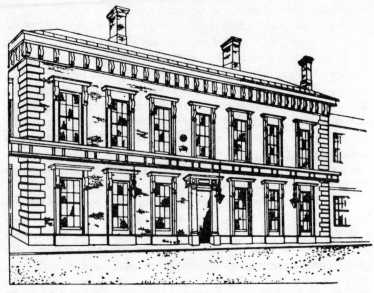

Greenwich Station of 1878; it is almost unchanged after nearly
a century

Only two tracks now run through the station instead of the
original four, and the up and down platforms are wide apart;
the bay, which formerly existed on the south side, has also gone,
although its site can still be traced. (This was originally a
temporary siding for the removal of materials from the demolition of the old station, and was connected by facing points to
what was then the down line.)

The company had been considering for some time the reversal
of the Greenwich lines once more, to bring them back to normal.
After the opening of the Charing Cross line all the Greenwich
trains had to cross over just east of London Bridge, so as to use
the normal up and down lines to Charing Cross and Cannon
Street; the congestion west of London Bridge was, from the
first such that no crossings could be contemplated there. It was
becoming a matter of some urgency that the crossing east of
London Bridge should be eliminated, and the fact that the
Greenwich trains would come on to the North Kent line near
Charlton, necessitating another crossing, provided an additional
reason for normal running to be restored throughout the branch.

However, it was found that, with only three tracks available, no alteration was practicable between London Bridge and North Kent East Junction, and that the easier course would be to reverse the running over the Maze Hill–Charlton section (which, since its opening in 1873 had been operated in the normal way), when this line was linked up with the Greenwich branch. This required the installation of a scissors crossing at Charlton to effect the reversal of the lines there, and the modification of a couple of stations which now had their booking offices on the wrong side. A minute of 5 September 1877 refers to the station to be erected at Combe Farm Lane, and states that it was '... proposed to change the up and down lines on the opening of the Greenwich and Maze Hill extension, which would necessitate the booking offices being erected on the north instead of the south side of the line'. The reference is to Westcombe Park station, which was originally built with the booking offices on the north, or up, side.

The Deptford Bridge–Maze Hill extension, as it was usually called, was practically completed in April 1877, and was inspected on 23rd of that month; permission to open for traffic was given, subject to the provision of a turntable at Charlton. In June the public protested at the delay in opening the line, and the company promised to open it as soon as the new Greenwich station was finished; this took another six months, however, as the stonemasons went on strike a few weeks later.

At just after 6am on 1 February 1878 the first train left Greenwich for Maze Hill on the line that the promoters of the old London & Greenwich Railway had been so desperately anxious to build more than forty years before. Then it would have probably developed into the main line to Dover, as Landmann and Walter had intended, and the pattern of the whole railway system of Kent would, no doubt, have been very different. By the time the line was built it was more of an embarrassment than an asset to the SER; although it had the effect of transforming the Greenwich Branch from an isolated, and virtually self-contained section of the system into part of yet another alternative route to the coast and elsewhere, it threw more traffic on to the already congested lines to London Bridge, Cannon Street and Charing Cross.

In the meantime the board's concern over the increasing congestion on the lines between Charing Cross and North Kent East Junction led it to commission Sir John Hawkshaw, Mr Brady and Mr J. Wolfe Barry to investigate the position. In their report, issued in 1880, they recommended widening of the line and the extension westwards of the Bricklayers Arms branch to join the Charing Cross and Cannon Street lines near Metropolitan junction, thus relieving the Greenwich viaduct of some of the pressure.

The company did not adopt the suggestion, however, but embarked upon the costly expedient of widening the river bridges instead. Various improvements at London Bridge station were also carried out, but none of these works resulted in any material relief since they did not increase in any way the capacity of the lines on the viaduct which fed the three stations. From 1868 the North Kent & Greenwich down line and the North Kent up had carried the SER long-distance traffic for the new main line via Sevenoaks and Tonbridge, opened in that year; these trains ran through North Kent East junction, and could not use the joint SER and LB&SCR lines. The opening of numerous branch lines over the years still further increased the pressure on these two tracks along the viaduct.

During April 1893 the question of altering the arrangement of the Greenwich lines again occupied the board, and the general manager, Sir Myles Fenton consulted Mr Birt, his colleague on the Great Eastern Railway on the subject. This matter was inseparable from the wider one of accommodating the traffic, however, and it was found to be impracticable to disturb the arrangements until further tracks could be laid. The company called for another report on the situation, this time from J. W. and A. J. Barry.

Their report, dated 8 August 1894,[29] dealt briefly with the obstructions to the free running of the traffic. These were enumerated under the following heads:

1 Ignoring the South Eastern and Brighton joint lines, only three lines existed between London Bridge and North Kent East junction, the central one for down, and the other two for up traffic. On the single down line the whole of the down traffic of the Greenwich, New Main, North Kent and Mid Kent lines was carried. Fast main line trains, as well as local and empty trains had to run along it. In one day 338 trains passed over this one line; at peak periods they ran at the rate of 48 an hour, or one every 75 seconds.

2 Up traffic could not be evenly distributed between the two up lines, for in order to prevent the up Greenwich line from

crossing the down line at North Kent East Junction on the level, the northern line was reserved exclusively for Greenwich trains. The Greenwich line, therefore, carried eighty trains a day, whilst the other took all the rest, amounting to some 300 trains daily. Furthermore, whilst the objectionable crossing at the junction was avoided, an almost equally objectionable one just east of London Bridge had to be made, since the up Greenwich trains had to reach the correct line in order to proceed to Charing Cross or Cannon Street.

3   Constant crossing on the level at North Kent East Junction, arising from the fact that four lines from St John's converged on to two lines at this point.

4   The large volume of shunting at Surrey Canal Junction on to the Bricklayers Arms branch. In addition to all the light engines, there were 35 goods trains, and 34 empty trains each way, daily passing over Surrey Canal Junction to and from Bricklayers Arms. The empty trains caused the greatest dislocation of traffic, as they were moved during the busy hours; they came from London on the down line, stopped at the junction, and then backed across the up line on to the branch.

The solution to the problem that was suggested in the report was the provision of an additional track between London Bridge and North Kent East Junction, with the reversal to normal running of the Greenwich lines, and the more even distribution of traffic over the four lines which would then be available. The viaduct had, however, by this time already spread itself northwards to occupy the land originally used by the London & Greenwich Railway for its footpath, and in the period of nearly half a century which had elapsed since the widenings of 1849 a number of factories had grown up alongside the railway. None of these could be disturbed without incurring great cost and inconvenience. To overcome this, the novel method of constructing the additional line above the existing lines was put forward. This 'second storey' as the report called it, was to run from North Kent East Junction rising at 1 in 100 to Surrey Canal Junction, where it would turn in over the existing viaduct; it was then to turn out again just beyond the Neckinger Mills, and commence to fall at 1 in 100, regaining the level of the original lines at London Bridge. To avoid possible objections on the grounds of the restriction of light, it was suggested that the new viaduct be constructed of open ironwork.

It was pointed out that if the South Eastern Railway, by means of the additional line recommended, could operate its traffic with the punctuality of the Brighton lines, London Bridge station would assume a new importance from the fact that the new Tower Bridge had relieved the congestion of road traffic over London Bridge, and had consequently made it far more accessible than it had ever been in modern times.

An alternative to the elevated viaduct was a proposal to widen the viaduct at North Kent East and London Bridge, but to run the additional track round the factories on a new viaduct which would have reached the Jamaica Road, Bermondsey.

The second part of the report dealt with the lines between London Bridge, Charing Cross and Cannon Street, where the problems of operation were even more acute. At Borough Market Junction, 300 yards from London Bridge, the lines diverged, three tracks running to Cannon Street, while two turned off towards Charing Cross; over this junction 674 trains passed daily. The line to Cannon Street curved sharply to the right, to another junction about a hundred yards from the south end of the bridge, made with a spur from the Charing Cross line. From this Stoney Street Junction five lines ran towards the bridge; after about thirty yards they spread out to eight lines over the bridge. Some 788 trains passed over Stoney Street Junction every day. At that time, most of the trains called at Cannon Street on their way to or from Charing Cross, and then came back over the bridge to resume their journey. These trains, of which there were 344, used Stoney Street Junction twice on each run; the remaining hundred included goods and empty trains. Every train passing in and out of Cannon Street fouled most of the running lines on the bridge; moreover, each train had to take on a new engine at Cannon Street, and be followed out by the engine which brought it in, an operation which further complicated a situation already abounding in difficulties.

The next junction was Southwark Street, where the Cannon Street–Charing Cross line joined the direct London Bridge–Charing Cross line. This, with Borough Market and Stoney Street Junctions, formed a triangle, and the situation here was similar to that at Borough Market Junction. At Metropolitan Junction, where the London, Chatham & Dover Railway from Blackfriars joined the South Eastern, there was no particular difficulty; only nine passenger trains in each direction daily used it, and the sixty goods trains which passed over it ran at times when there was little other traffic. At Waterloo Junction Station there was a single line connecting the South Eastern with the London & South Western Railway, but by 1894 it was very seldom used, and created no difficulties.

Before suggesting methods by which the difficulties might be removed, the engineers commended those responsible for managing the traffic so well that it had been carried on without accident – although at the cost of punctuality.

After discussing various schemes that had been put forward, the report recommended the adoption of a plan which was substantially the same as that suggested in 1880 by Sir John Hawkshaw. This consisted in the abandonment of the in-and-out running at Cannon Street, except in the case of the Greenwich trains, which would thus provide the local service between the three great South Eastern stations, and the division of all other trains at New Cross. Those trains bound for Cannon Street would then run over the Greenwich viaduct, through London Bridge, and into Cannon Street, terminating there; the Charing Cross trains were to be diverted to the Bricklayers Arms line, widened for the purpose, and extended to join the Charing Cross line near Blackfriars Road. Two new stations, one at Old Kent Road and one at Newington Causeway, to correspond with the London, Chatham & Dover stations at the Elephant & Castle and Borough Road, were suggested, and the extra traffic they would contribute, together with the rents from the new arches, would partly offset the cost of extending the line. Alterations at New Cross would have been necessary to enable trains to be divided there, and the repercussions of the plan would have been felt as far away as Ashford Junction, where facilities for making up the trains in two portions would be necessary.

Of the other plans noticed in the report, two seem worthy of mention. The first was the prolongation of the 'upper storey' suggested for the Greenwich viaduct, through London Bridge, across Cannon Street bridge, and into the station. Another elevated line was then to run out from Cannon Street, back across the bridge, and at Stoney Street Junction join the main line into Charing Cross. By this plan, all fouling of lines by trains going in the opposite direction at the three junctions would be avoided. Apart from the obvious objection on aesthetic grounds to the double bridge across the Thames, which alone might have been enough to defeat the Bill, there was the enormous cost involved.

The second scheme was the abandonment of Cannon Street station as a railway station, and the construction of a new main City station at the Borough Market; the Cannon Street bridge was to be converted into a private road bridge, with shops on either side. Passengers for Cannon Street would leave the trains at the new station, and be taken by shuttle train or tramcar over the bridge, to complete their journey as quickly, it was claimed, as they then did by the reversing trains.

The cost of any improvements to the Charing Cross line was reckoned in millions of pounds, and the above were no exceptions; as the original extension had cost about £2,000,000 per mile, it was probably considered that further expense of this order was not justifiable.

However, a programme of works was put in hand in 1896, and this went forward steadily until 1904, thus spreading the capital charges over a number of years. These works, which started west of London Bridge, included the provision of a fourth line on each of the curves into Cannon Street station, a fourth line from Cannon Street West Junction to Belvedere Road, the entire re-building of Waterloo Junction Station, the construction of a new depot and siding at Ewer Street and the replacement of the old Cannon Street Signal Box by a new one at Worcester Street, a little to the west. East of London Bridge the viaduct was widened for the fourth time, by two tracks between London Bridge and Spa Road, and by three on to North Kent East Junction.

By January 1901 the new Waterloo station was ready, and the widenings between Charing Cross and London Bridge were brought into use completely in March 1903 on completion of the new 167-foot four-track bridge across Southwark Street. The line was widened on the up side by the extension of the brick arches and the provision of nineteen steel girder underbridges.

At London Bridge supporting columns were placed under the great bowstring bridge across the station approach, and the old terminal portion of the station, which for many years had been used as a goods depot, was restored for use again as a passenger station, the goods traffic being transferred gradually to Ewer Street. This part of London Bridge Station was the original South Eastern main line terminus of 1851, and it was described in 1901 as '... a very venerable and archaic specimen of Railway archi-

tecture, its wooden roof in particular being quite a curiosity'.[30]
Footbridges were built to connect it with the high level station,
which had itself been reconstructed a few years before; the further
rearrangement of the high level station was completed in 1902.
The new works included the reorganisation of the whole signalling system.

Below London Bridge station the larger girder bridge across
Parish and Artillery Streets was built, and the railway was carried over the London County Council's new Tower Bridge Road
by another wide bridge of 60 foot span and incorporating twenty-
six girders; some of the original Greenwich Railway arches were
removed to make way for this latter structure. The bridges carrying the line over the East London Railway, the Surrey Canal and
Trundleys Road were widened by the addition of wrought iron
girder spans alongside the old arches, and although much of the
intermediate portion was still unfinished, by 1901 enough progress had been made for the Greenwich lines to be reversed.
The right-hand running was finally abolished during the night
of 25/26 May 1901. Some confusion was anticipated among the
regular passengers, and notices were pasted on the inside of
carriage doors of trains travelling over the section warning them
before alighting to see that they were alongside the platforms.

The widening continued through Bermondsey, entailing an
alteration to the Spa Road station approach which may still be
seen – the arch bearing the letters 'S.E.C.R.' – in Priter Way. The
only other modification here was the reversal of the up and down
platforms, a matter upon which a passenger complained to the
Board of Trade. The new arrangement meant that the small
narrow down platform became the departure platform for
London Bridge – '... situated in the middle of the railway, with
Expresses flying by every few minutes. It was built 40 years ago
for their requirements when the fare was 3d to London, and now
1d; and where 2 to 300 passengers leave every ten minutes from
8 to 8.40am ... how is it possible for all this crowd to get on to
the platform with safety?' Only 16 feet of the platform was
covered, and passengers stayed on the staircases when it rained.
The company replied that little could be done to remedy the
matter, short of erecting a hoarding on the North Kent side, and
this would have prevented the running of excursion trains for
the district, since they could not then stop at the platform on
the up main line; the cancellation of some other trains which

called at Spa Road would also have followed.

On 1 October 1902 the new Southwark Park station at Corbetts Lane was opened, on space provided by the extra wide arches built from a point 168 yards west to 680 yards east of Rotherhithe New Road. Two loop lines were laid through the station, and traffic was controlled by the former Corbetts Lane Signal Cabin, renamed Southwark Park Station Signal Cabin. The station consisted of two island platforms 170 yards long, each provided with waiting rooms and 220 feet of roofing. The booking hall and offices were at ground level, with ramped approaches leading to the platforms.

Deptford station was partially rebuilt in 1904 when the platforms were widened and lengthened, an additional exit provided on the up side, and new waiting rooms prepared. The old signal box was removed from the up platform, where it stood between the turret and the High Street bridge, and a new one was erected at the London end of the station, on the walls of the old engine shed. Greenwich station was not seriously affected by the reversal of the lines, beyond alterations in the signal box at the west end of the station. This frame of fifteen levers also contained a key which unlocked the Deptford Creek bridge, its removal breaking down the electrical locking for the acceptance of trains between Deptford and Greenwich. The bridge had been reconstructed in 1884, but by the end of the century it was rarely used, and could be opened only after a rail length had been taken up.

The opening of Southwark Park station coincided roughly with the coming of the electric tramcar, and little traffic developed. Together with Spa Road and Deptford stations, it was closed as a wartime economy measure on 15 March 1915, and, like Spa Road, it has never been reopened; its booking office remains closed and deserted in Corbetts Lane. The remains of the platforms of Spa Road station, near Peek Freans biscuit factory, have been a familiar sight to travellers over the viaduct for the past fifty years.

The South Eastern & Chatham Railway, which had been working the Greenwich line since 1899, became part of the Southern Railway at the grouping of the railways in 1923, and at this time, the London & Greenwich Railway Company, which had maintained its separate existence, was formally incorporated in the Southern Railway. William Henry Simpson was the chairman at the time of the winding-up, and the office was in

Winchester House, Old Broad Street – which could not have been far from the site of George Walter's office when he started the company ninety years before.

Plans for the electrification of the Greenwich line, as part of a much wider scheme, had been prepared by the South Eastern & Chatham Railway after the 1914-18 War, but the work was eventually carried out by the Southern Railway under its suburban electrification plan. Electric trains were put into regular service over the Greenwich line on 6 June 1926; on 1 December 1929 colour light signals came into operation between Spa Road and Greenwich.

Deptford station, which had been closed for eleven years, was partially reconstructed, and with its platforms lengthened at the London end, it was reopened on 19 July 1926. In August 1927 the exterior of the station in the High Street was modified, and the turret, then eighty-five years old, was removed. The stairs on the north side now turn and connect with a passage through one of the arches, to provide a single entrance and exit for the station. The platforms were last lengthened to accommodate ten-coach trains, and part of the up side was burnt out in the early morning of 15 January 1958, apparently as an act of hooliganism following a burglary.

The last work of major importance on the Greenwich line was the replacement, in December 1963, of the old Deptford Creek Bridge by a modern electrically-operated lift bridge. The 40-ton centre platform lifts vertically, clear of any vessel using the Creek, and one man can now raise the bridge in 3 minutes where 12 men previously took at least an hour. It was built to the designs of Mr A. H. Cantrell, Chief Civil Engineer, Southern Region, at a cost of £92,000 by Sir William Arrol & Co Ltd of Glasgow.

Today, after 135 years' continuous use, the old London & Greenwich Railway viaduct stands practically in its original form. The brickwork is now black with age and dirt, and many of the dingy arches have ramshackle old gates and woodwork across the entrances. Some are filled with heaps of rusty iron and other rubbish which appears to have been lying there for years; others have been made into well-lighted modern factories, sawmills and timber-yards, but almost every one is now occupied. Here and there one can see an old and faded SER notice-board affixed to the viaduct, and in some places the iron frame of an ancient gas-lamp protrudes from an arch over a road or alley. An occasional patch of new brickwork shows where the bombs fell thirty years ago.

Most of the surviving relics of the Greenwich Railway have been mentioned in the foregoing pages. Apart from the viaduct itself, there is now little to be found, although several sections of the original footpaths still exist; but they do not bear much resemblance to the 'dainty boulevards' of which the London & Greenwich Railway was so proud in 1835. Sometimes they appear as public thoroughfares, often they form the yard or forecourt to the arches, and between Corbetts Lane and Deptford on the south side of the line sections of the path have been roofed over to provide additional workshop accommodation. Here, and along a private road called Mechanic's Path, by Deptford Station, the old boundary wall separates the footpath from the back gardens of some houses; this has been built up in several places to a height of seven or eight feet, but it can be seen in its original state with its rounded coping where it divides the footpath from the pavement in Hamilton Street, Deptford.

From Silwood Street a path runs along the north side of the viaduct, with footbridges over the East London lines and the derelict Deptford Wharf branch, to Trundley's Road; there is little building at this point, and with a little imagination one can visualise the appearance of the line in earlier days. From the towing path at Trundley's Road the original arches over the Surrey Canal may still be seen, with the very obvious widenings on either side.

Corbetts Lane junction; L&GR on right, Croydon Railway on left and SER spur to Bricklayers Arms running beneath the Croydon line

The double row of heavy cast-iron pillars supporting the arches over Abbey Street (formerly Neckinger Road) and Spa Road are still there, but those under the Deptford High Street bridge were removed some years ago.

Very much heavier trains than those for which the viaduct was built now travel over it at high speed, and for over fifty years most of these have been electric trains. Seventy years ago it was said that '... in spite of the dank, foggy locality and the shaking of some two-and-a-half millions of trains ...' the structure was still sound. Since this time many more millions of trains have sped over the arches, and they are evidently just as firm and solid as ever. The engineer and builders did their work well, and provided a pattern for other railway companies with lines to construct in congested areas.

Over a century ago the London & Greenwich Railway was regarded as a major 'Metropolitan Improvement'; a century hence it may well have disappeared in some future 'improvement' or development plan. When the time for its removal does come, perhaps some enlightened authority will recognise in the old viaduct an ancient monument to industry and enterprise, and preserve at least a few of its arches to recall for future generations London's first railway.

POSTSCRIPT

Since this chapter was written, major works have been carried out in the London Bridge area, extending over the period of five years from 1973 to 1978 at a cost of some £24m, and culminating in the rebuilding of the London Bridge Station concourse. The present station, designed by the Board's Architect, N.D.T. Wikeley and the eighth to occupy the site, was opened by the Bishop of Southwark on 15 December 1978. It is a splendid example of modern railway architecture, and by replacing the old war-damaged stations of the SER and LB&SCR has, by means of footbridges connecting the 16 platforms, provided one convenient station for the 53 million passengers who use it each year.

The local authorities of Southwark, Lewisham and Greenwich, through which the London & Greenwich line runs, have co-operated in arrangements to celebrate, in 1986, the 150th anniversary of the opening of the L&GR. With the assistance of British Rail, Southern Region, stretches of the viaduct are being cleaned and the brickwork restored to its original appearance.

Appendix

Miscellaneous Pamphlets and other publications not mentioned in the text

London & Greenwich Railway Guide (Mansell), 1836

London & Greenwich Railway Guide, 1837; 6 pp

London & Greenwich Railway; Advantages and Reasons for supporting it, April 1833. Circulated to Members of Parliament

From a Morning Paper; The Yorkshireman Inn, Deptford High St, 17 October 1836. Pamphlet by John Stead 'late Assisting Engineer of the London & Greenwich Railway'. Refers to Walter, who lived at East Dulwich at that time as the '... French Cook from East Deluge'

G. Walter; numerous printed circular letters to shareholders, issued during the period of his dispute with the company. One of these, headed *A Letter from Mr Walter to Mr Wales, Barrister* ..., dated 13 February 1840, claims that the '... accounts of the money raised for the Company were correct', as detailed in his *Plain Statement*. Akerman's copy has a note in ink 'Yes, but the writer was a defaulter for £5,000!!! – upon shares which he had NOT PAID UP, though he had sold them at a premium'

Raillery on a very peculiar species of Railway Legislation, 1843

London & Greenwich Railway; List of Shareholders: also, curious facts stated in Explanatory Notes, February 1840

Widening of the Greenwich Railway; The earnest appeal of a Greenwich Railway Shareholder to the Justice and Consideration of Parliament, March 1840

Railroad Impositions Detected, 1834

Statistics of the Greenwich Railway, 1842

G. Walter; *Hints on the Management of the Greenwich Railway, 1841*

Extracts from various Publications and Reviews on the London & Greenwich Railway, 1833.

Railway Travelling and the Toll Question, 1843

T. Hammond; *A few cursory remarks on Railways, 1835*

A Serio-Comic, but very important little book, to be read by all Proprietors of the London & Greenwich Railway Unprivileged Shares, November 1842

G. Money; *Greenwich Railway Shareholders and Statistics*, June 1842

Will Watch, the Railway Caesar (Seizer), or the Miller and his Men, 1843. This was a burlesque performed at the Theatre Royal, Deptford, at the end of January 1843 and simultaneously published as a pamphlet

The Railway was the subject of some doggerel verse in 1836; *A Proper New Song of the Greenwich Railway* and *A New Christmas Carol* are two examples from *The Musquitto* of 5 November and 17 December 1836 respectively. The following is a specimen verse from the latter composition:

> 'The first good joy that W[alter] had,
>   It was the joy of one,
> To see the Greenwich Railway Trains
>   Like greas-ed lightening run,
> The cads and coachmen looked aghast
>   And cried that they were done,
>   etc.'

The Opening Day of the Greenwich Railway—comic song, 1836 (*see* plate 9). A pencilled note on the copy reproduced gives the second figure from the left as 'Mr Addinall' (John Addinall, a director of the Greenwich Railway Gas Co), but the statement cannot be checked in the absence of any portraits

References and Notes

Abbreviations
BM   British Museum   PRO   Public Record Office

Acts of Parliament
All Acts relating to specific railway companies are in the category
Local & Personal Acts. In addition to the principal L&GR Acts
mentioned in the text, the following were passed granting
'Further powers':

  1838 1–2 V c 4   1842 5–6 Vc 102
  1839 2–3 V c 19   1902 2 E7 c 254

Railway Magazine
All references in the text and notes are to the original journal
which began publication in 1835 and became known as
Herapath's Railway Magazine or *Herapath*.

Railway archives and other official records
Much of the information upon which this work is based has been
derived from the Board of Directors' Minutes of the London &
Greenwich Railway and, to a lesser extent, those of the Croydon,
Brighton and South Eastern Railways and the Joint Locomotive
and Station Committees of these Companies. References to these
sources have been omitted from the following list as they are too
numerous, but it will usually be apparent from the text where
this material has been consulted.

Chapter 1: The Formation of the Company (pp 11-26)

  1 Quoted in *The Engineer* Vol 70, 1890, p 300
  2 Newcomen Society *Transactions* Vol 2, p 43
  3 BM: Kentish Railway Prospectus 1825
  4 Surrey County Records
  5 Patent No 4618 of 1821
  6 Newcomen Society *Transactions* Vol 18, pp 16, 27

7 House of Commons Journal Vol 81, 1826, p 68
8 His office was at 42 Fish Street Hill, City, above a baker's shop
9 The *London Gazette* notices for the Southampton & London and London & Birmingham Railways appeared on 8 and 9 November respectively; the London & Greenwich appeared on the 7th
10 55 accidents, 17 deaths in 1832
11 BM: 'Collection of prints chiefly relating to Deptford and Greenwich' 578 m 11
12 Deptford Public library
13 *Railway Bell*, October 1844
14 *New Monthly*, March 1834 'Dolphin': coaching inn, Greenwich
15 A. J. Dunkin: *History of the County of Kent*, 1856
16 Surrey County Records
17 3 W4 c 46
18 G. Walter: *Origin and Progress of the London & Greenwich Railway*, 1837
19 F. Clifford: *History of Private Bill Legislation*, 1885
20 *The Musquitto*, No 1, 17 December 1833. A local Greenwich paper
21 *Origin & Progress etc*
22 The Surrey Iron Railway, incorporated 1801, opened 1803; the first public railway in the world (horse-operated)

Chapter 2: The Construction of the Viaduct (pp 27-45)

1 Patent No 6187 of 1831. A further Patent for improvements relating to railways was granted in 1832, No 6281
2 G. Walter: *A Plain Statement of Facts connected with the London & Greenwich Railway*, 1841, p 7
3 The writer was most probably George Walter
4 Section 80
5 *Birmingham Journal*, 27 August 1834
6 Aytoun Ellis: *300 Years on London River*, 1952
7 The property was a market garden between the Ravensbourne and Greenwich
8 In 1845 a number of arches under the London & Blackwall Railway were used as houses, and at least one as an infants' school. The remains of some houses built in the arches of an old LB&SCR viaduct are still to be seen from Coldblow

Lane, near New Cross. Reports of the Royal Commission on Railway Termini in the Metropolis, 1846

9 *Railway Magazine*, 3 June 1843

10 Between Blue Anchor Road and Surrey Docks

11 Section 46

12 The completed sections were London Bridge–Bermondsey Street and Neckinger Road–Deptford

13 *Mining, Railway and Steam Navigation Gazette*, 6 March 1837

14 *Journal of the Statistical Society of London*, 1839

15 *Civil Engineers' and Architects' Journal*, October 1837

16 The Act of 1836 for the Deptford Pier & Junction Railway contained a Section compelling that company to provide such screens

17 Movable bridges of other types existed in this country at the time; e.g. Soar Lift Bridge, Leicester & Swannington Railway

18 *Railway Magazine*, December 1838

19 7 W4 & 1V c 120

20 W. B. Paley, writing in the *Gentlemen's Magazine*, 1897, Vol 59, p 247, says 'Rails were not joined to each other in any way, further than having their ends resting in the same chair'

21 The Preston & Wyre Railway, 19 miles long, until May 1839, when he was succeeded by George and Robert Stephenson

22 In evidence before the Gauge Commission, 1845. Parl Papers 1846, XVI No 34

23 Between London Bridge and Deptford there were 842; *The Mirror* 17 December 1836

24 *Birmingham Journal*, 17 December 1836

Chapter 3: The Opening of the Railway (pp 46-62)

1 L&GR; *Advantages of Railways with Locomotive Engines*, 1833

2 *Public Ledger*, 18 and 23 February 1835

3 *Ibid*, 21 April 1835

4 'It gathers strength as it goes'

5 A. M. Broadly and R. G. Bartelot; *Nelson's Hardy; his Life, Letters and Friends*, 1909. In 1835 he was 67 years old, and Governor of Greenwich Hospital

6 *John Bull*, 15 November 1835

7 PRO: Admiralty Documents, Ad/1/5553

8 7 W4 & 1V c 50

9 A Naval officer, John Brothers, said in March 1837 that he had made a profit of about £2,000 by buying L&GR shares at par or £1 premium and selling at £10-11 premium. House of Commons Accounts & Papers 1837, Vol 18, Pt 1

10 George Walter: *Explanatory Notes on the Report of the Committee of Shareholders of the London & Greenwich Railway, 1837*, and *Greenwich, Woolwich & Deptford Gazette*, 23 July 1836. (The latter was generally known as the *Greenwich Gazette* until 1838, when it became the *Kentish Mercury*.)

11 Report of Select Committee on Danger by Fire from Locomotive Engines, 1836. House of Lords Papers, Vol 9, 1836

12 *London & Greenwich Railway and the Direct Brighton Railway*: Extracts from the Evidence of George Walter Esq, 1836. Another pamphlet, *The Examination Examined*, 1836, attempted to refute many of Walter's statements. On the title-page of J. Y. Akerman's copy is the pencilled note 'By the Right Honourable Lord Dundonald'

13 *The Political Economy of Railroads*, 1836

14 *The Musquitto*, No 2, 5 November 1836

15 *Ibid*

16 There were two versions of this ticket or invitation card; one, in black, had the badge of the Bridge House Estates and the Arms of the City of London and of the Company; the other, in blue, had the badge and the City Arms surmounted by the Company's motto 'Vires acquirit eundo'

17 Most accounts refer to six trains, but the *Railway Magazine*, January 1837, p 70, mentions four engines on four trains

18 The 'Scorpion'; *The Engineer*, 1895, Vol 80, p 39

19 The cost of the military bands employed on the opening day was £58

Chapter 4: Early Years on the Greenwich Railway – 1 (pp 63-88)

1 *Origin and Progress of the London & Greenwich Railway*, 1837

2 *The Examination Examined*, 1836

3 *Greenwich Gazette*, 15 March 1834 etc

4 1st Report of Select Committee on Railway Subscription Lists: *Deptford and Dover Subscription List*; House of Commons Accounts and Papers, 1837 Vol 18, Part 1

5 Typed note on copy of the print in Greenwich Public Library

6 *Railway Magazine*, 1 May 1835

7 *Morning Herald*, 10 June 1835

8 The question of taking the line through Greenwich Park is dealt with in Parliamentary Papers, 1846, Vol 38

9 *Deptford and Dover Subscription List*

10 John Yates joined the Board in January 1837 on the resignation of Thomas Philpotts

11 *Origin and Progress of the London & Greenwich Railway*, 1837

12 *Greenwich Gazette*, 5 October 1837. They probably charged him one shilling as he no doubt travelled first class

13 24 May 1838 at the Red Lion Hotel, Deptford

14 *Railway Magazine*, 23 November 1839, p 360. This is the medal illustrated in C. F. Dendy Marshall's *History of the Southern Railway*, 1936, and previously supposed to have commemorated the opening of the railway. Designed by J. Barber, it was 60mm in diameter, and bore on the obverse the head of Walter surrounded by the following inscription: 'Those connected with the Greenwich Railway thus record to whom the South of England is principally indebted the zeal and perseverance of George Walter Esq for the introduction of Railways. Late Resident Director. Caesari Quae Caesaris MDCCCXXXVIII.' The Corbetts Lane view appeared on the reverse, with dates of opening, names of the contractor, engineer etc. An example in bronze is in the BM

15 *Railway Magazine*, 5 December 1840, *and see* pp 84-5

16 £100 per annum for the first five years, £350 pa by 1845

17 His 2-volume *London Legends* under the pseudonym of Paul Pindar was published in 1842

18 Letter 17 November 1862, Albinus Martin to C. Manby; Phillimore Collection, Science Museum

19 Evidence before the Select Committees on Railways, 1839 and 1840

20 *Kentish Mercury*, 29 December 1838

21 *Ibid*

22 *Railway Magazine*, 3 October 1840

23 *The Times*, 17 February 1838

24 *Kentish Mercury*, 20 April 1840

25 Unidentified cutting, Greenwich Public Library; references to the 1st Afghan War date it c 1840. Conditions had not

changed very much eight years later – *The Puppet Show*, 1848

26 *The Times*, 6 October 1840; 'flats' = contemporary slang for dupes or duffers

27 *Railway Times*, 4 September 1840

28 *Meyer's Universum*, 1841, Vol 8, p 12 and Plate 333

29 *The Globe*, 18 March 1841; 'tram(s)' = railway track

30 The steps referred to were on the north side of the viaduct and on the London side of Blue Anchor Road (now South-wark Park Road)

31 Damages of £500 were recovered by the bus proprietor Shilli-beer from the Eastern Counties Railway for injuries sustained in an accident on 18 October 1845; *Annual Register*, 1846

32 The path crossed the Canal by a footbridge fixed to the south side of the viaduct at the height of the parapet wall, and reached by stairs on either side; Civil Engineer's plan of Rail-way, c 1842

33 *Kentish Mercury*, 31 March 1838; *Railways – their uses and management*, 1842

34 *Kentish Mercury*, 31 March 1838

35 An Act for regulating Railways; *3/4 Vict c 97*, 10 August 1840 Board of Trade Returns, 30 June 1842 – 30 June 1843

36 PRO; Board of Trade (Railway Department) Out Letters 21 July 1841. MT 11

37 *Ibid*

38 13-carriage trains were occasionally run at holiday times if extra rolling stock could be borrowed

39 *Railway Times*, 21 December 1839

40 *See* chapter 6

Chapter 5: Early Years on the Greenwich Railway – 2 (pp 89-107)

1 BM; Prospectuses of Railway Companies, etc. 5 Volumes, 1800-1856

2 F. Whishaw; *Analysis of Railways*, 1837

3 BM; Prospectuses of Railway Companies, etc

4 The use of coke as locomotive fuel was almost universal until the 1860s, since virtually all railway Acts prohibited the emis-sion of smoke from engines; it went out of use with the intro-duction of fireboxes modified to burn the much cheaper coal

5 *Hereford Journal*, 16 May 1827 and 5 January 1831

6 BM; Miscellaneous Papers relating to Kent – Railways and Greenwich Elections

7 The handbill referred to on p 75; a copy survives in the Greenwich Public Library

8 *Woolwich Advertiser*, 1 August 1840; the report adds that the passengers were '... packed like cattle in a manger'

9 *Railway Magazine*, 2 April 1842

10 *Railway Times*, 9 January 1840

11 Select Committee on Railways, 1840; Vol 13, 5th Report App 1 (24) p 378. Return dated 28 April 1840

12 *Railway Travelling and the Toll Question*, 1843; reprinted from the *Westminster Review*, 77, May 1843; and *Railways, their uses and management*, 1842

13 *2/3 W4 c 120*. Section 50 stipulated payment monthly after 10 October 1832 and required books to be kept; Section 52 provided for composition of the Duty. The Schedule laid down the rate at '... $\frac{1}{2}$d for 4 passengers per mile'. See also Second Report Select Committee on Railways, 1839, Q 3648 etc

14 Example in Greenwich Public Library

15 *Kentish Mercury*, 4 February 1843; W. W. Tomlinson, *History of the North Eastern Railway*, 1915

16 The penny was 1.35 inches in diameter, ie 34mm approximately

17 Six examples of tickets and 3 Directors' Passes are in the British Museum Collection; the Science Museum and Museum of British Transport, London, also have some specimens. Items 2, 3 and 4 on p 98 were in the Dendy Marshall Collection

18 *Gentlemen's Magazine*, Vol 59, 1897, p 247

19 *The Observer*, 30 October 1836

20 *Kentish Mercury*, 22 September 1838

21 'Veritas Vincit'; *Railway Locomotive Management*, 1847

22 F. Whishaw; *Railways of Great Britain and Ireland*, 1840

23 Evidence; Committee on Widening and Station Bills, House of Lords Record Office

24 *Greenwich Gazette*, 25 January 1837

25 Evidence of engine driver at inquest, March 1836

26 *Railway Times*, 30 November 1839

27 PRO; Board of Trade (Railway Department) letters, MT 11

Chapter 6: Relations with other Railways (pp 108-132)

1 Surrey County Records
2 *Ibid.* A print showing the proposed railway is in the Greenwich Public Library, and a drawing of the arcade planned to run beneath the arches is reproduced in C. B. Andrews' *The Railway Age*, 1937
3 2nd Report of Select Committee on Railway Subscription Lists, 1837 Vol 18, Pt 1 (132 pp)
4 First mentioned in *Borough Bubbles*, published by William Pooley, Bookseller, High St, Deptford, 5 November 1834:

> It will not only bring the Vauxhall people here,
> But with wonderful speed will take Deptford folks there,
> To sit in the gardens, eat ham and drink beer,
> Unless it should go to the wall, Sir.

The writer predicted that along with many other projects in the borough at that time, including a floating steam-driven cast iron church, it would '... go off pop, Like a Fifth of November sky-rocket'
5 Surrey County Records
6 6 W4 c 63
7 Surrey County Records. A second Act was passed on 19 July 1839, 2/3 Vict c 76. The railway would have cost £135,000 per mile had it been built
8 5/6 W4 c 10
9 6 W4 c 75
10 7 W4 and 1 Vict c 119
11 A month later, 23 May 1839, the London & Brighton Directors were taken by special train over the Greenwich and Croydon Railways
12 Copy in BM
13 Among the proposals was one to join the Croydon, Brighton and South Eastern trains, and run them as one long train with assistant engines between London Bridge and Corbetts Lane, always giving right of way to any Greenwich trains. Second Report, Select Committee on Railways, (9 August 1839), 1840
14 First Report, Select Committee on Railways, 1840, Q 210 etc
15 *Woolwich Advertiser*, 1 February 1840
16 The speeches of Charles Austin and William Page Wood,

counsel for the Croydon and Greenwich Railways respectively, were published as pamphlets by the companies in 1840

17 3/4 Vict c 127; 7 August 1840

18 BM; 'Miscellaneous Papers relating to Kent – Railways and Greenwich Elections'

19 Report of Select Committee on Railway Accidents, 1841

20 *Ibid*; Q 96 etc; 'On the Greenwich line you can see from one end to the other?' – 'Yes, except in foggy weather'

21 PRO; Board of Trade (Railway Department), Out Letters, MT 11

22 Z. Colburn and A. Holley; *The Permanent Way and Coal burning boilers of European Railways*, N.Y. 1858. Estimates of the cost of the early railways varied; the basis of Colburn's calculation is not known

23 A Committee of Directors of the South Eastern, London & Brighton and London & Croydon Railways, formed to administer their Joint Station at London Bridge

24 PRO; Board of Trade (Railway Department) Out Letters, MT 11

25 *The Toll Question on Railways Exemplified, in the case of the Croydon and Greenwich Companies*, 1841

26 6/7 Vict c 62

27 Joint Locomotive Committee engine No 83 *Forester*, built by Edward Bury, 1844

28 *Railway Bell*, 21 September 1844

29 R. S. Scrimgeour; *Railways, Cause of Property*, 1845

30 *Railway Bell*, 22 February 1845

Chapter 7: Stations 1836-45 (pp 133-162)

1 On leaning out of a second-class carriage window his '... head came with fearful violence against the station house, which is a wooden erection for the purpose of taking up and setting down passengers'. – Report of Inquest. A railway guard had been killed in similar circumstances a month previously

2 *Kentish Mercury*, 26 January and 16 February 1839

3 Report of Select Committee on Railways and Turnpike Trusts, 1839

4 A. J. Dunkin; *History of the County of Kent*, 1856

5 Patent No 8756 of 1840

6 G. Walter; *Addenda to Explanatory Notes*, July 1838

7 Supplied by Fox, Henderson & Co for £43 10 0

8 South Eastern Railway Board Minutes, 20 January 1848

9 Patent No 7773 of 1838

10 *Kentish Mercury*, 2 November 1839

11 *West Kent Guardian*, 29 February 1840

12 *Woolwich Advertiser*, 18 April 1840

13 *Railway Times*, 1 May 1840

14 S. C. Brees; *Railway Practice*, 1837-47

15 The refilling of locomotives was transferred from Deptford to Greenwich in 1840. In June 1844 a Mr Hicks was paid £50 for his 'water pumping process' and a large saving was expected on the cost of filtration

16 *Railway Times*, 1 May 1840

17 *Mechanic's Magazine*, 16 May 1840

18 *West Kent Guardian*, 27 June 1840

19 *Railway Magazine*, 7 October 1843

20 G. R. Corner; *History of Horseleydown*; Paper, 30 October 1855, GLC Members' Library

21 6/7 W4 c 121

22 Report of Select Committee on Railways, 1839, Q 1744 etc

23 R. Tyas; *The Croydon Railway and its adjacent scenery*, 1839

24 *Railway Magazine*, 7 December 1839

25 1/2 Vict c 20

26 O. Manning and W. Bray; *History and Antiquities of the County of Surrey*, 1804-14, Vol 3, Southwark, extra-illustrated copy in the City of London Guildhall Library

27 London Bridge Station Acts:
   London & Greenwich Railway: 3/4 Vict c 128
   London & Croydon Railway: 3/4 Vict c 129

28 Surrey County Records

29 *Civil Engineer & Architects' Journal*, Vol 6, 1843, p 403

30 *Illustrated Guide to the London & Dover Railway*, published by J. Mead, London, 1845

31 *The Penny Magazine*, 30 December 1843, p 498

32 Some of the prints of the Joint Station showing it in its final form are partly conjectural; one appeared in the *Illustrated London News*, 3 February 1844, some four months before the completion of the approach road enabled the station to be opened, and another was published in the *Stationers' Almanac* for 1845, prepared from the official drawings loaned for the purpose by the Joint Station Committee on 28 February 1844.

A view in Charles Knight's *London*, 1841-4, shows the section that was built, including five sets of windows instead of eleven, and another picture, in A. H. Payne's *Illustrated London, or a Series of Views in the British Metropolis*, 1845, shows the tower only, looking north, after the verandah had been built along the frontage of the station

33 Measom's *Official Illustrated Guide to the South Eastern Railway*, 1858. (Sir George Samuel Measom; many editions of the guide were published)

Chapter 8: Signalling (pp 163-168)

1 J. Moxon, Chairman of the London & Croydon Railway, referred to the lighthouse with '... three different coloured lights'. Second Report, Select Committee on Railways, 1839, Q 1502
2 *Ibid*, Q 2826
3 *Gazetteer of England and Wales*, 1841
4 PRO; Board of Trade (Railway Department) Out letters, 14 July 1841; MT 11
5 Resolutions of Railway Directors, Birmingham, 19 January 1841; House of Lords Papers 1841, 21
6 Select Committee on Railways, 1839

Chapter 9: Locomotives (pp 169-194)

1 The principles are outlined in a pamphlet by J. Ward; *A New Discovery whereby Manual Labour ... etc*, 1834
2 At about this time he '... ceased to be an engine-maker to the public', being fully occupied by the London & Birmingham Railway; Second Report, Select Committee on Railways, 1839, Q 3898
3 Maj S. Snell; *A Story of Railway Pioneers*, 1921
4 Board of Trade Report on Railways, 1841; Sessional Vol 41, 1842
5 White's *Staffordshire Directory*, 1834
6 Montagu, Deacon and De Gex; *Reports in Cases of Bankruptcy*, 1842-5
7 *The Black Country and its Industries*, brochure, Stourbridge, 1905
8 Institution of Civil Engineers; Sir John Rennie's Ms Reports. A printed description of *The Steam Engine simplified by the*

Earl of Dundonald (1833) in Robert Stephenson's papers, BM, Add Mss 38, 781

Wolverhampton Chronicle, 25 January 1834

9 Institution of Mechanical Engineers; *Proceedings*, 1848, *On the Fallacies of the Rotary Engine*. See also *The Engineer*, Vol 50, 1880, p 217: Royal Scottish Society of Arts, *Transactions*, 1835, Vol 1, p 43, Paper by David Stevenson: *Public Ledger*, 2 April 1835, quoting *The Cambrian*

10 Scottish Record Office: papers of the 10th Earl of Dundonald. The files include correspondence, depositions and affidavits sworn by Walter, Landmann, Fenwick and others

11 Patent No 6923 of 1835

12 William Bridges Adams; *English Pleasure Carriages*, 1837, reprinted 1971

13 *The Engineer*, Vol 80, 1895, p 39; C. F. Dendy Marshall: *History of the Southern Railway*, 1936

14 Academie des Sciences, Paris; *Comptes Rendus*, tome 4, 1837, pp 179, 335. See also, Institution of Mechanical Engineers, *Proceedings*, 1848, and *The Engineer*, Vol 22, 1866, p 297

15 *American Railroad Journal*, 14 September 1833

16 *The Engineer*, Vol 59, 1885, p 26, and Manchester Association of Engineers, *Transactions*, 1889

17 Royal Scottish Society of Arts; *Transactions*, Vol 1, 1885

18 F. Wishaw; *Analysis of Railways*, 1837 and *Railway Engineer* October 1893, p 313

19 *Civil Engineer & Architects' Journal*, Vol 1, November 1837

20 There is no evidence that he was ever employed as Locomotive Superintendent, as writers have sometimes claimed; in 1838 he was described as a Civil Engineer of Stamford Street, Blackfriars

21 *Mechanic's Magazine*, 30 April, 1836. The brake was demonstrated to '... Mr Rennie and several scientific gentlemen' on Saturday, 23 April. A more elaborate version was the subject of Patent No 7792 of 1838

22 W. Curtis; *Inventions for Railways*, 1840

23 *Mechanic's Magazine*, 10 October 1835

24 BM; 'Prospectuses of Railway Companies etc', 1800-56

25 *Deptford and Dover Subscription List*

26 G. Walter states that the first act of the new Board of Directors appointed in 1837 '... was to pass a public but pitiful insult upon some of their predecessors in office, by removing their

names from the Engines, upon which, as a compliment, they had been originally engraved. This ... must have cost the Company not less than £14, at a time when one of them had declared at a Public Meeting that the Treasury did not boast the wherewithal to purchase a single day's consumption of coke for the Engines.' *Addenda to Explanatory Notes*, 1838

27 *Morning Advertiser*, 26 April 1837

28 Adam Gordon & Co of Deptford experimented with locomotive constuction at this time and one of their engines ran trials on the London & Croydon Railway between New Cross and Croydon in November 1839

29 Cleveland Institution of Engineers; *Proceedings*, 1886. West was Chief Draughtsman on the North Eastern Railway

30 *The Engineer*, Vol 75, 1893, p 429

31 G. Walter; *Addenda to Explanatory Notes*, 1838

32 The Board decided on 12 January 1838 that a '... night watch be kept, and fires continued under the engines all night during the prevalence of frost'. See also *Kentish Mercury*, 20 January, 3 February 1838

33 G. Walter; *Addenda to Explanatory Notes*, 1838: copy in BM

34 Patent No 6791 of 1835 referred to a locomotive that could be guided at junctions by the driver from the footplate

35 Robert Stephenson & Co's engine No 191

36 Second Report, Select Committee on Railways, 1839, Q 5358-5365

37 West Hartlepool Railway, Board Minutes

38 Nathaniel Ogle was an engineer of note, having had an engine named after him on the Stanhope & Tyne Railway; he was also a Director of the original Southampton & London Railway

39 The Richmond, Fredericksburgh & Potomac RR

40 Stephenson Locomotive Society; *Journal*, July 1941, p 132

41 Charles Hutton Gregory; *Practical Rules for the Management of a Locomotive Engine*, 1841

42 *Railway Magazine*, 18 March 1843 and F. W. Hackwood; *Wednesbury Workshops*, 1889

43 Second Report, Select Committee on Railways, 1839, Q 4578

44 Letter, A. Martin to C. Manby – see note 18, Chapter 4

45 South Eastern Railway Account books etc; BRB Historical Records

46 PRO: Admiralty papers; letters in the files of the Secretary's, Surveyor's and Victualling Departments, 1845
Although the practice of using Locomotives as marine engines was not common, there were previous instances; one from the Wylam Waggonway was used to drive a tug on the Tyne in 1822, and in 1842 a steamboat, 'The Locomotive No 1', ran between Adelphi Pier and Greenwich, fitted with a locomotive engine removed from its wheels to drive the paddles

47 *Illustrated London News*, 24 May 1845

48 B. Bell; *Lieutenant John Irving, RN*, 1881

49 R. J. Cyriax; *Sir John Franklin's Last Arctic Expedition*, 1939

50 A modification of the original scheme was published in 1844 as 'Motley's Manual Railway'. The idea, said to have originated from Tate, Permanent Way contractor to the Grand Junction Railway, was to employ hand-propelled machines weighing 4 cwt; on the assumption that 8 men equalled '1 good horse', six sets or gangs could perform 112 trips daily on the L&GR. Forty-eight men at 2/- a day each would be cheaper than horses or steam. *Year Book of Facts in Science and Art*, 1844

Chapter 10: Carriages (pp 195-211)

1 William Bridges Adams; *English Pleasure Carriages*, 1837

2 F. Whishaw; *Analysis of Railways*, 1837

3 Coloured print published by J. Brown, Broad Street, entitled *London & Greenwich Railroad*, probably 1832, shows a train of first-class carriages in yellow, pink and black and one of second-class open carriages painted blue; Science Museum

4 M. Bineau (Ingenieur au Corps royal des Mines); *Chemins de fer d'Angleterre*, 1840

5 Patent No 6923 of 1835

6 The Bolton & Leigh and Leigh & Kenyon Junction Railways

7 *The Observer*, 30 October 1836

8 A shareholder alleged that Wright was a friend of one of the Directors, and had been allowed to purchase the company's carriages for £4,000 in order to hire them back to the company at £3,000 a year. Joseph Wright's business eventually developed into the Metropolitan-Cammell Carriage & Wagon Co Ltd

9 G. Walter in letter to the Ministry of Public Works, 30 May 1842

10 After May 1842 through the Joint Locomotive Committee

11 In October 1843, 13 ballast waggons were sold to the London & Brighton Railway at 30 gn each

12 PRO; letter to the Board of Trade (Railway Department)

13 Nathaniel Worsdell, '... a Liverpool coachbuilder in the service of the Railway', who, in 1838, secured a Patent for mail-bag apparatus. R. Pike; *Railway Adventures and Anecdotes*, 1884

14 A. R. Bennett; *The First Railway in London*, 1912 (*Locomotive Magazine Souvenir*). The South Eastern Railway carriages on the North Kent line are referred to in the Board of Trade (Railway Department) Returns, 1850

Chapter 11: 1845 and After (pp 212-245)

1 8/9 Vict c 80. (21 July 1845)

2 8/9 Vict c 186

3 8/9 Vict c 196

4 9/10 Vict c 234

5 9/10 Vict c 305

6 10/11 Vict c 230

7 10/11 Vict c 104

8 F. D. Bannister; *LB&SCR Co. and SER Co. – Historical Notes in reference to the lines of railway between Redhill and London, by means of which the LB&SCR and SER Companies obtain access to the London Bridge Stations of both Companies*, March, 1888

9 Board of Trade Report on Railway Termini, 1845, Vol 39

10 Report of the Royal Commission on Railway Termini in the Metropolis, 1846, Vol 17

11 By T. H. Shepherd, undated; City of London Guildhall Library

12 *Magazine of Science*, Vol 14, 1851

13 16/17 Vict c 116

14 The SER was asked to retain the London & Greenwich staff in a memorial containing 1,014 signatures; *Kentish Mercury*, 18 January 1845

15 G. Landmann; *Adventures and Recollections of Colonel Land-*

mann, 1852 (2 vol); *Recollections of my Military Life*, 1854 (2 vol)

16 *Post Office Railway Directory*, 1847. In 1847 he was living at 2, Hamilton Terrace, Hyde Vale, and in 1851 at 6, Egerton Drive, Greenwich

17 Board of Trade Report, 1855; Vol 54, 1856

18 *Annual Register*, 1856

19 22/23 Vict c 81

20 The Arbitration Report of 25 October 1861 is 177 pages in length. To secure the Hospital from noise and inconvenience, 'Every railway scheme that has been brought forward within the last 30 years they [the Hospital Governors] have opposed, and it has cost them a very considerable sum of money'

21 24/25 Vict c 93

22 *Railway Magazine (Herapath)* 21 May 1870, p 502

23 PRO; Board of Trade (Railway Department) MT 11

24 Measom's *Guide to the South Eastern Railway*, 1858

25 *South Ensign*, 30 March, 1878

26 House of Commons Papers on the subject were published as follows: —
    No 375, 19 May 1846
    No 436, 25 June 1846
    No 61, 27 March 1863
    No 67, 16 April 1863
    No 248, 3 May 1865
    No 259, 5 May 1865

27 *Autobiography of Sir George Biddel Airy*, Ed Wilfred Airy, 1896

28 The contractors for all the works between Greenwich and Charlton were Aird & Co

29 J. W. and A. J. Barry; *South Eastern Railway (Access to London)*, 8 August 1894

30 *The Engineer*, Vol 91, 1901, p 133

Index